THE EASTERN FATHERS
OF THE
FOURTH CENTURY

VOLUME SEVEN
in *THE COLLECTED WORKS* of

GEORGES FLOROVSKY
Emeritus Professor of Eastern Church History
Harvard University

General Editor
RICHARD S. HAUGH
Visiting Scholar
Andover Newton Theological School

Translated by
CATHERINE EDMUNDS

BÜCHERVERTRIEBSANSTALT
Postfach 461, FL - 9490 Vaduz, Europa
[Exclusive Sales Agent: Notable & Academic Books
P. O. Box 470, Belmont, MA {USA} 02178]

THE EASTERN FATHERS OF THE FOURTH CENTURY
ISBN 3–905238–07–1

THE COLLECTED WORKS OF GEORGES FLOROVSKY

[Additional forthcoming volumes. The final volume contains an Index to the entire *Collected Works,* Bibliography, Appendices, and Miscellanea]

PRINTED IN THE UNITED STATES OF AMERICA

THE EASTERN FATHERS OF THE FOURTH CENTURY

ABOUT THE COLLECTED WORKS

Fr. Florovsky devoted much attention to his *Collected Works*. Until shortly before his death, he had continued to supply a variety of materials. These included suggestions for the structuring of the volumes; changes in certain texts; new materials; updated materials; notes; revisions; suggestions for revisions; updated bibliography; and several outlines for a new structure to his work on the Byzantine Fathers. Substantial time has been expended to implement his suggestions and instructions. Some materials will be included in the final volume, a volume which also contains an Index to the entire *Collected Works*, Appendices, Notes, Bibliography, and Miscellanea. To publish *The Collected Works* in English has entailed the translation of his works from several languages, including Russian, Bulgarian, Czech, Serbian, German and French.

TABLE OF CONTENTS

IN MEMORIAM

FR. GEORGES FLOROVSKY
1893-1979

"Preeminent Orthodox Christian Theologian, Ecumenical Spokesman, And Authority on Russian Letters."

[All quotations are from pages 5 and 11 of the *Harvard Gazette* of October 1, 1982, written by George H. Williams, Hollis Professor of Divinity *Emeritus*, Harvard Divinity School and Edward Louis Keenan, Dean of the Graduate School of Arts and Sciences, Harvard University and "placed upon the records" at the Harvard Faculty of Divinity Meeting on September 16, 1982.]

"Archpriest Professor Georges Vasilyevich Florovsky (1893-1979), preeminent theologian of Orthodoxy and historian of Christian thought, ecumenical leader and interpreter of Russian literature . . . died in Princeton, New Jersey in his 86th year" on August 11, 1979.

Born in Odessa in 1893, Fr. Florovsky was the beneficiary of that vibrant Russian educational experience which flourished toward the end of the 19th century and produced many gifted scholars. His father was rector of the Theological Academy and dean of the Cathedral of the Transfiguration. His mother, Klaudia Popruzhenko, was the daughter of a professor of Hebrew and Greek. Fr. Florovsky's first scholarly work, "On Reflex Salivary Secretion," written under one of Pavlov's students, was published in English in 1917 in the last issue of *The Bulletin of the Imperial Academy of Sciences.*

In 1920, with his parents and his brother Antonii, Fr. Florovsky left Russia and settled first in Sophia, Bulgaria. He left behind his brother, Vasilii, a surgeon, who died in the 1924 famine, and his sister Klaudia V. Florovsky, who became a professor of history at the University of Odessa. In 1921 the President of Czechoslovakia, Thomas Masaryk, invited Fr. Florovsky and his brother Antonii to Prague. Fr. Florovsky taught the philosophy of law. Antonii later became a professor of history at the University of Prague.

In 1922 Georges Florovsky married Xenia Ivanovna Simonova and they resettled in Paris where he became cofounder of St. Sergius Theological Institute and taught there as professor of patristics (1926-1948). In 1932 he was ordained a priest and placed himself canonically under the patriarch of Constantinople.

In 1948 he came to the United States and was professor of theology at St. Vladimir's Theological Seminary from 1948 to 1955, and dean from 1950. From 1954 to 1965 he was professor of Eastern Church History at Harvard Divinity School and, concurrently (1962-1965) an associate of the Slavic Department and (1955-1959) an associate professor of theology at Holy Cross Theological School.

"Although Fr. Florovsky's teaching in the Slavic Department [at Harvard University] was only sporadic, he became a major intellectual influence in the formation of a generation of American specialists in Russian cultural history. His lasting importance in this area derives not from his formal teaching but from the time and thought he gave to informal "circles" that periodically arose around him in Cambridge among those who had read *The Ways of Russian Theology* [then only in Russian], for decades a kind of "underground book" among serious graduate students of Russian intellectual history, and had sought him out upon discovering that he was at the Divinity School . . . During a portion of his incumbency at Harvard . . . patristics and Orthodox thought and institutions from antiquity into 20th century Slavdom flour - ished. In the Church History Department meetings he spoke up with clarity. In the Faculty meetings he is remembered as having ener - getically marked book catalogues on his lap for the greater glory of the Andover Harvard Library! In 1964 Fr. Florovsky was elected a director of the Ecumenical Institute founded by Paul VI near Jerusalem." Active in both the National Council of Churches and the World Council of Churches, Fr. Florovsky was Vice President-at-Large of the National Council of Churches from 1954 to 1957.

"After leaving Harvard, Professor *Emeritus* Florovsky taught from 1965 to 1972 in Slavic Studies at Princeton University, having begun lecturing there already in 1964; and he was visiting lecturer in patristics at Princeton Theological Seminary as early as 1962 and then again intermittently after retirement from the University. His last teaching was in the fall semester of 1978/79 at Princeton Theological Seminary."

"Fr. Florovsky in the course of his career was awarded honorary doctorates by St. Andrew's University . . . Boston University, Notre Dame, Princeton University, the University of Thessalonica, St. Vladimir's Theological Seminary, and Yale. He was a member or honorary member of the Academy of Athens, the American Academy of Arts and Sciences, the British Academy, and the Fellowship of St. Alban and St. Sergius."

Fr. Florovsky personified the cultivated, well-educated Russian of the turn of the century. His penetrating mind grasped both the detail and depth in the unfolding drama of the history of Christianity in both eastern and western forms. He was theologian, church historian, patristic scholar, philosopher, Slavist, and a writer in comparative literature. "Fr. Florovsky sustained his pleasure on reading English novels, the source in part of his extraordinary grasp of the English language, which, polyglot that he was, he came to prefer above any other for theological discourse and general exposition. Thus when he came to serve in Harvard's Slavic Department, there was some disappointment that he did not lecture in Russian, especially in his seminars on Dostoievsky, Soloviev, Tolstoi, and others. It was as if they belonged to a kind of classical age of the Russian tongue and civilization that, having been swept away as in a deluge, he treated as a Latin professor would Terrence or Cicero, not presuming to give lectures in the tonalities of an age that had vanished forever."

Fr. Florovsky's influence on contemporary church historians and Slavists was vast. The best contemporary multi-volume history of Christian thought pays a special tribute to Fr. Florovsky. Jaroslav Pelikan of Yale University, in the bibliographic section to his first volume in *The Christian Tradition: A History of the Development of Doctrine*, writes under the reference to Fr. Florovsky's two works in Russian on the Eastern Fathers: "These two works are basic to our interpretation of trinitarian and christological dogmas" (p. 359 from *The Emergence of the Catholic Tradition: 100-600*). George Huntston Williams, Hollis Professor *Emeritus* of Harvard Divinity School, wrote: "Faithful priestly son of the Russian Orthodox Church . . . , Fr. Georges Florovsky – with a career-long involvement in the ecumenical dialogue – is today the most articulate, trenchant and winsome exponent of Orthodox theology and piety in the scholarly world. He is innovative and creative in the sense wholly of being ever prepared to restate the saving truth of Scripture and Tradition in the idiom of our contemporary yearning for the transcendent."

AUTHOR'S PREFACE (1978)

These four volumes on the Eastern Fathers of the fourth century and
the Byzantine fathers from the fifth to eighth centuries were originally
published in 1931 and 1933 in Russian. They contained my lectures
given at the Institute of Orthodox Theology in Paris from 1928 to 1931
and were originally published in Russian more or less in the form in which
they were originally delivered. They therefore lacked exact references
and appropriate footnotes. Another reason for the omission of reference
material in the 1931 and 1933 publications is that the books were orig -
inally published at my own expense and strict economy was therefore
necessary. In fact, their publication was only the result of the generous
cooperation and help of personal friends. These English publications
must be dedicated to their memory. The initiative of the original publi -
cation was taken by Mrs. Elizabeth Skobtsov, who became an Orthodox
nun and was later known under her monastic name of Mother Maria. It
was she who typed the original manuscripts and she who was able to
persuade Mr. Iliia Fondaminsky, at that time one of the editors of the
renowned Russian review, *Sovremennye Zapiski* [*Annales Contem -
poraines*], to assume financial responsibility. Both these friends
perished tragically in German concentration camps. They had been
inspired by the conviction that books in Russian on the Fathers of the
Church were badly needed, not only by theological students, but also by
a much wider circle of those concerned with doctrinal and spiritual
vistas and issues of Eastern Orthodox Tradition. Their expectation was
fully justified: the volumes in Russian rapidly sold out and were warmly
appreciated in the general press.

When I began teaching at the Paris Institute, as Professor of Patro -
logy, I had to face a preliminary methodological problem. The question
of the scope and manner of Patristic studies had been vigorously de -
bated by scholars for a long time. (There is an excellent book by Fr. J.
de Ghellinck, S.J., *Patristique et Moyen Age*, Volume II, 1947, pp. 1-
180). The prevailing tendency was to treat Patrology as a history of
Ancient Christian Literature, and the best modern manuals of Patrology
in the West were written precisely in this manner: Bardenhewer, Cayré,
Tixeront, Quasten, adherents to this school of thought, made only spor -
adic reference to certain points of doctrine but their approach was no
doubt legitimate and useful. However, another cognate discipline came
into existence during the last century, *Dogmengeschichte*, or the
school of the history of doctrine. Here scholars were concerned not so
much with individual writers or thinkers but rather with what can be
defined as the "internal dialectics" of the Christian "mind" and with types
and trends of Christian thought.

In my opinion, these two approaches to the same material must be
combined and correlated. I have tried to do precisely this with the re -
vision of some of the material for the English publications. I have written
some new material on the external history and especially on the
ecumenical councils. But in essence Patrology must be more than a
kind of literary history. It must be treated rather as a history of Christian
doctrine, although the Fathers were first of all *testes veritatis*, wit -
nesses of truth, of the faith. "Theology" is wider and more com -
prehensive than "doctrine." It is a kind of Christian Philosophy. Indeed,
there is an obvious analogy between the study of Patristics and the
study of the history of Philosophy. Historians of Philosophy are as
primarily concerned with individual thinkers as they are interested
ultimately in the dialectics of ideas. The "essence" of philosophy is ex -

hibited in particular systems. Unity of the historical process is assured because of the identity of themes and problems to which both phil - osophers and theologians are committed. I would not claim originality for my method, for it has been used occasionally by others. But I would underline the theological character of Patrology.

These books were written many years ago. At certain points they needed revision or extension. To some extent, this has been done. Re - cent decades have seen the rapid progress of Patristic studies in many directions. We now have better editions of primary sources than we had forty or even thirty years ago. We now have some new texts of prime importance: for example, the Chapters of Evagrius or the new Sermons of St. John Chrysostom. Many excellent monograph studies have been published in recent years. But in spite of this progress I do not think that these books, even without the revisions and additions, have been made obsolete. Based on an independent study of primary sources, these works may still be useful to both students and scholars.

GEORGES FLOROVSKY
SEPTEMBER, 1978

CHAPTER ONE

THE BASIC FEATURES OF THEOLOGY IN THE FOURTH CENTURY

Introductory Background

With the beginning of the fourth century a new epoch opened in the life of the Church. Caesar, the "equal of the apostles," was baptized and in his person the empire accepted Christianity. The Church came out of hiding and offered its solace to the dis - satisfied classical world, a world filled with anxieties, doubts, and temptations. This world brought with it both a great longing, which the Church had to satisfy, and a great pride, which the Church had to subdue. The classical world was reborn and be - came part of the Church but only after a period of confusion and struggle. A spiritual excitement gripped not just ecclesiastical circles but all of society, from the top to the bottom. The calcula - tions of rulers and politicians, personal ambitions, and tribal dis - sensions all found their way into the religious upheaval.

This time of great and victorious triumph was also a time of trial and sorrow for the Church. During this epoch Orthodox believers frequently had to make their way in bonds and fetters, scorned and persecuted, and often reached the end of their path by ac - cepting the crown of martyrdom. The lives of Athanasius and Chrysostom are typical.

It was too early to speak of a definite victory, for the world still re - mained "outside" the Church, and paganism continued to flour - ish immediately beyond the Church's confines. Pagan temples were still open and pagan teachers were still arguing against Christianity. Culture and domestic life were filled with survivals of heathenism and remained pagan. It is not surprising that the monastic movement and the attraction of flight to the desert were so strong. These were motivated by more than a desire for seclu - sion and solitude. The life of a Christian in that world was truly dif - ficult.

The restoration of paganism under Julian cannot be con - sidered fortuitous. On the contrary, it clearly demonstrates that the old world had not yet died. Pagan culture experienced a revival in the fourth and even in the fifth centuries, which cul - minated in Iamblichus and the Athenian school of Neoplatonism. The quarrel about the Altar of Victory during the reign of Gratian shows that the same thing was happening in the West. During the collision between the two worlds of Hellenism and Christianity the Church never rejected classical culture but the Hellenes refused to accept the Church. A similar situation had existed earlier during the era of the Gnostic school of Plotinus and Por - phyry, when Porphyry had resolutely opposed Christianity. (We know of his objections from the refutations of Macarius of Magnesia). Now the resistance became even stronger. The sig - nificance of this struggle is not in the external or political events of the period. The internal struggle was even more painful and more tragic because every Hellene had to experience and overcome this division within himself. Some became reconciled too early. Synesius of Ptolemais (also known as Synesius of Cyrene) is typical in this respect, for, although he was made a bishop, he remained a Neoplatonist and maintained his faith in dreams and divination. The spiritual regeneration of classical society began in the fourth century when the majority of men were still living in a spiritual environment made up of two distinct cultures. The spiritual temperament of classical man was trans - formed very slowly and this process was not completed until much later when a new Byzantine culture was born. The fourth century is significant as a time of transition. It was the end of a previous age, not the beginning of a new period.

The whole of the fourth century was an era of continuous theological debate, which primarily centered around the Church's struggle against Arianism. The Arian movement was not homo - geneous and it is necessary to distinguish the problem of the origin of Arius' teaching from the reasons for the positive response which his theology drew from different sides. There is good cause for connecting Arius with Lucian of Antioch and even with Paul of Samosata. Alexander of Alexandria pointed to this from the very beginning: "(His ideas were) were fermented by the impious Lucian." This does not mean that Arius simply borrowed his teaching from Lucian. There is no foundation for denying Arius' independence as a theologian.

Lucian of Antioch

Little is known about Lucian and his image has a mysterious duality. Apparently he was connected with Paul of Samosata and he lived under interdiction for many years "during the age of the three bishops." He died as a martyr, however, and his name was entered in the Church canons. He was an outstanding Biblical scholar and continued the work on the correction of the Greek Biblical text which had been begun by Origen. For this he used a Hebrew text, possibly the Syrian *Peshitta*, which he studied in Edessa with a certain Macarius. It is Lucian's recension of the

Septuagint which received general recognition in the churches of Asia Minor and in the environs of Constantinople.

Lucian as an exegete was a resolute opponent of Origen. He tried to replace the allegorical interpretation of the Alexandrian school with a more direct and literal "historical-grammatical" meth - od. More than anything else it was disagreement about exe - getical methodology which divided the Antiochene and Alex - andrian theologians. Just like the classical interpreters of ancient texts, they belonged to completely different schools of philol - ogy. At the same time, Lucian in his theological views was not very far from Origen. In this respect it is significant that many of his students were Origenists, which is true of Arius himself. The Arians frequently referred to Origen and to Dionysius of Alex - andria because, while they were opposed to Origen in their exegesis, they remained Origenists in their theology.

Origen's System and Arianism

Thus, the problems of Arian theology can be understood only in terms of the premises of Origen's system. Origen's fear of Modalism can also be discerned among Arian theologians. Since the Arian movement was possible only on the foundation of Origenist theology, the struggle against Arianism was actually a struggle against Origenism. However, the teacher's name was rarely mentioned in this controversy because the opponents of Arianism, especially Alexander, were Origenists themselves. Ori - gen was not an Arian but it is easy to see how the Arians reached their conclusions not merely from misunderstandings of his teachings but from his actual premises. Historically, therefore, the defeat of Arianism proved at the same time to be a defeat of Origenism, at least in trinitarian theology.

At that time the system of Origen as a whole had not yet been subjected to debate and the general question of its validity was raised only at the very end of the century. Origen's trinitarian doctrine was silently renounced, and even such a consistent Origenist as Didymus was completely free from Origen's in - fluence in his dogma of the Trinity. He was even further from Origen than Athanasius. Thus, Origenism was not only rejected but overcome, and this is the positive contribution which the Arian controversy made to theology.

Arius bases his theology on the conception of God as a perfect unity and a self-enclosed monad. For him this Divine monad is God the Father, and everything else in existence is alien to God in its essence. The absolute nature of the Divine Being makes it impossible for God to give or endow His essence to anyone else. Therefore, the Word, the Logos, the Son of God, as an hypo -

stasis and as one who has actual existence, is unconditionally and completely alien and unlike the Father. He receives His Being from the Father and by the will of the Father, just as all other creatures do, and He comes into being as a mediator for the sake of the creation of the world. Thus there exists a certain "interval" between the Father and the Son, and the Son is not coeternal with the Father. If He were, there would be two "eternals" or two ultimate principles, and the truth of monotheism would be abrogated.

In other words, "there was a then, when the Son did not exist." He did not exist, but He came into being and had an origin. This means that the Son comes into being "out of things that do not exist" (ἐξ οὐκ ὄντων). He is a creature, something which is generated and therefore like all generated things He has a "mutable" nature. He is endowed with Divine Glory in advance, from outside, "by grace" and by God's foreknowledge of the future.

Such are the general features of the teaching of Arius, as much as we are able to judge by the fragments of his compositions which have survived and by the evidence of his contemporaries. His doctrine is basically a rejection of the Divine Trinity. For Arius the Trinity is something derived and generated. It has an origin and its members are separated by "temporal intervals" (διάστημα). Its hypostases are not coeternal and are not similar but alien to each other. "They are eternally dissimilar." It is a type of dimin- ishing Trinity, a union or, in the words of St. Gregory the Theo- logian, an "association" of three essences which are not alike. It is a union of three hypostases which are united by essence. It is three essences and three coexisting wills which are distin- guished by essence.

In his theology Arius is a strict monotheist, almost a Judaizer, and for him a Trinity cannot be a single God. There is a one and only God, and that is the Father. The Son and the Spirit are the highest and first-born creatures who are mediators in the creation of the world. In this doctrine Arius approaches Paul of Samosata and the Dynamic Monarchians, but he is even closer to Philo. It is not difficult to understand why his arguments found supporters among the Alexandrians and Origenists.

The connection between Arius' dogma and the problems of time and the creation of the world are immediately evident. Creation implies origination. That which is created is that which has a beginning, which exists not from itself or through itself, but from another. It is that which does not exist before it comes into being. In Arius' system "creation" is indistinguishable from "gen- eration" because for him both entail origination, which in his understanding can only take place in time.

This difficulty arises because of the ambiguity of the conception of "origination." That which is generated has an origin, a reason for its being outside of and before itself. But "origin" can have two meanings: it can be the cause or source of being, or else it can be a moment in time. For Arius both meanings coincide. For him "eternity" or timelessness means ontological primacy, and therefore he refuses to grant that the existence of the Son is "without beginning" or eternal. This would be a denial of His "generation" and the fact that He is begotten, and, if this were not true, then the *Logos* or Word would be a second and independent God. If the Word is from the Father, then He must have been begotten. Otherwise, He is not from the Father. From tradition Arius knows that the Word is the God of revelation and the most immediate cause of creation. But a creature is subject to change, since it is temporal, and this gives him another reason to connect the existence of the Word with time.

It thus seems that Arius was in sharp disagreement with Origen. In Origen's doctrine the generation of the Word is eternal and this proves that the Divine Being is immutable. However, Origen inferred too much from this. Because he believed that origination is incompatible with the immutability of God, he posited that the creation of the world is also eternal. In his system the generation of the Son and the creation of the world are united by the concept of origination, and to protect the immutability of God Origen essentially denied that any origination ever takes place. There is nothing in existence about which he was willing to say "there was a then, when it did not exist."

In this way Origen concluded that all existence is eternal and that everything coexists with God, a dogma which is similar to Aristotle's doctrine of the eternity of the world. For Origen the world was not a created thing. This conclusion was unacceptable to his followers who, although they rejected his conclusions, did not deny his premises. Arius also reasoned in this way. He denied that the world is eternal, and the entire emphasis of his system is in affirming the temporal character of everything which is generated or which has the "origin" of its being in another. However, from this he concluded that the Son also is generated in time. Arius differed from Origen in his conclusions but agreed with him in his premises. Within the bounds of Origen's system there was an inescapable dilemma: it was necessary to either admit the eternity of the world or to reject the eternal generation of the Son. This dilemma could be avoided only by denying Origen's premises. For this reason Arius' system attracted those disciples of Origen who did not accept his idea of an eternal world.

Eusebius of Caesarea

Against this background the theology of Eusebius of Caesarea becomes clearer. Eusebius is far from agreeing with Arius on everything and he flatly rejects Arius' basic idea about the "generation" of the Son from "things that do not exist." At the same time, however, he denies that the Son is "coeternal" with the Father. As the cause or source of origin of the Son, the Father precedes Him, although not in time. Even before His actual generation the Son exists "in the Father," but "in potential" alone. Only later is He generated by and from the will of the Father as a real and independent hypostasis, and even as a "second essence" ["*vtoraia sushchnost'*] (or "second being" ["*vtoroe suschestvo*"]) with the Father.

In the doctrine of Eusebius the Son in His objective reality is turned toward the world, and in this sense He is the "first-born of all creation." He is the demiurge and the creator of all visible and invisible beings, the first among which is the Spirit of the Comforter. Since He is a direct creation of the Father, the Son is inherent in Him but since He is generated from the Father, He is less than the Father and is an "intermediate" force between the Father and the world. He is the "second God" but not the first, in spite of all His honor from the Divinity. Although He is "not like other creatures," He is still a creature.

Like Arius, Eusebius is essentially dealing with a problem of cosmology, not theology. He continually refers to "generation," and he almost identifies the existence of the Son "in His own hypostasis" with the existence of the world. In order not to efface the boundary between God and the world, he maintains a sharp separation between the Son and the Father: "the existence of the Son is not necessary for the completeness of the being and the divinity of the Father." For Eusebius the existence of the Son is connected with time because the existence of the world is also temporal. He does make a distinction between the generation of the Son and the creation of the world, $\gamma\acute{\epsilon}\nu\epsilon\sigma\iota\varsigma$ and $\delta\eta\mu\iota\upsilon\rho\gamma\acute{\iota}\alpha$. but even this does not completely resolve the problem.

The Divine "generation" and its relation to time were the main subjects of debate in the Arian controversies. In a certain sense both Arianism and Origenism can be called heresies about time because this was the basic doctrine on which both systems were built.

Alexander of Alexandria

During the period of the Arian controversies the Church was faced with problems of a philosophical nature and, in answering the heretics, theologians developed systems of philosophical conceptions and terminology. In the words of the Church his - torian Socrates, Alexander of Alexandria "theologized like a philosopher" in his refutation of Arianism. Alexander's theology is mainly concerned with the problem of time. His basic doctrine is also that the Divine is immutable and unchanging, and for this reason he stresses the complete indivisibility of the Father and the Son. "God has always existed and the Son has always existed; the Son and the Father are together; the Son coexists with God." ἅμα and ἀεί : this definition excludes the idea of gradation within the Trinity. "The Father does not precede the Son by the slightest instant." He has always and unchangingly been the Father of His Son. The Son is generated "absolutely from the Father" and is His "indistinguishable Image." He is completely and exactly the Image of the Father and is perfectly similar to Him in everything. It is only "unoriginateness" which is the attribute and "personal property" of the Father alone and which does not extend to the Son. But since the Son's gen - eration is eternal, this does not abrogate the complete inherence of the Son in the Father.

Alexander was also an Origenist, but he developed different aspects of Origen's system. He ignored cosmological problems and tried to understand and explain the being of the Son as an internal event within the Divinity, and not as a moment or act of "generation." From his theological creed it is clear that the prob - lem of time and eternity was connected with his doctrine on the being and essence of God. This was tremendously significant at the beginning of the Church's struggle against Arianism. The anathemas appended to the Nicene Creed reject all definitions of the Divinity which suggest any limitation in relation to time, such as "there was a then, when He did not exist," or "(He has being) out of things which do not exist," or which involve the concepts of mutability or a created nature. The Nicene Creed also rejects the idea of origination "from another essence or hypostasis." Socrates reports that Ossius (Hosius) of Cordova, who was sent by the emperor to Egypt to settle the Arian conflict, was the first to raise the question of essence and hypostasis, making these the subject of a new controversy.

'Ομοούσιος and ἐκ τῆς οὐσίας

The fathers at the Council of Nicaea refuted the doctrine of
Arius by means of philosophical terminology and argumentation.
The entire meaning of the Nicene acts, the "dogma of the 318
holy fathers," can be expressed in two words: ὁμοούσιος and ἐκ
τῆς οὐσίας, "of one essence" and "from the essence." The
teaching authority of the Church determined the use of these ex -
pressions. According to Eusebius of Caesarea these terms were
subjected to "careful analysis" at the council: "Questions and
answers were given on this subject and the meaning of the
words was thoroughly examined." It is possible that the term "of
one essence" was suggested at the council by Ossius who, in
the words of Athanasius, "set forth our faith at Nicaea." If
Philostorgius is to be believed, Alexander and Ossius decided to
concentrate on the word ὁμοούσιος while still travelling to Nicaea.

In the West this term, or rather its Latin analogue, was a
common expression. Tertullian used it in his trinitarian theology in
the definition *tres unius substantiae*. In Greek this word had to be
translated as *homoousios*. Novatian also spoke about "one
substance" and "a common substance" (*communio substantiae
ad Patrem*)" in the Trinity. Dionysius of Rome reproved Dionysius
of Alexandria for his failure to use the term "of one substance."
This was remembered in Alexandria and was later mentioned by
Athanasius: "The ancient bishops, who lived almost 130 years
ago, the bishop of great Rome and the bishop of our city,
condemned in writing those who asserted that the Son is a
creature and not of one essence or substance with the Father."
Although they were not found in Scripture, these expressions
did occur in Church usage, and Athanasius made it clear that the
Nicene fathers borrowed them "from ancient times, from their
predecessors," "having witness to this from the fathers." How -
ever, the Latin term did not fully coincide with the Greek, and
unius substantiae did not protect Tertullian from subordination -
ism. In the East the term "of one essence or substance" had long
been familiar but it was not satisfactory to the fathers and had
been condemned at previous councils.

This expression appeared in philosophical literature only in -
frequently. Aristotle spoke about the consubstantiality of the
stars among themselves. Porphyry speculated as to whether the
souls of animals are consubstantial with the souls of men. For him
"consubstantiality" meant both "of one matter" and "of one kind."
Plotinus used the word in the same meaning. The term was first
introduced into religious usage by the Gnostics and Valentinians
to designate the unity and community among aeons. In their

conception that which is of one essence or substance is generated within the bounds of one nature. It seems that this term entered the language of the Church primarily for the translation of Gnostic texts. As used by the Gnostics, it clearly entailed emanation, and this explains the negative or at least cautious attitude that Origen had toward the expressions "from the essence of the Father" and "of one essence." It seemed to him that their meaning was too specifically material and that they introduced into the Divine Being the idea of division, "similar to that which is understood of pregnant women." Dionysius of Alexandria also avoided this word, probably for the same reasons. For the later defenders of *homoiousia*, "consub - stantiality" designated a material union, or uninterrupted matter. Like Origen, they considered the term unsuitable for theology.

It is not entirely clear why the use of the expression "of one essence" was rejected and condemned at the Council of Antioch in 269, which was convened against Paul of Samosata. Athan - asius and Hilary of Poitiers offer different explanations. Probably Hilary is more accurate, and the term was banned because Paul had imparted a Modalistic meaning to the expression by asserting the complete singleness of the Divinity and the purely nominal distinction of persons. "*Quia per hanc unius substantiae nun- cupationem solitarium atque unicum esse Patrem et Filium praedicabat.*" In Paul's conception "consubstantiality" desig - nated the modalistic unity of the Godhead. This is the way the *homoiousians* explained the Antiochene anathema, and Hilary borrowed their explanation.

Generally speaking, the word "consubstantial" allowed for a variety of interpretations, and from the history of the dogmatic controversies of the fourth century we know that it called forth great disagreement. In this respect a letter written to Apollinarius of Laodicea and attributed to Basil the Great is typical. Even if this letter is not the work of Basil, it dates to his era and clearly depicts the contemporary state of mind. The author asks about the meaning of the term *homoousios*. Does "consubstantial" des - ignate a "common kind," of which the Father and the Son are "aspects," or does it designate the unity of a preexisting, "cor - poreal" substratum, from which both the Father and the Son are generated through separation?

In his book on the councils Hilary of Poitiers, defending the Nicene Creed, explains that *homoousios* may have, and had been given in the past, an "incorrect significance." He points to three examples or types of false and unorthodox understanding of "consubstantiality." In the first place, "consubstantiality" can be understood in the Monarchian sense as an expression of ab - solute monotheism in such a way that the Father and Son differ only in name and as modes of the same person. In the second place, "consubstantiality" can be interpreted to mean the "dis - tribution" of a single Divinity between the Father and the Son as co-heirs, or in the manner of two torches from a single flame. Finally, the concept of "consubstantiality" can be understood as a part of the Father or as something "cut off" from the Father, in the same way that a single "thing" is divided and split up into two things, or between them. It must be noted that even Tertullian's dogma of the Son as a derivation of the Father, as something which has been separated ("*derivatio*" or "*portio*"), is not entirely free from this.

All these inexact shades of meaning in the conception of "consubstantiality" had to be isolated, refuted, and excluded from theological usage. At the Council of Nicaea the strictly literal Arians drew attention to just these nuances. "To call someone consubstantial" meant, in their view, "to indicate the fact that he is generated from another, either by grafting, like a plant from a root, or by flowing out, like children from fathers, or by separation, like two or three golden vessels." It seems that by "consub - stantiality" they understood co-materiality.

All of this explains the cautious attitude which contemporary theologians took toward the Nicene doctrine. It needed to be elucidated and interpreted, and this was possible only within the structure of an integral system of religious instruction. Only then could its exact meaning be explained and protected from unor - thodox interpretation. In order to achieve this it was first of all nec - essary to define the concept of essence or substance, *ousia*.

In classical philosophy this word had different meanings for different schools. In Platonism and Neoplatonism "essence" meant that which is general or common. For the Stoics also the term "substance" (*substantia*) designated a common, unqualified substratum, or matter in general, in opposition to the forms which distinguish it. For Aristotle and the Aristotelians, on the other hand, *ousia* meant primarily individual and indivisible existence, an individual and single thing in the fulness of its immutable attributes, πρώτη οὐσία. Only in a secondary sense was a common kind, uniting and comprehending individual existences, called an essence. This was what Aristotle called δευτέρα οὐσία or "second essence." However, for Aristotle himself *ousia* did not have an exactly defined significance, and occasionally in his usage it coincides with the concept of existence, "that which is underlying." Also, essence for Aristotle was connected with the idea of origin, of coming into being, γέννεσις. By the fourth century it was this narrow Aristotelian meaning which was widely in use. In this sense οὐσία is not only essence but also being.

Ὑπόστασις

The other term of the Nicene Creed, ὑπόστασις, came into use in philosophy comparatively late, in any event after the age of Aristotle. For a long time this word was used in its literal sense, "that which stands under." It was even then not without a par-ticular significance, since for Aristotle καθ' ὑπόστασιν meant the reality and actuality of a thing, as opposed to its outward ap-pearance. In the *Septuagint hypostasis* was used in various meanings and designated, among other things, "foundation" (foundation of a house, or foundation or base of hope), com-position, and so forth. In the works of Philo *hypostasis* meant, apparently, independence and uniqueness. It signified "es-sence" for St. Paul (*Hebrews* 1:3): "Image of the Father's *hypo-stasis*"). Its significance elsewhere in St. Paul's writings was varied: it meant confidence (*II Corinthians* 9:4; *Hebrews* 11:1), composition, etc.

"*Hypostasis*" was first defined as a term by the Neoplatonists. Plotinus called the forms in which the One reveals itself "*hypo-tases*" and, possibly, distinguished οὐσία as τὸ εἶναι and ὑπό-στασις from τί εἶναι. Porphyry, in any event, maintained such a distinction. It is characteristic that Plotinus considered the term "hypostasis" inappropriate to describe the ultimate principle, as is also the idea of "essence," because the One "is higher than any essence." Apparently for him it implied the act of generation.

At this same time Origen also referred to "three hypostases," as did Dionysius of Alexandria after him. However, "hypostasis" remained indistinct from the concept of essence and this is why the terminology of Dionysius' theology was so disturbing to the Roman theologians. In general it can be said that until the middle of the fourth century "essence" and "hypostasis" were inter-changeable both as ideas and as terms. Jerome said bluntly: "the school of worldly science knew of no other meaning for the word 'hypostasis' than substance." In the anathemas pronounced by the Nicene Council "essence" and "hypostasis" were clearly identical ("from one hypostasis *or* essence"). Athanasius also identified them. However, it should be noted that both of the Greek terms could be expressed in Latin by only one word. Both *ousia* and *hypostasis* were translated as *substantia*.

There remained one major ambiguity in the Nicene Creed. The confession of consubstantiality entailed the complete "identity of essence" of the Father and the Son. Was it possible, then, to speak of the generation of the Son "from the essence of the Father?" This difficulty was later eliminated when "from the es-sence of the Father" was omitted from the Creed of Constantinople. The works of Athanasius make it clear beyond doubt that in the minds of the Nicene fathers there was no contradiction or hesitation. For them the expressions "from the essence" and "of one essence" affirmed from different viewpoints one and the same thing: the true, immutable co-belonging of the Father and Son in an identity of unchanging life which was common to both of them. By opposing the Arian terms "from the desire" or "from the will" with their own definition "from the essence," the Nicene fathers tried to express the immanent and ontological character of the Divine generation as an internal, everlasting and essential condition, rather than an act, of the Divinity.

"From the essence" for them meant "in essence" or "by essence," and excluded the idea of an act of the will from the concept of Divine generation. Generation and "being from the essence" coincided in the Nicene interpretation, and were opposed to the concepts of creation and being as a result of desire or will, which had frequently been linked together. The shortcoming of the Nicene Creed lay elsewhere: there was no common term to name the three which made up the unity of the Godhead. The unity and indivisibility of the Divine Being had been expressed more clearly than the distinctions of the Trinity. The Divine Being was one essence yet three . . . there was a number, but no noun to follow it.

The Nicene and Anti-Nicene Positions

Soon after the council an intense theological debate flared up around the Nicene Creed. The political, social and personal motivations which complicated and exacerbated the passionate argumentation are not of particular interest for the history of dogma. There were enough purely theological reasons for the conflict without these. The manner of expression used in the creed was confusing to many because it was not familiar and seemed to be inexact. By the standards of contemporary usage, it appeared that the language of the Nicene statement did not express with sufficient strength and precision the hypostatic distinctions, especially in relation to the Son as Word. In addition to this, there was the danger of the Marcellian heresy, which Athanasius and the Nicene fathers regarded with perhaps too much tolerance.

The members of the so-called "anti-Nicene opposition" held various doctrinal positions. Numerically predominant among them were the conservative bishops of the East, who refrained from using Nicene terminology in favor of the older, more familiar expressions of Church tradition. They were united by their com - mon fear of Sabellianism. The most active group of opponents were the "Eusebians," as they were called by Athanasius, who remained firm supporters of Origen and his dogma of sub - ordinationism, and openly rejected the language and creed of Nicaea. They were joined by more extreme heretics who had not previously enunciated their views.

According to Socrates, after the bishops had made the term "of one essence" the subject of their discussions and examination, they declared war on each other, and this war "was like a battle at night, because neither side understood why it was abusing the other." Some rejected the expression "of one essence," claim - ing that those who accepted it were guilty of the heresy of Sabellianism and were blasphemers who denied the personal being of the Son of God. Others, defending consubstantiality, considered that their opponents were polytheists, and turned away from them "as from pagans." The anti-Nicene factions feared Sabellianism to such an extent that they became careless with regard to Arianism. They tried to protect themselves with sweeping anathemas that were stated in very general terms, and they attempted to replace the Nicene Creed with a new doctrine. Thus arose what Socrates called "a maze of creeds."

It is enough to point out the basic features of these arguments without going into their finer points. In the first place, the de - liberate rejection of Nicene terminology is immediately apparent in all the creeds written at this time. In the second place, their main purpose was to make clear the doctrine of the distinction and individuality of the different hypostases. The second creed of Antioch (341) contained the expression "three hypostases," which was qualified by the weaker definition "one by agreement."

At the end of this long and confused struggle, which was complicated by deceit, duplicity, treachery, and the military inter - vention of various emperors, it turned out that no creed except the Nicene was capable of expressing and protecting the true and orthodox faith. It was in this sense that St. Athanasius called the Nicene Creed "the expression of the truth." He predicted that the dissent and confusion would not end until the "anti-Nicenes" came to their senses and said: "Let us arise and go to our fathers and say to them, 'We proclaim our anathema on the Arian heresy and recognize the council of Nicaea'."

St. Athanasius clearly saw the danger that was latent in the op - position to the Nicene doctrine. Given the prevalence of Arianism which existed at that time, this opposition, in the form of Sabel - lianism, was a threat to orthodoxy. The older, traditional systems of theology now seemed ambiguous, and a sound, new system could be established only on the basis of the Nicene doctrine of "consubstantiality." The whole structure of theological reasoning had to be rebuilt and regulated by this concept.

The Creation of a New Terminology

It was first of all necessary to present and clarify the premises and doctrines of the Nicene Creed, and this was the task of St. Athanasius. What was left incomplete by him was finished by the great Cappadocians. Their work also culminated in the creation of a new terminology. The differentiation of the concepts of es - sence and hypostasis, and the exact definition of the attributes of the hypostases, gave both completeness and flexibility to the orthodox doctrine of the Trinity.

About 360 the ill-considered and imprudent struggle against the Nicene terminology resulted in the reemergence and apparent victory of extreme Arianism. The symbol of this victory was the so-called Second Formula of Sirmium of 357, which Hilary referred to as "the blasphemy of Ossius and Potamius." This was a daring attempt to end the discussion of the problem by declaring that it had in fact been decided. The purpose of this "Arian treachery," which was inspired not by sincere doctrinal motives but by tactical considerations, was to discredit the Nicene formulations on the grounds that they were not found in Scripture, that they were "incomprehensible to the people," and that the Nicene doctrines in general exceeded the measure of human knowledge and understanding. Catholic teaching was limited to the confession of "two persons" (not two Gods), of which the Father was greater in honor, dignity, and divinity by the very name of Father, while the Son was subordinate to Him together with everything over which the Father had given Him dominion.

Aëtius and Eunomius

However, this attempt to silence the argument proved fruitless. The controversy soon burst out again with new force. The prop - agation of "*Anomoeanism*" ("unlikeness") began in 356 in Alex - andria, where Aëtius had established a circle of disciples. Soon he moved on to Antioch, where his preaching was very suc - cessful and was furthered by his pupil Eunomius.

According to Sozomen, Aëtius was "strong in the art of deduction and experienced in logomachy." "From morning until night he sat over his studies," wrote Epiphanius, "trying to define God by means of geometry and figures." Aëtius turned dog - matics into a dialectical game and he boasted that he "knew God better than he knew himself."

Eunomius gave logical definition to the dialectics of Aëtius. His main doctrine is that the Father is an "eternally unique God," Who "does not transform Himself from one essence into three hypostases" and Who "does not have a partner in His Divinity." His basic and "essential" positive definition of God is that He is unoriginate, *ἀγεννησία*. Therefore the essence of God cannot be endowed to anyone else. The "consubstantial" generation of the Son, His generation "from the essence of the Father," is impossible, since this would entail the division or breaking down of that which is simple and immutable. For this same reason a trinity of hypostases, which would abrogate the singleness and uniqueness of God, is inconceivable. Therefore, the Son is "of another essence" and "not similar" to the Father because any comparison or comparability is incommensurate with the absolute uniqueness of the Father, Who is superior to everything. The Son is a creature and does not exist prior to His origination.

For Eunomius the ideas of "generation" and "creation" are identical. The Son is distinct from all other creatures in that He is the *immediate* creation of the Father, while everything else, including the Holy Spirit, is created indirectly, *through* the Son. Therefore, the Son is similar to the Father with a "primary simi - larity," in the same way that a completed work bears the reflection of the artist. He is the image or stamp of the energy and will of the Almighty.

Homoiousia and the Homoiousians

When the opponents of the Nicene Creed were confronted with the resurgence of Arianism, the inadequacy of their ir - resolute pronouncements was immediately evident. The anti-Nicenes who had remained orthodox became alarmed and their anxiety was expressed first of all by the movement of the so-called "*homoiousians*," which was concentrated around St. Basil of Ancyra. The teaching of the *homoiousians* was first set forth at the Council of Ancyra in 358 when the fathers stated that they "wanted to express the creed of the Catholic Church as thor - oughly as possible," hoping at the same time to introduce into this explanation "something of their own."

This new element "of their own" was the concept of the kinship or the unity by relation, *γνησία*, of the Only Begotten Son and the Father. This was a milder form of consubstantiality. The main concern of the fathers of Ancyra was not to emphasize the separateness and distinction of the persons but to make clear their commonness and unity. By stressing the mystery of the Sonship, St. Basil of Ancyra (who was apparently the sole author of the doctrinal "Epistle" of the council) distinguished the "gen - erating energy" of the Father from His "creating energy." In the act of generation not only the will and power of the Father are revealed, but his "essence" also is made manifest. What is essential in generation is *likeness by essence*. Being a father means being the father "of a like essence."

St. Basil of Ancyra also tried to define the conception of "hy - postasis" and the individuality of the Divine Persons. He writes that it is necessary to consider the Son "as an independent 'hypostasis', different from the Father." As they later explained, in using the word "hypostasis," as well as the word "person," the *homoiousian* theologians wanted to express the "independently and actually existing properties" of the Father, Son and Spirit, and also to avoid Sabellian Modalism in doing so. Although they were not always precise, they tried to maintain a distinction between the concepts of "essence" and "hypostasis," which was understood as the individual existence of an essence. The "individuality" of the Second Person is His Sonship and His gen - eration from the Father. The unity of the Persons was designated by the common term "Spirit." This theological system on the whole was a successful refutation of Arianism, although the *homoiousians* weakened its impact by their anathema against the term "consubstantiality," which in their understanding implied the identity of the Father and the Son.

The Councils at Sirmium and Ancyra

The *Anomoeans* and the supporters of the *homoiousian* doc - trine (The Third Formula of Sirmium of 358) met with hostility and opposition. The *homoiousians* were forced to replace the expression "of like essence," ὁμοιούσιος, with the ambiguous "like in everything," ὅμοις κατὰ πάντα. Although he signed the so-called "Dated Creed," St. Basil of Ancyra insisted on spec - ifying what he understood by "like in everything": "That is, not only by desire, but by hypostasis and essence." He ana - thematized those who limited this likeness "to any one thing." This "Dated Creed" (the Fourth Formula of Sirmium of 359) was largely a repetition of previous doctrinal statements, but it also contained a particular prohibition against the use of the term "essence" in defining God. The authors of the creed justified themselves by claiming that this expression was not found in Scripture and that it could lead to error among the faithful. Later at the council of Constantinople of 361, the explanatory κατὰ πάντα, "in everything," was omitted from the new creed, and the generation of the Son was declared inaccessible to human understanding. The prohibition against the term *ousia* was re - peated, and a new prohibition against *hypostasis* was added. Thus, from the testimony of unorthodox groups we learn that those who were orthodox deviated from the *homoiousian* formulas. This was the opinion of the supporters of the Nicene Creed.

St. Hilary of Poitiers, who was exiled to the East for his role in the struggle against Arianism in Gaul, saw in the council of Ancyra and the *homoiousian* doctrine a light in the darkness and a ray of hope. In his interpretation, "of like essence"meant the same as the Nicene term "of one essence," that is, unity of nature, but not person. In his writings about the councils, St. Athanasius admitted that "it is not necessary to treat people like Basil (of Ancyra) as enemies. They should be considered as brothers who differ from us by one word alone but who think the same as we do." Although by itself the concept of "like essence" is vague and inadequate, when qualified by the affirmation of generation "from the essence," it is equal to "consubstantiality" in the Nicene sense. The expression "like in everything" is found in the writings of Alexander, and Athanasius himself had earlier used it to elucidate "consubstantiality."

The Council of Alexandria (362)

The term "of like essence" was used in spite of the fact that as a philological device it was awkward, for, as Aristotle had demon - strated, "likeness" refers to the "qualities" or properties of ob - jects, not to their "essence." In dealing with a unity of essence it is necessary to speak about identity and not likeness. This had been pointed out by Athanasius. But here the meaning of "like essence" was related to "one essence" in the way that a recog - nition of an "identical essence" is a recognition of "one es - sence." In the first case it is the separateness of the compared elements which is being emphasized. After the council of Alexandria of 362, which was presided by St. Athanasius, the question was again raised as to the meaning of the concepts *ousia* and *hypostasis*. After heated argument it was recognized that the same orthodox truth is professed by those who speak about "one hypostasis" in the sense of a "single essence" and the "identity of nature," and those who teach "three hypostases" with "one ultimate principle," in order to express the knowledge of the Trinity "not only in name, but as truly existing and enduring."

After the Alexandrian council the expressions "of one essence" and "from the essence of the Father" entered the theological usage of many of the eastern churches: for example, in Laodicea, Antioch, Cappadocia. At the same time, the dis - tinction of the concepts and terms *ousia* and *hypostasis* as something general and something individual was affirmed. The historical and doctrinal achievement of the great Cappadocians consists in their justification and propagation of this new usage. They were "the trinity which glorified the Trinity." The formula "one essence and three hypostases, μία οὐσια, τρεῖs ὑποσ- τάσεις, has been maintained in general Church usage since their time.

Unexpectedly, much time and labor was required to prove to the West the validity of this formula and its identity with the time-honored western expression *tres personae*. In the words of St. Gregory the Theologian, "because of the poverty of their lan - guage and its lack of designations, the Westerners cannot distinguish between essence and hypostasis." Both were ex - pressed in Latin as *substantia*. In the confession of three hypostases Westerners seemed to detect tritheism, a recog - nition of three substances or three gods.

The Classical Languages' Lack of Terminology for the Mystery of Personal Being

A dangerous ambiguity remained in the formulation "three persons," in both Latin and Greek, for the Easterners and even partially for St. Basil the Great. *The classical world did not know the mystery of personal being* and in the classical languages there was no word which exactly designated individual person - ality. The Greek πρόσωπον meant mask rather than person and, moreover, it was tainted through its association with Sabellianism. Therefore, St. Basil the Great considered that it was inadequate and dangerous to speak of "three persons" and not of "three hypostases." "Person" was too weak, as was also the Latin *per - sona*.

Around 370 St. Jerome came under suspicion in Antioch for his refusal to confess "three hypostases." He avoided the new term of "three substances" and confessed instead one sub - stance and three *persons*. Only after the work of St. Gregory the Theologian, who identified the concepts of hypostasis and person, and after the Second Ecumenical Council was an agreement finally reached between the East and West about theological terminology. But by the fifth century St. Augustine was objecting to Cappadocian theology and searching for new paths.

The theological movement of the fourth century had a Christological character. The focus of Church thought was the dual image of Christ as the God-man and Word Incarnate. The consubstantiality of the Son-Word with the Father meant the confession of the completeness of the Divine nature in Christ, which was necessary for the understanding of the Incarnation as the basis for man's salvation. The correlation of these dogmas was fully and clearly developed in the theological system of St. Athanasius. The denial of consubstantiality would invalidate the Redemption, which is based on the true union between creation and God. It was from this point of view that the doctrine of the Pneumatomachi, who detracted from or denied the consub - stantiality and complete Divinity of the Holy Spirit, was debated and rejected. Since the Spirit is the principle and power which sanctifies and deifies creation, the sanctification which He brings is of no avail if He is not truly God. This movement also had its source in Arianism.

The doctrine of the Holy Spirit became the subject of debate in 350. This dogma was first examined in the works of St. Athanasius and later in the resolutions of the council of Alexandria of 362. It was set forth in its entirety in the writings of the Cappadocians, especially St. Gregory the Theologian. The elaboration of the doctrine of the Divinity of the Word made a clear understanding of the significance of the Incarnation indispensable, but the problem of the manner in which the Divine and human were united in Christ was not immediately raised. This dogma was not developed until the Creed of Chalcedon in 451, and more than two centuries of theological activity were still necessary before it was completely accepted.

Apollinarius of Laodicea

The Christological debate had begun in the fourth century in connection with the heretical doctrine of Apollinarius of Lao - dicea. Of the "countless" works of Apollinarius only a few have been preserved. Among these are a series of fragments and citations which have been taken from writings denouncing him, and several of his compositions have survived under the names of other writers, including Gregory Thaumaturgus and Pope Julian.

In the first years of his activity Apollinarius was a zealous de - fender of the Nicene resolutions. But even before 362 he had begun to express his own Christological views, apparently in order to counteract the teaching of Diodore of Tarsus, who at that time was the leader of the Antiochene school. Apollinarius tried to define the conditions in which the Incarnate Word could be recognized as a complete union of Divine and human natures within the person of Christ. Since he did not distinguish between "nature" and "hypostasis," Apollinarius saw in Christ not only a single person and hypostasis but also a single nature. "God and flesh made up a single nature, complex and composite." For Apollinarius, unity of person is possible only in conjunction with unity of nature. A "complete unity" cannot be formed "from two complete entities."

If God was united with a complete man, who consists of a spirit or intellect, soul, and body, then an irreconcilable duality would be formed. In the conception of Apollinarius, if the Word as-sumed a human intellect, which has the properties of freedom and self-determination, then no true union would take place, for there would remain two center points, two ultimate principles. Redemption, which is the goal of the Incarnation, would not be achieved because it would be a man who died and not God as man. Furthermore, a human intellect, in maintaining its freedom and self-direction, would not be able to overcome sin within the soul. This is possible only for the Divine Intellect.

With this in mind, Apollinarius denied the presence of the complete triad of human qualities in the Incarnate Word. He as-serted that Christ did not assume a human "intellect," but that this was replaced by the Word, which was united with an animate body. Christ became flesh, but He did not become man. Apol-linarius held that the animate body of Christ "coexisted" and indivisibly "grew together with" the Word, Who became the principle of action in it, and thus took on a new manner of existence "in the unity of a complex incarnate Divine nature," $\mu i\alpha$ $\phi \acute{v}\sigma\iota s$ $\tau o\tilde{v}$ $\Theta\epsilon o\tilde{v}$ $\lambda \acute{o}\gamma o\upsilon$ $\sigma\epsilon\sigma\alpha\rho\kappa\omega\mu\acute{\epsilon}\nu\eta$.

Apollinarius had many followers and the struggle against his teaching began at the Alexandrian council of 362. About 370 a two volume treatise against Apollinarius was written by an un-known author and included among the works of St. Athanasius. At this same time Apollinarius was denounced by St. Basil and, after a series of condemnations by various Church councils, Apollinarianism was officially rejected at the Second Ecumenical Council. In order to oppose him, the fathers of the fourth century, in particular St. Gregory of Nyssa and St. Gregory the Theologian, developed the orthodox doctrine of the unity of two natures in one hypostasis. It is the completeness of the human nature in Christ that makes salvation possible. Christ is "one from two."

All of this prepared the way for the Creed of Chalcedon. *Once again the main problem was terminology.* The concepts of "nature," "person," and "hypostasis" had to be distinguished and the nature of "the union of God and man" had to be precisely defined. In the fourth century this theological work was just beginning. At the same time in Antioch an extreme position was being developed in opposition to Apollinarianism by Diodore of Tarsus and Theodore of Mopsuestia, who were later regarded as the precursors of Nestorianism.

The Importance of the Concern for Terminology

These theological arguments developed the consciousness of the faithful and made it strong. The apostolic tradition was elaborated and recognized as the highest form of wisdom and philosophy, as the reason of truth and the truth of reason. Through both speculation and the assimilation of experience, modes of thought were transformed and a new system of concepts was developed. The Church fathers had good reason for devoting so much attention to *problems of terminology* . They were trying to find and establish words that would be adequate to their conceptions of God and which would precisely express, and thus protect, the truths of their faith. *Their concern for termin - ology was not excessive. A word gives outer form to a thought and verbal precision is necessary for the full expression of intellectual conception.* The patristic theologians tried to form - ulate their creeds with clarity because they hoped to establish the living traditions of the Church by expressing them in a versatile system of theology. This task was not easily fulfilled and theological speculation in the patristic age developed in many different directions. But all coincided in their basic principles and all were united by the common experience of the Church. "That is the mystery of the Church, that is the tradition of the fathers."

CHAPTER TWO

ST. ATHANASIUS OF ALEXANDRIA

I
LIFE

St. Athanasius was born into a Greek Christian family in Alexandria at the end of the third century, probably in 295. During his
youth he witnessed the persecutions which took place under
Diocletian. In the words of St. Gregory the Theologian, he spent
"little time" in getting a general education or in studying the
secular sciences but he had some knowledge of classical philosophy and of Neoplatonism in particular. He gave most of his
attention to the study of Scripture, which he knew extremely well.
Possibly he studied at the Catechetical School in Alexandria.

St. Athanasius was noticed by Alexander, bishop of Alexandria, when still very young. He lived in Alexander's home and
was instructed in grammar and rhetoric under his guidance. St.
Athanasius was appointed deacon and became secretary to the
bishop not long before the beginning of the Arian controversy.
He accompanied Alexander to Nicaea where he "boldly rose up
against the impiety of the Arians." Alexander died soon after the
council. Apparently he had designated St. Athanasius as his successor. At the Alexandrian council of 339 it was stated that "all
the multitude of inhabitants, everyone belonging to the Catholic
Church, had gathered together and unanimously, as if in one
body, cried out demanding Athanasius as bishop of the Church.
Throughout the land they prayed to Christ for this for many days
and many nights." In 328 St. Athanasius was consecrated bishop
of Alexandria at a large gathering of prelates.

St. Athanasius was persecuted throughout his administration.
He spent more than 15 of his 47 years as bishop in exile and banishment. The Arians and Meletians responded to his elevation
with hostility and slander and the Eusebians saw him as the main
obstacle to their attempts at compromise. Athanasius cleared
himself of all the accusations brought against him at the council of
Tyre in 335 but his enemies managed to convince Constantine
that he was responsible for the dissension. The emperor ordered
Athanasius to leave Egypt for the West and sent him to Trier, but
he did not give permission for anyone to succeed him to the
Alexandrian see. Athanasius was received at Trier with honor and
love. During his short stay he exerted great influence on

ecclesiastical circles and he was long remembered with veneration. After the death of Constantine in 337 Athanasius and other exiles received permission to return to Alexandria, where he was greeted with popular rejoicing.

However, the intrigue against St. Athanasius was immediately resumed. Eusebius accused him of having returned to his see illegally, since his deposition by the council at Tyre had not been overturned by a new council. An Arian presbyter Pistus, who had been made bishop by Secundus of Ptolemais, also an Arian, was sent to take his place, but he was anathematized by the Egyptian bishops.

In spite of the unanimous defense which St. Athanasius re - ceived at the council of Alexandria in 339, at the council of Antioch in 340 he was again deposed, and a Cappadocian named Gregory was installed in the Alexandrian see. Gregory and his armed supporters rushed to Alexandria and seized the churches after much bloodshed. Athanasius considered it necessary to leave Egypt and went to Rome, where a local council cleared him of the accusations made against him and received him into their community. Pope Julius also interceded on his behalf. Roman supporters of monasticism, who were attracted by the renown of the Egyptian anchorites, gathered around Athanasius. In 343 he attended the council of Sardica. In 345 Constantius invited him to come back to Egypt, and in 346 Athanasius returned to Alexandria.

The Arian controversy broke out again toward the middle of 350, and St. Athanasius was deposed at the councils in Arles (353) and Milan (355). At the beginning of 356 the military com - mander Sirian was sent to Alexandria with orders to seize Athanasius, but Athanasius went into hiding and withdrew into the desert. The see of Alexandria was usurped by a new bishop, George, who subjected the orthodox to cruel persecution. Alex - andria temporarily became the center of Arianism, and Aëtius and Eunomius began their preaching at this time.

During this period Athanasius hid in the desert among the hermits in complete seclusion. It was at this time that he wrote and circulated his most important denunciatory and apologetic works. His enemies continued to look for him, but he was not found. Athanasius was not able to return from this exile until the reign of Julian in 361, but again for only a short time. During the few months of his tenure in Alexandria he succeeded in calling and leading a large council in 362, which made important defin - itions of doctrine.

At the end of 362 Athanasius was again exiled. He went to upper Egypt and stayed there until the death of Julian. After a preliminary meeting in Antioch with the new emperor, Jovian, Athanasius returned to Alexandria in 364. He again had to leave in 365 when Valens ordered the banishment of everyone who had been exiled under Constantius and returned under Julian. In four months this order was revoked by popular demand and Athanasius spent the rest of his days in Alexandria, occupied with literary and pastoral affairs. He died on May 2/3, 373, having ordained his successor, Bishop Peter, shortly before his death.

II
WORKS

Oratio contra Gentes and Oratio de Incarnatione

Only two of Athanasius' apologetic works date from the early years of his life: *Oratio contra gentes* [*Discourse against the Pagans* (λόγος κατὰ ἑλλήνων)] and *Oratio de incarnatione Verbi* [*Discourse on the Incarnation of the Word* (λόγος περὶ τῆς ἐνανθρωπήσεως)]. They were probably written c. 317-319. There is no trace in these two works of the Arian controversy or of Nicene theology. These are interconnected by theme and con-tent and Jerome united them with the common title *Adversum gentes duo libri* [*Two Books against the Pagans*]. The first discourse or oration demonstrates the falseness of paganism and outlines the path of ascent to the true knowledge of God and the Word through introspection and through the contemplation of the external world in its harmony and beauty. In this discourse certain elements of Hellenism and Neoplatonism are very strong, especially in the criticism of idolatry and in the depiction of the fall and return of the soul.

The second discourse or oration deals with the truth and significance of the Incarnation. Athanasius demonstrates that it is a fulfillment of prophecy and that it marks the moral rebirth which took place in the Christian world. He concludes his argument with references to Scripture, which was set forth by God through wise and holy men. He adds that "without a pure mind and without imitating the lives of the saints, no one can comprehend these holy words."

The Lost Exegetical Works

Many of Athanasius' exegetical works were known in antiquity but only fragments of his interpretations of the *Psalms* and the

Gospels of Matthew and Luke, which were preserved in catenae, have survived to our time. His commentary has an Alexandrian character and deals primarily with moral problems. In his *Epistula ad Marcellinum de interpretatione Psalmorum* [*Letter to Marcellinus on the Interpretation of the Psalms*] Athanasius expresses his general view of the Old Testament. It was written by one Spirit and was written about our Savior. The *Psalms* have a particular and primary grace because the law and the prophets are combined in them. At the same time, they were written about each of us, as examples for our edification.

Orationes contra Arianos

Athanasius set forth his theology as a polemic in the struggle against Arianism. Most of his dogmatic and polemical works were written during his third exile (356-362). Most important are the *Three Discourses against the Arians* [*Orationes contra Arianos*]. A fourth is frequently added to these but it was probably not written by Athanasius.

The first discourse or oration refutes the rational and exegetical arguments of the Arians. Here Athanasius cites and analyzes a series of excerpts from the *Thalia* [*Banquet*] of Arius. He defends the definition of faith of the Council of Nicaea (325) that the Son is eternal, uncreated (ἀγέννητος), unchangeable, and of one Divine Essence with the Father. The second discourse deals mostly with the interpretation of *Proverbs* 8:22, the text which the Arians used as one of their main proofs for the created nature of the Son-Wisdom ("He created me at the beginning of His works"). In both the second and third discourse he analyzes other Scriptural texts used by the Arians to refute Arian exegesis – *Hebrews* 3:2; *Acts* 2:36; *Matthew* 26:39; 28:18; *John* 3:35; 12:27; *Mark* 13:32; and *Luke* 2:52. The third oration explains divine consubstantiality, and also the significance of the pas-sages in Scripture which seem to detract from the divinity of Christ.

Epistulae IV ad Serapionem, Episcopum Thmuitanum

At this time Athanasius wrote *Epistulae IV ad Serapionem episcopum Thmuitanum* [*Four Letters to Serapion, Bishop of Thmuis*] on the divinity and consubstantiality of the Holy Spirit. These four letters comprise an integrated work. Not only are they addressed to the same person but they deal with the same subject – the Holy Spirit. Serapion had written to Athanasius about "certain persons, who, although having left the Arians because of their blasphemy against the Son of God, oppose still the Holy Spirit; they claim the Holy Spirit is not only a creature but actually one of the ministering spirits; that the Holy Spirit differs from the angels only in degrees." [I,I]. Athanasius called this group the "tropicists" (τροπικοί) because they used tropical or metaphorical exegesis to explain away Scriptural texts not in accord with their doctrine. In these letters Athanasius stresses that our knowledge of the Spirit is derived from the Son. His theology of the Holy Spirit is expressed very clearly in these important letters.

Dogmatic Writings

An oration on the words: "Everything has been given to me by my Father" may very well prove to be authentic and to have been written in the early part of his life. The authenticity of *De Trinitate Libri XII* and *De Spiritu Sancto* (which have survived only in a Latin translation) is questionable. Both the work against the Arians and the work against Apollinarius on the appearance of God in the flesh are dubious. Several of his letters, including some to Epic - tetus of Corinth [*Epistula ad Epictetum episcopum Corinthi*], Adelphius the Confessor [*Epistula ad Adelphium episcopum et confessorem*], and to Maximus the Philosopher [*Epistula ad Max - imum philosophum*] have a dogmatic content and deal mostly with Christology.

Athanasius was more than once forced to defend himself against libel. He wrote three apologetic works to justify himself: *Apologia contra Arianos* [*Apology against the Arians*], which includes all the documents relating to his case from his first two exiles (probably written c. 357); *Apologia ad Constantium impera - torem* [*Apology to Emperor Constantius*] (probably written c. 357); and *Apologia pro fuga sua* [*Apology for His Flight*] (probably written c. 357) which Athanasius addressed to the en - tire Church and has, as such, remained one of his most famous works.

The historical and polemical works of Athanasius were also intended as apologies. *Historia Arianorum ad monachos* [*History of the Arians for Monks*] was written probably in 358 at the invitation of the monks with whom he had found refuge. In this work he attacks Emperor Constantius as a precursor of the Antichrist, as a patron of heresy, and as an enemy of Christ. However, in his *Apologia ad Constantium imperatorem* Athan - asius utilized his most dignified language to the emperor. His *Epistula de decretis Nicaenae synodi* [*Letter concerning the Decrees of the Council of Nicaea*] was probably written about

350/351 and is a defense of the Nicene definition. The *Epistula de synodis Arimini in Italia et Seleuciae in Isauria celebratis* [*Letter concerning the Synods of Ariminum in Italy and Seleucia in Isauria*] was written in the autumn of 359 and constitutes an extensive report and analysis. His *Epistula de sententia Dionysii episcopi Alexandrini* [*Letter on the Opinions of Dionysius, Bishop of Alexandria*] is authentic; there may be merely a question as to whether it was a later addition to his work on *The Decrees of the Council of Nicaea*, but that it is authentically from Athanasius is not seriously questioned. To these can be added the encyclical epistles from the Alexandrian councils: *Tomus ad Antiochenos* [*Tome to the People of Antioch*]; *Epistula ad Afros episcopos* [*Letter to the African Bishops*], and others.

The Vita of St. Antony

Contemporaries are unanimous in ascribing *The Vita of St. Antony*, the father of monasticism, to Athanasius. During Athanasius' lifetime it was translated into Latin by Evagrius, a deacon and later bishop of Antioch, probably in 371 or 382, but in any event before 383, which was the year of the death of the youth Innocent, to whom the translation was dedicated. Doubts about the attribution of the *Vita* to Athanasius, which have existed since the time of the Centuriators of Magdeburg, have no foundation.

The *Vita* was written soon after the death of Antony (356), during the "Arian invasion" which forced Athanasius to leave Alexandria and take refuge in the remote desert. It was written for "our brothers in another land," in a country where monasticism had only recently begun to appear. Athanasius saw in St.Antony a "worthy model of asceticism." *The Life of St. Antony* had great influence on the development of hagiographic literature, and especially on Jerome's *Life of Paul of Thebes*. Recently an ancient Syriac adaptation of the *Life of Antony* has been published.

Ad Amunem, Ad Dracontium, and De Virginitate

Athanasius' *Epistula ad Amunem monachum* [*Letter to the Monk Amun*] (written before 356) and his *Epistula ad Dracontium* [*Letter to Dracontius*] (written about 354 or 355) were intended to instruct them in the practice of ascetic discipline. The authenticity of *De virginitate* [*On Virginity*] is highly doubtful, despite the testimony of Jerome in his *De viris illustribus*, 87. However, there is another treatise *De virginitate* that may be recognized as genuine; a substantial Syriac fragment of it has been edited and the complete text is extent in Armenian.

The Paschal Letters

A particular place in the works of Athanasius is occupied by his paschal letters – ἐπιστολαὶ   ἑορταστικαὶ. Only insignificant fragments have been preserved of the original Greek, but a large collection has survived in Syriac translation. These letters are important for the chronology and history of the epoch. A frag - ment of the thirty-ninth letter (367) contains a list of the canonical books of Holy Scripture. This is supplemented by a list of books which were not included in the canon but which the fathers did not condemn for reading by the faithful: the *Wisdom of Solomon*; the *Wisdom of Jesus,   Son of Sirach*; *Esther*; *Judith*; *Tobit* (Athanasius omitted the books of the *Maccabees*); the so-called "Doctrine of the Apostles" or *The Didache*; and *The Shepherd*. This is the first time that the 27 books of the New Testament were enumerated as a single whole.

III
THOUGHT

THE DOCTRINE OF REDEMPTION

The theology of Athanasius is based on the historical figure of Christ, the God-man and Savior. The trinitarian question of the generation and consubstantiality of the Son of God is for him primarily a Christological and soteriological problem. He is con - cerned not with speculation, but with living religious experience. The reality of salvation is Athanasius' proof of the divinity and consubstantiality of the Incarnate Word, for only the Incarnation of the Only-Begotten brings salvation. He sees the significance of salvation in the fact that a created human nature is united (or, more exactly, reunited) with God. This is possible only if it is truly God who takes on flesh and becomes a man. Salvation is "deification," θέωσις. In this respect St. Athanasius follows the teaching of St. Irenaeus and the tradition of the Church of Asia Minor.

Creation and Created Existence

In the theology of Athanasius there is an absolute opposition between God and creation. "Everything which is created is not at all like in *essence* to its Creator," for created things originate from that which does not exist and can have no similarity with that which has independent being. Created from nothing, creation exists above the abyss of nothingness and is ready to fall back into it. The created world is generated and has an origin, and therefore its nature is "fluctuating and subject to dissolution," since it has no support or foundation for existence within itself. True being belongs only to God, and God is first of all Being and Existence because He was not generated but is eternal. However, creation exists and at its origin it receives not only being but also stability and harmony. This is possible through participation in the Word, Who is present in the world. Creation, illuminated by the dominion, works, and order of the Word, can attain stable being by "participating in the Word, Who truly exists from the Father."

The Word of God as the Strength and Wisdom of the Divinity is the source, builder, and guardian of the world. God in His goodness does not let creation "be enthralled or enslaved by its own nature," but the one and only Word of the Father descends into the universe and spreads His power. He enlightens all things visible and invisible. He supports and strengthens everything in Himself, and He gives life to and preserves every individual thing and all things as a whole. The Word is the source of the order and unity of the world. Everywhere in the world there is symmetry and proportion, the harmonious combination of opposite things. God is revealed in this unity and harmony: "No one dares to say that God's invisibility is harmful to us or that it is completely impossible for us to know God. On the contrary, He has brought such order to His creation that, although He is invisible by essence, He is knowable by his works."

The God of revelation is the Word. "For the Word has spread everywhere, both above and below, into the depths and in all directions: above in creation, below in Incarnation, into the depths of hell and everywhere in the world. Everything is filled with the knowledge of God." "The stamp and likeness" of the Divine Word and Wisdom have been placed on all creation and on every individual creature in the world, and this preserves the world from decay and disintegration. Here Athanasius' ideas seem similar to the teaching of Plotinus about the ordering of matter by Intellect, but there is a sharp distinction between them. According to Plotinus, Intellect imprints itself on unqualified matter and remains in it. For Athanasius, the origination and existence of creation is based on the presence of the Word within it. He rejects the Stoic concept of "seminal" words, λόγοι σπερματικοί. The source of the order of the world is the Word of the Father.

For Athanasius the origination of the world and its impression by the Word are not separated in time. He wants to stress the duality of creation, which has its own fluctuating and created nature, and also bears the preserving stamp of the Word, through Whom it exists. Thus, creation has both "nature" and "grace." Athanasius' system is built on the distinction and opposition of these two elements. He developed his teaching about the Word as sovereign and creative Wisdom before the Arian controversy. His work is a continuation of the pre-Nicene tradition but his cosmology remains completely free of sub - ordinationism. "Coexisting with the Father as Wisdom, and gazing at Him as the Word," the Son of God "creates, brings into being, and gives order to the universe, and, as the Strength of the Father, maintains all creation in its being . . . As the true Son, begotten of the Most Good, He is the Father's Strength and Wisdom and Word, not just by participation, as though everything were given to Him from outside, as it is to those who participate in Him . . . but in such a way that He is the very Wisdom, the very Word, the very Strength of the Father, the very Light, Truth, Justice, Virtue, Imprint, Radiance, Image. In short, He is the most perfect fruit of the Father, the Only Son, the unchanging Image of the Father." This means that the Father is completely knowable in the Son.

Athanasius developed his teaching about the Word at the height of the Arian controversy. He stressed the close con - nection between the creative action of the Word and the Incarnation, the work of salvation. He united these in the concept of the entry of the Word into the universe. In Scripture the Word is called the First-born in relation to creation "because the Word, Who created the world at the beginning, came down to the things that were created so they could come into being, and also because all creation was adopted by the Word at His descent." The Son was placed as the foundation before the beginning of time, "at the beginning of His works."

In keeping with his general teaching on the dual nature of every created being, Athanasius distinguishes two logical (not chronological) stages in the creation of man: the creation of human nature from nothing, and the imprinting or anointing of creation with the image of God. This "genesis" or adoption is made possible by the Son in the Spirit. God through His grace became the Father of those whom He created. Creation, main - taining its createdness, was adopted by the Father through its participation in the Son. At the moment of creation man, who had been led out of nonexistence, was anointed by the Spirit. The "breath of life" which God blew into Adam was not a soul but the holy and life-giving Spirit, and the first man was a "spiritual man" because he had the Spirit within him. By making him like Himself, God enabled man to contemplate and observe the true Divinity, and introduced him to the bliss of true life.

The Fall of Man

But the grace and gifts of the Spirit were given to the first man from outside. Therefore it was possible for them to be lost, and indeed man did lose them at the Fall. Man turned away from the contemplation of God, ceased his intellectual striving toward Him, and became shut up in himself, giving himself over to "self-consideration." It was then that passions and desires flared up in him, and his life disintegrated and became fragmented. People fell into "self-love" and the soul turned from the intellectual to the corporeal, forgetting that it had been made in the image of God, Who is good. The soul "turned its thoughts to that which does not exist," gave it form, and thus became the inventor of evil. For evil is nothingness. It has no example for itself in God and is derived by human reasoning. The multitude of corporeal desires which crowded together in the soul hid the mirror it contained by which it could and should have seen the image of the Father. The soul no longer saw or contemplated the God of the Word, in Whose image it was created, but gave its thoughts to a variety of things and saw only what was subject to the senses. This was the intoxication and bewilderment of the mind.

By breaking God's commandments the first man was deprived of the light of intellect and was returned to his "natural condition." He became the slave of the "natural" law of decay. Man's mind turned to vanities and was poisoned by sensual desires, and humanity was lost in the darkness of paganism.

Grace and the Renewal of Creation

At the Fall man was impoverished and nature was deprived of grace. In this way it became necessary for a "reunion," a "re-newal" of creation, "which was created in the image of God," to take place. The lost grace of God's image had to be restored. The Word, as the Creator or Demiurge, had to "take on Himself the re-newal of creation." And this was accomplished" "The Word be-came flesh." The Word assumed human nature which, while remaining similar to our nature, was enlightened and freed from the weaknesses that are natural to it. "In this same way a straw, if it is covered by asbestos to oppose the action of fire, will no longer be afraid of fire, since it is safe in its nonflammable covering."

Although it is condemned to decay "by its essence," human nature was created and called to immortality. Indirect participation in the Word, which had existed from the beginning, was insufficient to preserve creation from decay. Repentance and forgiveness would be adequate only if transgression were not followed by decay, for "repentance does not lead man out of his natural condition, but only stops sin." Death, however, had become established in the body and had taken power over it.

God, of course, is omnipotent and could have driven death from the world with a single command, but this would not have healed man, who had become accustomed to disobedience. It would not have been in accord with divine justice. Such a complete forgiveness would show the power of the one who ordered it but man would remain the same as Adam, and once again grace would be given to him from outside. In that case the possibility of a new Fall would not be excluded. But through the Incarnation of the Word grace was given to humanity immutably. It became inalienable and remains with man constantly. The Word was clothed in a body in order to dress the body anew in life, in order to preserve it from decay not only externally but also to truly join the body to life. In this way "the body is clothed in the incorporeal Word of God and thus no longer fears death or decay, for it has life as a robe and decay is destroyed in it."

The Word was in the world from the beginning. As if the world were some large body, the Word gave it life and order. It was fitting for the Word to also appear in a human body and give life to it as well. The image of the Word was already outlined on man but when it became dirty and invisible "it was fitting to restore it." This was accomplished by the Incarnation of the Word.

The Word Became Man

The Word became man, similar to us in all respects. Athanasius employs the term "incarnation" and by this he means that in assuming flesh the Word became a full man, taking on an animate body with all the senses and sufferings that are proper to it. By virtue of its union with the Word, "because of the Word, which was in a body," the body was freed from its weakness and subjection to decay. The life-giving strength of the Word freed the body of the Savior from natural weaknesses: "Christ thirsted, since that is an attribute of a body, but He did not perish from hunger."

The body was subject to suffering but the impassible Word was within it. The body experienced weakness by the permission and will of the Word and not by necessity or against His will. The Lord tolerated everything proper to the body: He thirsted, wept, and even accepted death. But the death of the Lord took place because of His humility and love and not from necessity. He had the power to separate Himself from the body, and His body was able to die. However, it could not remain dead, for "it had become the temple of life." Therefore it immediately revived and arose from the dead "by virtue of the life that dwelled within it."

The Word was not bound by the body but freed the body from its limitedness and its inclination to sin. By the strength of the unchanging Word, the mutable human nature in Christ became immutably good, and all delusions were powerless over it. "Wis - dom caused humanity to flourish, and humanity gradually rose above human nature, became deified, and acted as the agent of Wisdom in the service of the Divinity and its radiance." "The works proper to the Word were achieved through the body." The flesh was deified by serving the works of God, and the humanity in Christ was without sin.

The human nature in Christ was fully anointed by the Spirit even before His baptism in the Jordan. Through Him we also were anointed by the Spirit and received Its imprint and presence within ourselves. Flesh was sanctified for the first time in the Spirit. The radiance of the human nature in Christ is the radiance of all human nature in its Source. In this way the Word through the Incarnation again stands ("is created") "at the beginning of His works," and is therefore called the First-born. The Lord "be - came our brother through the likeness of the body," and His flesh "was saved and liberated before the others." Since we "share in His body," we also are saved and our life is renewed "because our flesh is no longer earthly but has been made identical with the Word by the Divine Word Himself, Who became flesh for our sakes."

Destroying Death and Renewing Nature

Redemption and salvation were achieved not only at the moment of the Incarnation but were accomplished throughout the earthly life of the Lord. The Lord revealed His love for humanity in two ways, by destroying death and renewing nature, and by "revealing Himself in His works" to show that He is the Word of the Father, the Leader and Emperor of the universe. By his visible appearance the Lord showed His invisible Father to mankind, which had abandoned intellectual contemplation. By fulfilling the law He removed from us its curse and condemnation. But "decay could not be halted in men other than by death," and therefore the "ultimate goal" of the saving Incarnation must be seen as death itself. "He had a body in order to accept death, and it was not fitting to prevent death, lest the resurrection also be prevented." The death on the cross was an "offering," the ful - fillment of a common obligation. But the body of the Lord "could not be held by death and rose from the dead." "Two things were marvelously accomplished in this one action: the death of all was carried out in the Lord's body, and death and decay were des - troyed in it because of the Word which was inherent in it."

The Lord died not by the weakness of nature but by His own will, for the sake of the resurrection of all. "His body did not cast off its own death, but accepted death from men in order to completely destroy death." The body of the Lord did not ex - perience decay but arose whole, for it was the body of Life itself. The death of the Lord was a true death, but a brief one. "He did not leave His body in that condition for long, but showed that it was dead and immediately resurrected it on the third day. Thus He raised the sign of victory over death by showing that His body did not decay and did not participate in suffering." All humanity was resurrected and exalted in Christ: "Through death immortality was given to all." The Lord rose from the grave "in the flesh, which had been deified and had cast off mortality." The flesh had been glorified and "this grace belongs to us and this exaltation is ours." We who share in a body with Him have been admitted to heaven.

Thus, Athanasius' teaching on redemption is primarily concerned with the Resurrection, the resurrection of man by Christ and in Christ.

Christ's Unity of Divinity and Humanity

Holy Scripture tells us two truths about the Savior: He has always been God, Son, and Word, and He became man. This occasionally leads to ambiguity in passages dealing with Christ because, although He is glorified, His human nature is under-emphasized.

The Word did not simply "desire to become incarnate" or "manifest Himself in a body." He did not descend to man, but He *became* man, He made Himself the Son of Man. In this respect Athanasius sometimes uses incomplete or inexact expressions: the Word "clothes Himself" or "dwells within," and He is a temple, dwelling-place, or agent. However, Athanasius carefully distin - guishes the appearance of the Word in Christ from His ap - pearance and presence in saints. Christ *became* man. The visible body of Christ was the body of God, not man. He made the body "His own," and the weakness of the flesh became "proper" to the

Word. Christ's works were not separated in such a way that one was accomplished by His divine nature and another by His human nature, but "everything was achieved in combination" and indivisibly.

The very saliva of Christ was divine, healing, and life-giving because the Incarnate Word "adopted" all the properties of the flesh and made them His own. It was He Who both grieved for Lazarus and then resurrected him. God was born in the flesh from the Virgin, and Mary is the Bearer of God (Θεοτόκος]. The flesh, which was born from Mary, did not become consubstantial with the Word, and the Word was not joined to it. Mary was chosen so that the Lord could receive "from her" a body that would be "sim - ilar to ours" and not consubstantial with the Godhead. "From Mary the Word received flesh, and a man was engendered whose nature and substance were the Word of God and whose flesh was from the seed of David, a man from the flesh of Mary."

Athanasius clearly emphasizes both the *unity* of Christ the God-man and His unmerging two natures. Christ has a Divine nature, by which He is consubstantial with the Father, and also a human nature, by which He is similar and related to us. For this reason He is the Savior, the Word, and the Second Adam all at once.

The Word became man so that we could "become divine," "in order to deify us in Himself." Deification is adoption by God, and "human sons have become the sons of God." We are "received by the Word and are deified through His flesh" by virtue of the Incarnation. Born from the Virgin, the Word was not united with only one man, but with the whole of human nature. Therefore everything that was achieved in the human nature of Christ is immediately extended to all men because they have a body in common with Him. There is no coercion involved here. Men are more than similar to Christ; they are truly participants in the human nature of the Word. Christ is a vine and we are the branches, "united with Him by our humanity." In the same way that the ten - drils which grow from a grapevine are consubstantial with it, so are our bodies consubstantial with the body of the Lord, and we receive what He has accomplished. His body is the "root of our resurrection and salvation." Everyone is renewed, anointed, healed, and exalted in Christ, for "He has taken everyone on Himself." This is not merely similarity or substitution, but actual unity. Therefore all humanity is anointed by the Spirit in the Jor - dan, dies on the cross, and is resurrected to immortality in Christ because "He Himself bears our body."

Humanity's Participation in Christ

This participation in the humanity of Christ must also be realized in the actions of men. Because the Word assumed flesh, human nature has become "spiritual" and actually receives the Spirit. We are a "temple of God," a temple of the Holy Spirit which lives with - in us and we become "friends of the Spirit." In receiving the gifts of the Spirit we are united with Christ. "The Spirit gives us to drink and we drink Christ." "The Spirit anoints Christ and is the breath of the Son," and in the Spirit "the word glorifies creation, deifies it and adopts it, and leads it to the Father." The Word anoints and seals everything through the Holy Spirit, and in the Spirit we be - come "participants in the Divine nature." The Spirit is the "ener - gy" of the Word, and therefore in receiving the Word we win the Spirit. The Word received flesh and men received the Spirit, becoming "bearers of the Spirit." By virtue of the presence of the Spirit in human nature sensual desires burn out, temptations to sin are driven away, and men are given the ability "not to be deceived by worldly things." After the coming of Christ the devil is "only a sparrow, a toy for children." Men have been given power over demons and temptations and the sign of the cross, as a sign of victory, can destroy all magic and charms and show demons that they are dead.

What is most important here is that the sting of death has been removed from creation. Because they have been received by the Word, men have "inherited eternal life." "They do not remain sin - ful and dead in their passions but they arise by the strength of the Word and become immortal and free from decay." Death is no longer terrible, for we have been promised that we will arise from the dead and become rulers with Christ in heaven. This is the path followed by Christian ascetics, who conquer the mysteries and become bearers of God. Their accomplishments testify to the victory of Christ over death, and every day the host of martyrs laughs at death and rejoices in Christ. Let those who doubt ap - proach Christ with faith and they will see the feebleness of death in His victory over it. Christ "instills strength against death in all who come to Him." Christ is the cornerstone which has been laid "so that we can be built up on Him, like precious stones." Deifi - cation is the foundation for the complete union of men by love for one another in the image and by the example of Divine consubstantiality, all by the strength of the Spirit.

Redemption, the work of the Word, is the completion and renewal of creation. But the grace it offers man is much more than a simple return to the original condition which was lost at the Fall.

For the Word became flesh, and man became a permanent participant in God. Decay was overcome and creation received its final stability through the "body of God." In this way a new cre - ation was achieved. This was revealed in Scripture in the pas - sages on the "First-born" and "the beginning of His works." "Born before the hills," the Wisdom of God "was created at the beginning of His works" (*Proverbs* 8:22-25). Thus was an - nounced before the beginning of time the creation and salvation by the Word and in the Word, the saving Incarnation of the Word as the source of a "new creation," superior to the "original cre - ation." Every intention of God will be fulfilled at the second coming of Christ: Christ will come in glory "to render to all the fruit of His Cross: resurrection and immortality.

THE TRUTH OF THE CONSUBSTANTIALITY OF THE TRINITY

Athanasius' explanation of the mystery of the Trinity was called forth by the Arian controversy. His work is largely an examination of the Scriptural passages which the Arians used to support their arguments, which Athanasius refutes. At the same time, Athan - asius' trinitarian doctrine is the result of his own personal needs. It is the foundation of his faith and hope for salvation.

The false teaching of the Arians negates the work of Christ. A creature could not have true knowledge of God, could not over - come death, and could not unite us with God. "If the Word which became man was a creature, then men would not be deified and joined with God." It is only the Savior's consubstantiality which establishes the contact between men and God. Only a consub - stantial Spirit unites us with the Father. In his dogma of consub - stantiality Athanasius is defending the reality of salvation.

God as the Goodness and Fullness of Being

The starting point of Athanasius' trinitarian doctrine is the con - cept of God as the goodness and fullness of being. As a simple, holy and incomprehensible Being, which is higher than any essence, God is beyond human understanding. The perfect sim - plicity and inner fullness of Divine Being and Life is the basis for Athanasius' teaching on the eternal generation and consub - stantiality of the Only-Begotten, the Son and Word. The Word is generated by the Father and from His essence: He is the "proper generation of His essence." Everything which is generated is always consubstantial with that which engenders it. This is the basic feature of generation which distinguishes it from other modes of origination, and especially from creation. That which is created always originates either from some preexisting matter or from nothingness. It always remains unlike and external to its creator, "of another essence."

The Son is generated. His being is a necessity of the Divine nature, which is fertile and fruitful in and of itself. "The substance of the Father has never been incomplete, and that which is proper to it has never come to it at a later time." The denial of the Son's eternity and coeternity with the Father is blasphemy not only against the Son but also against the Father. It diminishes the dignity of the Father and negates His immutability. It supposes that "He once was without His own Word and Wisdom, that there was light which had no rays, that there was a spring which was dry and without water."

God is eternal, the source is eternal, and therefore the Wisdom-Word and His generation must also be eternal. If there was a time when the Son did not exist, then there was a time when God the Father and the Trinity did not exist. It would be as if "at one time the Trinity did not exist, but a Unity existed; as if there once was an incomplete Trinity, which at one time became complete." In this way the Trinity would be divided and com - posed of things which once had no existence, "of natures and essences that were alien among themselves." If this were true, the Trinity would have had an origin. It would be a complex "cre - ation" which was composed through connection and adhesion. Athanasius uses this reasoning to show that the "mystery" of Arianism is a denial of the Divine Trinity. In fact, Arianism is a reversion to abstract monotheism. It rejects the knowledge of God as the Trinity, which is the highest truth of Christian rev - elation.

Athanasius stresses that the Father is immutable. He has al - ways been the Father of "His own Son." There can be no ques - tion of succession in the relation of Father and Son, and there is not "interval" or "distance" between them. They are completely and perfectly coeternal. The possibility of a temporal relationship is excluded because it is impossible to designate the eternal and unchanging Father and the Son Who always abides in Him with temporal definitions. This eternity and coeternity means that the Son is generated, not created. Since He is generated, He is "from the essence," ἐκ τῆς οὐσία. The Son is thus consub - stantial with the Father, ὁμοούσιος. "That which proceeds from someone by essence is truly generated." Generation takes place "by nature," and not by will or desire.

The Free Necessity of Divine Generation

The necessity of Divine generation does not entail coercion or involuntariness. Athanasius was frequently accused of this, but he consistently denies it. He does not mean to replace free de - sire by compulsion, but he points out that "that which is entailed by essence is higher than free choice and antecedes it." Therefore, that which cannot not be does not have a source from which it came to be. God had no beginning. He did not begin to be good and merciful, nor was an act of His will necessary for Him to become good, for God *is* Good. However, He is good not by compulsion or against His will. In this same way God is the Father without His willing to be so, and it is impossible to consider God not having a Son. The Father desires His own Hypostasis and He also desires His own Son, Who is from His essence. Being is be - fore will, and only in will does the uncertainty of choice become possible. The generation of the Son is a condition within Divine Life, not an action. This explains the perfect closeness and unity of the Father and the Son. The Father is in the Son and the Son is in the Father. The "essence of the Father belongs to the Word." "The being of the Son is a property of the Father's es - sence . . . The being of the Son, since it comes from the Father, is in the Father. And the Father is in the Son, for that which is from the Father is the Son. He is in the Son, as the sun is in radiance, as intellect is in the word, as the spring is in the stream."

Therefore the Son is the "Image of the Father," the true and "indistinguishable Image," and the "form of the Divinity" in which the Father is known and contemplated. "As soon as there is the Father, there is also the Son." "Since there is the Hypostasis (of the Father), then without doubt there must also be His Image and form because the Image of God is not drawn from outside, but God Himself engenders His Image, and seeing Himself in it He rejoices in it." "When did the Father not see Himself in His own Image?"

This line of reasoning contains many elements of Neo - platonism, but Athanasius manages to free Origen's concept of the eternal generation from subordinationism. Athanasius devel - ops the idea of the Trinity as self-enclosed and complete Being and Life, which has no relation to the Revelation of God in the world, and which is unconditionally and ontologically prior to any Revelation.

The Living Unity of Divine Essence

Athanasius bases his theology on the living unity of the Son and Father. "The divinity of the Father unceasingly and permanently abides in the Son, and the divinity of the Son is never exhausted in the bosom of the Father." The Father and Son are united in the unity of essence, in an identity of nature," and in the indivisible "identity of a single Divinity." The Son has the Father's nature without change, and the Divinity of the Son is the Divinity of the Father. Athanasius expresses this identity as a property or attribute, ἰδιότης. He considers that its most exact definition is the Nicene "consubstantial," ὁμοούιος.

This signifies more than equality, identicalness, or likeness. For Athanasius it means the complete unity of being, the indissoluble and immutable identity, and the absolute inseparability of the Son and the Father. Likeness, similarity, and coincidence in definition are the results of this unity. The concept of likeness is too weak to express this, and furthermore it is used not of essences but of external appearances and qualities. Moreover, this concept gives too much weight to the separateness of the elements that are being compared. Consubstantiality means not only likeness, but identity in likeness. "The Father and the Son are one, not in the sense that one is divisible into two parts which compose a whole, nor in the sense that one bears two names. On the contrary, They are two in number because the Father is the Father and not the Son, and the Son is the Son and not the Father, but their nature is one. The Son has been generated, but He is also God."

The Father and the Son "are two, and together form an inseparable and indistinguishable Divine unity," μόνας τῆς θεότητος. The difference and distinction of the Father and Son exists within a single Divine Being. Athanasius has no particular terms to describe the three which make up the Divine unity. He never uses πρόσωπον, a "face." The meaning of "hypostasis" coincides with the meaning of οὐσία for him, as it did for the fathers of the Nicene Council. Athanasius never distinguishes them as the Cappadocians were doing even during his lifetime. He restricts himself to the proper names of Father, Son, and Spirit, and explains their mutual relation by such expressions as "the One who generates" and "the One who is generated," "One who is from someone" and "the One from whom He is."

This leads to a certain lack of clarity in Athanasius' distinction of the three hypostases. He concentrates his attention on refuting attempts to divide or negate the consubstantiality of the indivisible Trinity. In his interpretation of the Nicene formulation "from the essence of the Father," he stresses the internal nature of the Divine generation and being. This expresses the "truth and immutability" of the Sonship, its "indivisibility and unity with the Father," and the "true eternity of essence from which the Word is generated." Athanasius refers equally to "natural generation," "Sonship by nature," and "generation from the essence."

The Logos of the Father

The Word of the Father, the Son of God, is primarily the Creator and organizer of the world and the source of Divine Revelation in the world. "He is the life which pours forth from the Father as if from a spring, giving life to everything." All creation comes into being through the Word, and nothing exists outside of the Word or is not created by the Word. The Father creates nothing without Him. At the same time, the being and generation of the Son is not connected with God's will to create the world. The Son is not generated so that the world can be created through Him and in Him. "The Word of God did not receive being for our sakes . . . He, the all-powerful, did not receive being because of our weak - ness, or to be the Father's instrument in creating us. If God had chosen not to create the world, nevertheless the Word was with God the Father."

There is no cause for the being of the Son: "Just as the Father has no cause for His being, it is also not necessary to try to find the reason for His radiance. It is written: in the beginning was the Word, and the Word was with God, and God was the Word. The reason for this has not been stated." There is no cause by which the Lord is the Word except that He is generated by the Father and is the Father's Wisdom. This "causelessness" entails eternal being. Causes exist only for things which have an origin or source. But Divine Being has no beginning. One can only say that It *is*. It is impossible to consider Its causes, for there is nothing which existed before that *is*.

Athanasius decisively rejects and demonstrates the futility of the teaching of the Arians on the Word as the mediator in cre - ation. God does not need an assistant or helper because He can accomplish everything by a single movement of His will. God is not so conceited or fastidious that He would consider creation beneath His dignity and entrust it to another. God needs no in - strument to create in the way that a carpenter needs a saw and axe. Furthermore, if it is not unsuitable for God to create, why should He create even one creature as an instrument for Himself? The creation of one Mediator would entail the creation of another, and so on for eternity, and creation would thus be impossible. Since God can create, why should He need a mediator?

The Son is not generated for the sake of Revelation but God is revealed in Him and through Him. The being of the Son precedes the will to create the world. "Creation for God is secondary. Generation, being the Father of His own Son, comes before it." If there did not first exist in God that which is from His nature, how could there exist that which is from His will, that which is secondary?" That which is created by God's will "comes into being and is composed from outside, and is built by that which God has generated from His own essence. The Word builds and creates; He is the "living will of the Father, His own energy." At the same time creation is the common work and common revelation of the whole Trinity, which creates and builds as one. "The Father creates everything by the Word in the Spirit, for where the Word is, there is also the Spirit. That which is created by the Word has its being from the Spirit through the Son." Everything which is given, including being, is given "in the Trinity."

Theology of the Holy Spirit

According to St. Gregory the Theologian, Athanasius in his teaching on the Holy Spirit "is the first man who alone, or with very few others, dares to state the truth clearly and openly by confessing the single Divinity and the single essence of the Trinity." Athanasius develops his theology of the Spirit with clarity and vigor. He starts with the concept of the completeness and perfect unity of the Holy Trinity: "The whole Trinity is one God." "It is indivisible and similar to Itself." It is identical to Itself and con-centrated within Itself. "The Trinity is holy and perfect. It is knowable in the Father, the Son, and the Holy Spirit, and has nothing alien to Itself or given to It from outside." It is not a Trinity in name only, but in essence and in truth.

There exist two possibilities for the Trinity. If the Spirit is a creature, there can be no Trinity, for "what kind of theology would that be, composed of Creator and creature?" Or, God is triune and the Spirit is completely unlike a created thing. He is "proper to the one Word, proper and consubstantial to the one God (the Father)." Since the Trinity is such a union and such a unity, who can separate either the Son from the Father, or the Spirit from the Son and from the Father Himself?

The Holy Spirit is the principle of renewal and sanctification, the Spirit of Life and Holiness. He anoints and seals. Because of the

Spirit we are all participants in God. If the Holy Spirit were a cre-ature, it would be impossible for us to communicate with God: "We would be joined with a creature and would remain alien to God's nature, and would not be in communion with Him at all." The reality of deification testifies to the Divinity of the Spirit: "If the Spirit makes us gods, then there is no doubt that His nature is God's nature."

The Holy Spirit comes from and "proceeds from" the Father, τὸ ἐκπόρευμα τοῦ πατρός. He is the Father's Spirit. Athanasius does not explain the meaning of "procession," claiming that it is beyond the bounds of human understanding. However, he clearly distinguishes this mode of being from "generation" by stressing the complete uniqueness of generation. The Son is the Only-Begotten and is therefore unique. "The one Father is the Father of His one and only Son." This is more than a matter of words. Genuine and immutable Fatherhood and genuine and immutable Sonship exist only in the Divine Trinity. Only the Son of God is a Son and nothing else. He is generated as a son and not in order to become a father, as is the case for other created beings. The Father is only a father, "for He Himself is not from a father."

The Spirit is not generated and therefore is not called the brother of the Son, but is always known by the name of the Holy Spirit. At the same time the Holy Spirit is not "outside the Son, but is called the Spirit of the Son," the Spirit of strength and wisdom. God's Strength and God's Wisdom is Christ. "Where there is the Word, there is also the Spirit." The Spirit has the "same unity with the Son that the Son has with the Father," and the same properties. Where there is light, there is radiance. Where there is radiance, there is also its effect and shining grace. The Spirit is the "proper Image of the Son," His "living effec-tiveness and radiant grace." He unites creation with the Word, and in Him the Word gives to creation the "gift of the Father." "For the Father Himself acts and distributes all things through the Word in the Spirit."

In his explanation of the Holy Spirit Athanasius tries to demonstrate the complete unity and consubstantiality of the Holy Trinity and Its sanctifying action. Therefore he insists on the indivisibility of the actions of the Son and the Spirit.

The Trinity and Holy Baptism

Holy Baptism, which according to the traditions of faith is per-formed in the name of the one and indivisible Trinity, brings salvation. The mystery takes place in the name of the Trinity, and "whoever takes anything away from the Trinity and is baptized in the name of the Father alone, or in the name of the Son without the Spirit, receives nothing. Those who are baptized in this way and those who think they are giving baptism remain empty and unsatisfied."

In spite of the fact that the necessary words are spoken, Arian baptism "in the name of the Creator and His creation" "is only apparent and not real" because the words must be accompanied by true faith. Baptism takes place in the name of the Trinity because grace is received from the Trinity. "God as Father founded the world through His Wisdom, and by this He did not dishonor the world. He creates everything through His own Word, and He affirms the holy font through His Son. In the same way that everything that is done by the Father is done through the Son, so too in baptism everyone baptized by the Father is also baptized by the Son. Whoever is baptized by the Son is sanctified by the Holy Spirit." The persons of the Trinity act as one.

CHAPTER THREE

ST. CYRIL OF JERUSALEM

I
LIFE

There is much about Cyril's life which still remains unclear, and even during his lifetime he was regarded with doubt and suspicion. He was born about 315 in Jerusalem or its environs, and it is not precisely known when he entered the clergy. By 348 he was a deacon and in that year during Lent and on Holy Saturday he delivered his famous *Catechetical Lectures* (divided into the introductory *Procatechesis*; eighteen *Catecheses*; and five *Mystagogical Catecheses*). Sometime between 348 and 351 he became bishop of Jerusalem. Cyril's elevation was questioned by Jerome and Rufinus, and it has long been the subject of controversy because he was probably consecrated by Acacius of Caesarea and Patrophilus of Scythopolis; that is, by prelates whose orthodoxy was doubtful. In a letter addressed to Pope Damasus Cyril had to prove to the fathers at the council of Constantinople in 382 that his installation was legal and according to canon law (Theodoret, *Historia ecclesiastica* 5.9).

About 355 Cyril and Acacius quarreled over the precedence and jurisdiction of their respective metropolitanates. They probably disagreed on dogmatic matters as well. Cyril was deposed, and under pressure he withdrew first to Antioch and then to Tarsus. There he became a supporter of the *homoiousians* and sat with them at the council of Seleucia in 359. The council reinstated him as bishop of Jerusalem, but in the next year he was exiled again and returned only during the reign of Julian in 362. In 367 under Valens he was again forced to leave Jerusalem until 378, and nothing is known of his life during this period. In 381 Cyril participated at the Second Ecumenical Council. He died in 387. These few facts are all that is definitely known about his life.

The difference of opinion regarding Cyril is understandable in view of the religious controversies which raged during his lifetime. Cyril supported the anti-Nicene movement, first as a "Eusebian" and then as a "*homoiousian*," and this would be enough to make his orthodoxy questionable. He sided with Meletius in Antioch, which explains why Jerome regarded him with such extreme suspicion. However, the testimony of the fathers at the council of 382 dispels all doubt: "At various times he greatly struggled against Arianism." Theodoret later refers to him as a "defender of the apostolic faith."

II
WORKS

Cyril is not an original theologian, but he is important as a teacher and witness of the faith. His literary remains are few. Most important among his works are the *Procatechesis*, the *18 Catecheses for Candidates for Baptism*, and the *Five Mystical Catecheses*. These instructions are a rich source for the history of the ancient rite of baptism, and since they were delivered in the name of the Church they also provide a reliable summary of the faith confessed at Jerusalem. Cyril also delivered a sermon, the only one we possess in its entirety, on the cure of the paralitc, *In paralyticum iuxta piscinam iacentem*. Three fragments from a sermon "On the Marriage at Cana in Galilee" and one quotation from a sermon on the text "I am going to My Father" have been preserved. Cyril frequently preached in Jerusalem and during his exile in Tarsus but there is no reason to presume that he wrote down his sermons or collected them into a systematic work of exegesis.

Cyril's *Letter to the Emperor Constantius* on the miraculous appearance of the luminous cross in 351 should also be mentioned. The concluding doxology which contains the ex-pression "consubstantial Trinity" is a later addition. This com-pletes the list of Cyril's known works.

III
THOUGHT

Catechism in the Early Church

In ancient times catechumens were already considered members of the Church. Eusebius of Caesarea distinguished "three orders" within the Church, and catechumens were among them. Great circumspection was used in the admission of catechumens. Candidates needed to have the permission of the bishop and were required to undergo a period of testing, during which they were sponsored by baptized believers. Catechumens received the laying on of hands and were signed with the cross, and prayers were read over them. In the West they were also anointed and were allowed to taste consecrated salt. The Apostolic Constitutions contained a particular prayer "by which a catechumen is accepted." The imposition of hands made a Christian but a Christian was not yet a baptized believer (Canon 59, Council of Elvira). According to the seventh canon of the Second Ecumenical Council, a candidate was called a Christian even before he was called a catechumen.

Catechumens were subject to Church supervision and dis - cipline. They were required to attend special services where prayers were read for them, and they had to testify to the firm - ness of their desire for salvation by their general behavior and by performing acts of contrition. In later centuries the discipline pre - scribed for catechumens was confused with the discipline im - posed on penitents, and the categories or degrees among catechumens became less clear. In ancient times there were two. After a relatively lengthy period of preparatory instruction, a candidate for baptism made his decision known and his name was entered in the Church records. In the East he was then called "enlightened," or "signed with the cross," and in Jerus - alem he was immediately considered a "baptized believer." In the West he was called a "petitioner" or a "chosen one." He then began to prepare to receive baptism. This preparation usually lasted for forty days and coincided with the Lenten fast.

We can get a clear picture of the rite of instruction by combining the information given by Cyril with the evidence of the famous Western pilgrim Etheria (earlier called St. Silvia), who traveled in Palestine during the fourth century. A candidate had to practice fasting and continence, and express penitence in words and deeds. For him this was a time of exomologesis, of public con - fession. Invocations and exorcisms were performed over him. Invocations consisted of prayers "taken from divine Scripture," in- breathing of the Spirit, and the signing with the cross. His face was covered so that "his mind would be free, and so that his eyes in their wandering would not cause him to stray." Inspiration symbolized "purification from sins" and the driving out of the "shameless and primordially evil devil." It was also symbolic of the action of the Holy Spirit, and therefore had a "fiery strength" against invisible enemies. "Just as goldsmiths," writes Cyril, "first stoke up the fire by means of their tools, and then melt the gold which is put in their crucibles by intensifying the flames so that they may find what they seek, so do those who perform invo - cation instill terror in man and, with the help of the Holy Spirit, fire the soul in his body. The devil runs off, but salvation and hope for eternal life remain. Finally the soul is purified from sins and receives salvation."

Invocation delivers the catechumen from the kingdom of this world and from the power of demons. Catechesis also has a pos -

itive and sanctifying effect. "The fragrance of bliss is upon you and you are enlightened," Cyril writes in his *Procatechesis*. "The fragrance of the Holy Spirit pours forth. You are at the gates of the heavenly kingdom. Your names have been counted and you have been included among the hosts of heaven . . . You are being prepared not externally, but within, for the Holy Spirit has come to you and made you a temple of God."

At this same time candidates were also instructed in the faith, and the creed and the Lord's Prayer were explained to them. (Cyril explains the Lord's Prayer only after baptism, in mysta - gogical terms, as it is read during the liturgy.) The catechetical works of Cyril are intended for this prebaptismal instruction. Their contents must be kept secret. "Here is your command: learn by heart what is said and follow it always. Do not think that these words are ordinary. When this teaching is finished, if they try to find out what your teachers have told you, say nothing to those who stand outside. We will give you the mystery and the hope of a future life. You are already standing at the very threshold. Be careful not to divulge what is being said. Not because it is un - worthy to be told but because the ear is unworthy to hear it." There must be a strict gradation, a "harmonious order," in the explication and mastery of the saving truths.

Catechesis is a process of building. The stones must be placed in order, and each corner must be fitted together with another. Haste is dangerous and premature knowledge can result in obscurity. Prebaptismal instruction must be kept secret not only from outsiders but also from junior catechumens. Therefore, the creed which is finally revealed and explained to them "must be engraved on the heart by memory." It must be repeated orally, not written on paper, and it must be read in secret where no one can overhear. This *disciplina arcani*, the "concealing of the secret," was especially widespread in the Church during the fourth century. It had a pastoral and pedagogical purpose, and may reflect the Alexandrian theory of the degrees of knowledge. It is possible that it also shows the influence of the ancient pagan mysteries. It was more for the protection of creeds and rites than doctrine, and is expressed by the term "mystagogy," μυσ - ταγωγία.

The Principle of Faith

The content of prebaptismal instruction was primarily dogmatic. "The study of dogma is a great undertaking, and an earnest soul is necessary for this." In setting forth dogma Cyril follows the order of the baptismal creed or confession which catechumens were expected to recite at the font with a complete under-standing. In order to "conceal the secret," the text of the creed is never fully quoted in his sermons. (Sozomen also did not include the Nicene Creed in his history "so that the uninitiated might not read it"). The text of the creed which Cyril explicates must be ap-proximately reconstructed from superscriptions, which probably were added later, and from quotations. This is undoubtedly the Nicene Creed. Whether or not this "Jerusalem" baptismal creed formed the basis for the creed of Constantinople remains un-clear.

Cyril does not try to set forth the "holy and apostolic faith" in its completeness. He admits that "we have omitted much." How-ever, he does strive to be exact. "The doctrine of the faith has been composed not by human reason, but has been made up of what is most essential in Scripture." Therefore, every statement made in the creed expresses the whole content of Scripture in just a few words.

Since the study of doctrine requires an earnest soul, Cyril be-gins with a call to repentance, purification of conscience, for-giveness, and prayer. He then presents a brief summary of "indispensable dogmas." This summary is more extensive than the creed itself. Besides the doctrines of the Holy Trinity and redemption, Cyril includes teachings on man, on the soul and body, on moral life, and on Holy Scripture. After this, he follows the order of the creed. He warns against distraction by "simple probability or by the conclusions of reason." A confession of faith must rest on proofs from Scripture and on the teaching of the Church, which is conveyed by the creed itself. In the process of examining and rejecting false opinions, however, Cyril some-times relies on logical reasoning to support his arguments. This is because there are two degrees of faith. The "dogmatic faith, the agreement of the soul," is from man, but it is only the means to winning another faith, "the gift of grace, which is given by Christ." This faith is higher than human reason. It illuminates the soul and allows it to contemplate God and the rewards of future life.

God and Trinity

God is one, without beginning, and eternal. "He did not begin to live in time and He will never have an end," and "He will have no successor." The essence of God is beyond comprehension and "we cannot explain what God is." The whole of creation, "all the members of the whole Catholic Church, both present and future," are not able to praise the Lord as He deserves. "Our highest wisdom in relation to God is to admit that we know nothing." Only the Son and the Holy Spirit can see the Father as He should be seen, for They "share the Father's Divinity." However, to a certain extent God is knowable from creation, and a conception of God's power can be formed from His works. God has many properties, but He is one. "We must confess God both as the Father and as the sole creator of all things, and believe not only in one God, but recognize with devoutness that this one God is the Father of our Only-Begotten Lord Jesus Christ."

By simply uttering "the name of the Father we gain an under - standing of the Son," "for if He is a Father, He must be the Father of a Son. If there is a Son, then He must be the Son of a Father." There is no distance between Them. The Fatherhood is eternal. God did not become the Father, but He is the Father "before any hypostases, before any sensation, before time and all the ages." Even though he does not use Nicene terminology, Cyril con - fesses the apostolic faith as defined at Nicaea and he sets forth his teaching on the eternity of the Trinity with complete precision.

The Son is the Son by nature, not by an arbitrary act of will. "The Son is eternally generated in a way that is unknowable and incomprehensible." Neither time nor an act of reason are relevant in the generation of the Son from the Father, and there is no de - velopment in the being of the Son. "That which He is now, He also was in the beginning, for He is generated eternally." The mode of this generation is incomprehensible to us and we should not try to understand that which is not revealed in Scrip - ture by the Spirit, Who alone knows the profundity of God's nature. The Father generates the Only-Begotten, the "true God," before the ages. They are united in Their divinity, for "God engendered God," Who is "truly like in everything" to the Father. The Son has the "immutable dignity of Sonship," and by es - sence and in truth He is the Lord, one with the Father in Their indivisible authority.

The Father creates and orders everything through the Son, "through Christ." "Christ is the Only-Begotten Son of God and the Creator of the World." The Son creates everything "by the will of the Father," by the Father's authority, and the Son has power and dominion over that which He has created. Christ creates everything not because the Father cannot do so, but because "God wished the Son to rule over everything He created, and God Himself gave Him the design for what He established." In this Cyril strictly follows Scripture. In order to stress the complete unity and likeness of the Father and Son he emphasizes that the Son has everything (He did not "receive," for there was never a time when He was without anything) from the Father, and that He creates "by the will of the Father." He creates as the Son, but this

does not destroy the unity of their indivisible power and au -
thority. "He rules with the Father, and through the Father He is
the creator of everything. But this does not impair the dignity of
the Divinity." "He is the rich and inexhaustible source of all good,
the river of all blessings, the eternal, unceasing, shining light."

The Son is revealed in the Old Testament and was seen by
Moses and the prophets. (The concept of the manifestation of
the Word in the God of the Old Testament had been elaborated
long before Cyril). Cyril uses the name Christ to designate the
Son as Creator, and this is connected with his teaching on the
Son as the eternal High Priest. The Son was anointed by the
Father to "the High Priesthood, which exceeds the priesthood of
men." "He did not begin His priesthood in time, He did not as -
sume the High Priesthood as a successor in the flesh, and He
was not anointed with oil prepared by men, but His priesthood is
from the Father before the ages." Apparently Cyril is here re -
ferring to the Eternal Counsel of God, and he probably spoke
about this in greater detail in a sermon "On the Order of Mel -
chizedek" which has not survived.

Cyril speaks of the Holy Spirit only briefly. He should be
thought of in the same way that the Father and Son are thought
of, since they all share the single "glory of divinity." The Spirit is
"coeternal" with the Father and the Son, and concern for our
salvation is common to all of them. The Son reveals the Father
"together with the Spirit and through the Spirit." The Holy Spirit is
the Spirit of revelation and enlightenment, the "unique and
good" sanctifier, helper, and teacher of the Church, the Spirit of
grace "Who marks the soul as His own" and Who gives "sanc -
tification and deification to all." "The Spirit has one aspect" and is
not divided by the multiplicity of His gifts. It is not the Father Who
gives one gift, the Son Who gives another, and the Spirit Who
gives another, but salvation, strength, and faith are common to
all, and their dignity is indivisible. "We proclaim one God with the
Holy Spirit through one Son," without merging and without
division. "The Father gives to the Son, and the Son gives to the
Holy Spirit."

"For our salvation it is enough for us to know that there is a
Father, a Son, and a Holy Spirit." Nothing has been written about
anything else, and it is not fitting for us to speculate beyond what
can be found in Scripture "on the essence of the hypostases."
Thus the trinitarian theology of Cyril is distinguished by its strict
adherence to the Bible, and Cyril constantly strives to support his
arguments with quotations from Scripture. In spite of this, in
several instances he refers to the Father, Son, and Holy Spirit as
hypostases, recognizing three hypostases in one God. How -

ever, he does not clearly explicate the concepts of "*hypostasis*" and "*essence*." He uses both terms to express existence which is enduring, as opposed to transient or diminishing being. "Christ is not a Word which is spoken and then dissipates, but a living Word, an hypostasis." The Holy Spirit "is not exhaled by the lips of the Father to spread out in the air, but is an hypostasis, and speaks and acts Himself."

Redemption

The Only-Begotten Son assumed a human nature similar to ours and was born from the Virgin Mother of God. "Let us worship Him as God, and believe that He became man," for if Christ is only God "then we are outside of salvation." To call Him only God does not do Him full justice and does not bring us salvation, and to call Him only a man brings us no advantage. Cyril opposes Docetism by stressing the real human nature of Christ. The eternal Word became man "really, and not only in semblance." It is not a mere man who was crowned and deified, but the Word and Lord Who assumed a nature similar to our own.

Christ has a double nature. He is both God and man in complete unity, and therefore Cyril can speak of the blood, humiliation, and crucifixion of the Only-Begotten. "The One Who died for us was not just a simple man, nor only an angel, but God Who became man." Therefore the whole world is saved "because the Only-Begotten Son of God died for it." Christ came for the sake of salvation. He came in the flesh, "otherwise He would be inaccessible to us," and "we would not be able to see and rejoice in Him." The visible manifestation of divine glory struck the prophets with trepidation. God covered His divinity with the heavens, and thus veiled His unendurable radiance so that it would not destroy the world. In the Incarnation of the Word "grace is proportionate to us," for the Word has clothed itself and veiled itself in the flesh.

Christ came "so that the Father could be known," and the Son is the only door to the true knowledge of God. He puts an end to pagan delusions. "When people falsely began to worship the image of a man as God, God became a man to destroy the lie." He came "so that sinful men could enter communion with God and free themselves from the power of demons."

The Lord suffered for us, but the devil would not have dared to appear to Him if he had known Him. Therefore, "the body became a lure for death, so that the serpent, which was hoping to swallow it, vomited forth that which had already been swallowed." In this Cyril follows Origen.

The Lord descended into hell alone, but He left with a multitude. "Death was terrified to learn that Someone new, Who could not be held in fetters, had descended into hell." "The Lord was born from the new Eve, from the new Virgin, to fulfill the prophecies. He sanctified baptism by His own baptism." "The beginning of the Gospel is the Jordan." Christ worked many miracles, but the greatest of all was the miracle of the Cross. Christ's death on the cross was not in appearance only. "If salvation is from the cross, but the death on the cross was only a semblance, then our salvation also is only a semblance, and then so was the resurrection. If the resurrection was no more than an appearance, then so too is the second coming. And nothing would be real."

The cross is the indestructible foundation and hope of sal-vation, the glory and "praise of all praises." The voluntary suf-fering of Christ was real, and the Son of Man was glorified by accepting the crown of thorns. "He Who suffered and endured was not an insignificant man, but God Incarnate." All men were in bondage to death because of sin. Christ raised the sins of all in His body on the cross to pay the "ransom," and God's anger was satisfied. The justice of the sentence was maintained, but the strength of love for mankind was made manifest. Sin came from a tree and lasted until another tree. Christ was buried in the earth "so that the accursed earth received a blessing instead of curses, for the tree of life was planted in it."

During His life the Lord symbolically reenacted, and thus abrogated, the events of the Fall. "I confess the cross, for I know the resurrection." He ascended into heaven, "crowned by His victory," and sat at the right hand of the Father. "We will not concern ourselves with the nature of His throne, for that is beyond our understanding." Although He has left the earth in the flesh and is seated on high, the Lord is still with us. He will come again in glory for the judgment and the final victory, "wearing the crown of the kingdom of God." The eternal heav-enly kingdom will be at hand, but the eternal fire will also be prepared. The cross is a sign of victory, "a crown which does no dishonor." This is Cyril's brief but striking presentation of the saving work of Christ.

The Church

The Lord arose in fulfillment of the promise, and at Pentecost the Spirit, "the Comforter and Sanctifier of the Church," de-scended into the world. This is the same Spirit Who spoke to the prophets and came down to the righteous men of the Old

Testament. The "grace of the New Testament," however, is an even greater grace. "Grace was also among the fathers, but now it is overflowing. Then they were in communion with the Holy Spirit, but now we are completely baptized by Him."

At Pentecost the apostles received "complete" baptism by fire. "This grace was not partial, but perfect and complete." In the same way that fire penetrates metal and makes it burn and shine, so does the Spirit penetrate the depths of the soul, illuminating it and burning out the thorns of sin. At Pentecost an abundance of "spiritual water" was poured out into the world, and since that time the grace of the Spirit has been with the apostles and the whole Church.

The Church receives its name "because it gathers and unites all," just like the cross on which the Lord stretched out His arms. The Church is a Catholic Church because it is spread throughout the universe. All men should revere it because it reveals "com - pletely and without omission" the doctrine of all heavenly and earthly things. It heals the soul and the body and it teaches vir - tue. The Church opens the gates of eternal life through holy baptism and the other sacraments.

"Baptism is the end of the Old Testament and the beginning of the New," and without baptism there is no salvation. Man and baptism both have a dual nature. Baptism by water is for the body, and baptism by the Holy Spirit is for the incorporeal soul. All of man is purified, for "there is nothing bad in human nature unless we make it bad by adultery and incontinence." The body which houses the soul is not "a vessel that is alien to God," and it is not responsible for sin. "It is the soul that sins by means of the body." The body will be made eternal, and at the resurrection "we will all receive bodies that are immortal, but not identical." Therefore the body should be cherished and kept pure for the Lord, "so that the Lord might look upon the body with favor." The body, "our corporeal robe," is healed in baptism and "receives grace through the water." Through the flesh we will participate in the second coming of Christ.

At baptism we symbolically reenact the life and works of Christ. By removing our clothes we shed our old selves, and we imitate Christ on the cross Whose nakedness conquered the power of darkness. When we are led to the baptismal font, we depict the deposition of Christ from the cross to His tomb. The triple immersion signifies the three days of His burial. "You have died and been born again at the same time. The saving water has become a tomb and a mother for you."

This commemoration is not only symbolic. "Commemoration," ἀνάμνησις, is the objective reproduction of the action being remembered. At the sacramental "commemoration" the action is genuinely accomplished. This is the realism and reality of the sacrament, the "mystery." "This is new and extraordinary. We die and are buried, we are crucified and rise from the dead, but not in reality. Our imitation is only an outer form, but our salvation is real." When we share His passion through "imitation, μίμησις, Christ gives us salvation. For us this is only the "likeness" of suffering and death, "but our salvation is a reality."

Baptism gives not only remission of sins but we are also sealed by the Holy Spirit. At baptism we are "united with the spiritual Bridegroom." "Our soul is reborn. We receive bright clothes, the holy indestructible seal, the chariot of heaven, and the bliss of paradise. The heavenly kingdom is prepared for us." We are united in a single body: "You become sons and daughters of one mother when your names are entered." This is the "impression of the mysterious seal" by which our Lord knows us.

"We receive holy baptism not by necessity but by an act of free will," "not before faith but as a result of our faith which we choose freely." Man is completely free, and God waits for each man to make a sincere choice. We are just or sinful by our will alone and therefore repentance and good works are necessary. A man becomes elect by his own will. "Evil is the product of free will," and therefore a new act of will is required to overcome it. The will is strengthened by God. At baptism we must renounce Satan and his works, and we reject sin and hell. We are then given grace, but this grace must be guarded. "God gives, but you must preserve and protect." "You must give grace your assistance."

The Sacraments

Because of their character and purpose the sermons of Cyril do not offer a detailed explanation of the sacraments. However, he did explain those sacraments which were received by cate - chumens upon entering the Church. He deals mainly with bap - tism. Baptism by water is necessary for salvation. Only martyrs, who "baptize themselves in their own blood when they suffer persecution," are exempt from this. "They will find the kingdom even without water." The water in the baptismal font "bears Christ." It is "made holy" through the invocation of the Trinity of Spirit, Christ, and Father. Baptism cannot be repeated. "If once you have failed to achieve success, this cannot be corrected." Cyril considers that the baptism of heretics is merely apparent.

Baptism in water is made complete by "baptism in the Spirit," by anointing with oil. The oil used for anointing is not simply oil. Cyril compares it to the Eucharist: "In the same way that by the in -

vocation of the Holy Spirit the bread of the Eucharist does not remain simply bread but becomes the body of Christ, so is this holy oil no longer simple or ordinary but it is the gift of Christ and the Holy Spirit. It has its effect through the presence of the Divinity." The sacramental oil represents the Holy Spirit. The anointing of a believer is a recreation of the "inspiration of the Spirit" which Christ received after His baptism in the Jordan. "The image of all this is enacted over you because you are the image of Christ . . . By being anointed with oil you have entered communion with Christ and have become participants in Him." The Chrism gives spiritual protection to soul and body.

Believers "share the body and blood of Christ" through the Holy Eucharist. This is by virtue of the real presence of the Body and the Blood. "Although it seems to your senses that this is bread and wine, let your faith strengthen you. Do not judge things by their taste, but assure yourself through faith that you are honored by the Body and Blood of Christ." The form [$\tau \acute{\upsilon} \pi o s$] of bread and wine remain but in this form the Body and Blood are present. "We become bearers of Christ because the Body and Blood of Christ are given to us." It may seem to the senses that these are bread and wine, but the Lord has testified that they are His Body and Blood. Cyril explains the manner in which the sacramental transformation takes place by referring to the miracle of Cana in Galilee. Our knowledge of this miracle makes it pos- sible for us to believe that Christ also transforms wine into His Blood.

The Gifts are sanctified by the invocation of the Holy Spirit. "We pray to God that in His love for man He will send the Holy Spirit down to these gifts and that He will make this bread the Body of Christ and this wine the Blood of Christ. For it is certain that whatever the Holy Spirit touches is sanctified."

Cyril relates the request made in the Lord's Prayer for "our daily bread" to the Holy Eucharist. "Our daily bread" is bread which is suited to our substance, $\dot{\epsilon} \pi \iota o \acute{\upsilon} \sigma \iota o s$, and this bread "has an influence on the substance of our souls." It feeds not only our bodies, "but is imparted to our whole being."

The Eucharist is the "bloodless and spiritual sacrifice," and the Eucharistic Gifts are "holy and awesome." Before the sanc- tification of the Gifts believers pray for their souls to be united in gratitude. The Eucharistic prayers are said for all creatures and for the ranks of angels, and they include the angelic words which were heard by Isaiah: "By singing our hymns let us enter com- munion with the hosts of peace." At the completion of the sacrament prayers are said for all the living and the dead. "By bringing prayers to God for the dead, even if they were sinners, we are not weaving them a crown. We are offering to God Christ, Who was sacrificed for the sins of the world. We do this for the sake of the dead and for our own sakes as well, and we hope that God in His love for man will be merciful." One should receive the Eucharist frequently. "Do not deprive yourselves of these holy and spiritual mysteries because of spiritual pollution."

As much as we are able to judge by the brief essay on the liturgy in Cyril's fifth mystagogical sermon, the liturgy as cele - brated in Jerusalem was similar to the liturgy found in the eighth book of the Apostolic Constitutions, which was apparently based on the Palestinian tradition.

CHAPTER FOUR

ST. BASIL THE GREAT

I
LIFE

Basil the Great was born into a Cappadocian family which was wealthy and distinguished, and there was always something aristocratic about his spiritual outlook. His father, Basil the elder, was a well-known rhetorician in Neocaesarea, and it was he who introduced his son to intellectual pursuits. Basil's religious attitudes were formed largely under the influence of his grandmother, Macrina the elder, who was a disciple of Gregory Thaumaturgus. Basil was educated first in Caesarea and later in Constantinople and Athens, where he met Gregory the Theologian. A close friendship and spiritual intimacy, which was later described for us by Gregory, grew up between them. Basil was at this time drawn in two directions. On one hand he was interested in philosophy and secular knowledge, but he was also attracted by the idea of an ascetic life of quiet contemplation in isolation from the world. He grew restless and dissatisfied in Athens and finally left the city "for a more perfect life."

Before leaving Athens Basil completed a broad course of studies and he was later renowned for his enormous erudition. He was a brilliant orator and his eloquence, which "breathed with the strength of fire," seemed effortless. He studied philosophy, dialectics, and medicine. Basil returned to his native land in 354 and began to teach rhetoric, but he soon renounced his secular activities in favor of a life of asceticism. He was baptized and traveled through Syria and Egypt in order to witness the ascetic feats of the Eastern fathers. His later memories of this journey were unhappy because the East at this time was torn apart by religious controversy and the unity of the Church was threatened by schism.

After his return Basil again withdrew to the desert near Neocaesarea where he organized his first communal monastery. He was joined by his friend Gregory, with whom he had earlier shared the ideal of ascetic renunciation, and together they worked on the compilation of a cenobitic rule. They also took an interest in theological problems, read Scripture, and studied Origen, from whose works they compiled the *Philocalia*. The majority of the original Greek texts of the Alexandrian teacher's writings have

been preserved for us in this collection. Gregory later remem -
bered with great emotion this period when he and his friend
"luxuriated in tribulation," that is, in their feats of asceticism.

Basil spent almost the entire reign of Julian in the desert. The
accession of Valens marked the beginning of the Arian con -
troversy, which was a difficult era for the Church. Basil was
recalled by his compatriots. He returned, although not without
hesitation. In 364 he was ordained priest and became the chief
advisor to Eusebius, the bishop of Caesarea. He began his work
as a spiritual leader at that time.

Basil was a pastor by vocation and by temperament. Although
he was a man of strong will, he did not have the militant heroism
which distinguished Athanasius, who was actually rejuvenated by
controversy. Basil was exhausted by conflict. It was easier for him
to defend himself on a daily basis than to take part in any major
struggle which could prove to be decisive. He was, however, a
man who fulfilled his duties and he tried to overcome his weak -
nesses by obedience and by humbly bearing the responsibilities
which had fallen to him. His will was made strong by stringent
ascetic exercises and its strength is evident in his very style,
which is terse and abrupt.

Basil's character was severe and authoritative and many people
found him difficult to deal with. Even his affectionate and loving
friend Gregory occasionally complained about him. However,
Basil was not a cold man. He was easily moved and deeply hurt by
disappointment and treachery on the part of his friends. He was
particularly grieved by the betrayal of Eustathius of Sebaste.
Sometimes he allowed himself to express his bitterness, but us -
ually he hid his feelings and overcame them, subordinating his
personal emotions to his vows and duties. His courage was the
result of his will. Basil was never physically strong and since his
youth he had suffered from frequent illness. He was inclined to
be melancholic and could not easily overcome the painful
impressions produced by the life around him. All of this makes
the strength of his will even more remarkable.

As presbyter Basil was Eusebius' chief assistant in the ad -
ministration of the church of Caesarea. Eusebius, who had been
appointed from the laity, had little understanding of the difficult
position in which the Church found itself. According to Gregory
the Theologian, Basil came, taught, observed, gave advice, and
"served in all ways. He was a good counselor, skillful assistant,
interpreter of divine Scripture, mentor in all undertakings,
support to the aged, protector of the faith, the most reliable of
clergymen, and more experienced than all the laymen." It was at
this time that Basil's polemic with Eunomius took place.

When Eusebius died in 370, Basil was elevated to his see, although not without difficulty and opposition. Several prelates refused to give him their obedience. First of all the new bishop had to pacify his flock, and he achieved this by a combination of authority, eloquence, and charity: earlier, during a terrible famine, Basil had sold the property he had inherited and given all of his money to help the hungry. In the words of Gregory, Divine Providence called Basil to be the bishop not only of Caesarea but "through one city, Caesarea, he is lit up for the whole universe."

Basil was truly a universal pastor who brought peace to the whole world. When at first he had to fight for his see, it oc-casionally seemed that the concessions he was making were too great. However, these sacrifices were deliberate because Basil considered that nothing could be worse than a heretical bishop. Basil was forced to keep silent for a long time. He refrained from openly confessing that the Holy Spirit was God because, in the words of Gregory the Theologian: "They were trying to catch him clearly proclaiming that the Spirit is God." In spite of both Scrip-ture and his own beliefs, Gregory continues, "Basil for a long time hesitated to use the proper expression, asking both the Spirit and the true supporters of the Spirit not to take offense at his circumspection. At a time when orthodoxy was threatened, an uncompromising position taken on a matter of mere words could have ruined everything. The defenders of the Spirit could suffer no harm from a small variation in wording, since they would recognize the same concepts behind different expressions. Our salvation is not so much in our words as in our works." Although he was forced to impose caution on himself, Basil "granted the freedom" to speak to Gregory, "who, by reason of his fame, would not be condemned or exiled from his homeland."

As a result of this policy Basil was the only orthodox bishop in the East who managed to keep his see during the reign of Valens. He also succeeded in gradually reuniting the divided Eastern bishops. This, however, did not completely resolve the problem. The shadow of the past still lay on the Church and Basil himself agreed that in view of their previous actions some prelates might not be completely trustworthy. Their prede-cessors had fought against the Nicene Creed and had exiled Athanasius, and they themselves were now in contact with the *homoiousians*. Many of them had been appointed by Acacius. Finally, not all of them followed an orthodox liturgy, even if only because of misunderstanding. It was necessary to explicate unclear theological concepts in order to dispel suspicion and to combine the truth of those who supported Nicaea with the truth of the "Eastern" conservatives. This problem was resolved by

Basil in his theology, which was based on a new theological terminology. This became universal throughout the Church, and the Nicene doctrine was set forth in the language of the Cappadocians.

This theological achievement was only the first step in Basil's struggle. He was required not only to teach but also to bring peace to his flock. He had to unite the Easterners in a single, firm faith, and he also had to win for them the tolerance of the "Old Nicenes" and the West. These difficulties resulted from both theological and canonical problems: most of the "Easterners" in the Antiochene schism were Meletians, but Athanasius and the Westerners were supporters of Paulinus.

Basil managed to accomplish a great deal. He received the support of Athanasius, who testified to Basil's orthodoxy and to his wisdom as a spiritual leader. "The Cappadocians should thank God for having given them such a bishop, who would be desired by any country." It was more difficult for Basil to reestablish relations with the West. He was hindered primarily by the diversity of opinions within the Antiochene church. Furthermore, the West generally had little sympathy for the problems of the East. However, the reunion and mutual recognition of the Eastern and Western churches which took place later was primarily brought about by the efforts of Basil the Great. Basil had one direct and definite goal throughout the course of his activity as a pastor: he wanted to gather together the divided forces of the Church in order to oppose heresy with a strong and organized body, united by strength of faith and purpose. During his life he was abused, denounced, and condemned, but even Athanasius was able to foresee that "Basil became weak for the sake of the weak, and thus truly won the weak."

Basil died some time before the Second Ecumenical Council and thus did not live to see his victory. We know that the exact date of his death was January 1, 379. He was not yet fifty years old. He had burned himself out in the terrible fire which raged in the East and which was extinguished by his self-sacrifice. His achievements were recognized at once and his immediate suc - cessors called him "Great." Much of his work as a spiritual leader dealt with the immediate problems of the day. It was soon for - gotten when the storms were over or, more exactly, when new storms arose and the past was forgotten in new conflicts. But Basil has always been remembered as a great teacher and theologian.

Basil was one of the great organizers of monastic life and the father of monasticism in Asia Minor. He primarily supported the cenobitic ideal of communal life, although he did not actually re -

ject anchoritic monasticism and even founded several secluded monasteries. However, he saw the purest type of monasticism only in community living, and in this respect he was a precursor of Theodore of Studios.

Basil considers that monasticism is the evangelical ideal, "the image of life according to the Gospel." The primary means to achieving this ideal is renunciation, not from disgust with the world, but out of love for God. Such love cannot be satisfied in the vanity and confusion of the world, and the ascetic must renounce and escape this confusion and noise. However, the Gospel does not separate love for God from love for one's neighbor. Therefore, for Basil, hermitic seclusion, inspired by the desire to find personal salvation in isolation, is insufficient. It is even opposed to the law of love which, according to the Gospel, "seeks nothing for itself." Furthermore, the spiritual gifts of the anchorite are of no benefit to his brothers. Finally, isolation fre - quently leads to arrogance. For all these reasons Basil summons ascetics to communal life and stresses the importance of love. "By living in a community the gifts given by the Spirit to one will also be given to the others."

In connection with this Basil refers to the description of the early Christian brotherhood in Jerusalem which is found in the *Acts of the Apostles*. He describes the early Church as the "body of Christ," and urges a return to this type of communal life. A monastery should be a smaller Church, a smaller "body." In order to achieve this ideal Basil advises monks to take vows of obedience and subordination to their abbots "even until death." The abbot is Christ Himself, and the organic integrity of the body requires that all of the body's members be subordinate to its head. In this type of community an ascetic, surrounded by his brothers, can follow his path of purification, love, and self-sacrifice, his "service of words" ("mental service"). Basil considers that the vow of chastity is extremely important as a way to the "single Bridegroom of pure souls." Although he did not require monks to perform works of charity outside the monastery, Basil himself built a hospice near Caesarea. "Here sickness teaches wisdom, misfortune is not despised, and everyone is shown compassion."

The ascetic's basic vow is love. From this intense love, strengthened by spiritual exercise, Basil hoped that peace would return to mankind. Possibly his enthusiastic advocation of the communal ideal came from his desire to oppose the dissension which he saw in the Christian world around him. Speaking of this disintegration, he said, with pain and bitterness, "In everyone love has grown cold. Unanimity among brothers has disap -

peared, and even the name of accord has become unknown." Basil hoped to restore agreement and to reestablish "bonds in the world" through asceticism and communal life, even if only for a select minority.

II
WORKS

St. Basil's Rule

Basil exerted an enormous influence on the later development of monasticism in both the East and the West, on both Theodore of Studios and Benedict. This was due more to the popularity of his writings on asceticism than to his direct example. These writings have been gathered together to form a "book of ascetic practice," which may some day be revised. In any event, Gregory the Theologian has described the composition of Basil's *Rule*, so there is no doubt that this is authentic.

The *Rule* exists in two forms, a short version and an expanded one. The first was compiled by Basil during his years of isolation in Pontus and contains forty-five canons or short explanations. The second was written in Caesarea and contains 311 canons. These are possibly based on the oral instructions which, ac - cording to Gregory, Basil delivered to the Caesarean monks. There is also a collection of eighty *Moral Rules* which were intended not only for monks but for priests and Christians in general. Two sermons, *On God's Judgment* [*De judicio*] and *On Faith* [*De fide*] , form an introduction to these. The authenticity of other rules and instructions for ascetics which have been ascribed to Basil is doubtful. One of Basil's letters to Gregory the Theologian contains a brief characterization of his ideal of mon - asticism.

St. Basil's Work on the Liturgy

Basil's work on the liturgy must be dealt with separately. Gregory the Theologian ascribed to him a "rite of prayer." From a letter of Basil to the clergy at Neocaesarea it appears that he was accused of making innovations in the liturgy by introducing antiphonal hymns at vespers. Basil deals with liturgical customs and observances in his book on the Holy Spirit. In fact, the book is essentially a single theological argument drawn from liturgical tradition. One of Basil's instructions is that during the period from Easter to Pentecost prayer should be performed standing, with -

out bows of genuflections, as a sign of joy at the resurrection and as a reminder of the "age which will not end" (cf. Canon 20 of the First Ecumenical Council).

The following remark made by Basil is very significant: "Our fathers in their wisdom decided not to accept the grace of the evening light in silence but to give thanks as soon as it appeared. We cannot say who is responsible for this expression of grat - itude, but the people sing this ancient hymn and no one con - siders that those who proclaim 'We praise the Father and the Son and the Holy Spirit of God' are lacking in reverence." Basil is referring to the hymn "*Gladsome Light* [φῶς ʼιλαρὸν] and thus asserts the antiquity of the hymn, which by its theological ter - minology dates to the pre-Nicene era and most probably to at least the second century.

Basil undoubtedly devoted much attention to the liturgy. It is difficult to say to what extent the liturgical rite known by his name can be ascribed to him, especially in the form in which it has sur - vived. But the fact that it is based on Basil's own "rite" is un - questionable. The Trullan Synod refers to Basil "who gave to us in writing the religious rite of the sacraments" (Canon 32). The oldest copy of the rite of Basil is found in a Greek euchologion from the eighth century in the collection of Bishop Porphyry (it was in the St. Petersburg public library at the time of the Russian Revolution).

In spite of his great ability as a theologian, Basil was not a writer by vocation and he did not express his theology systematically. He wrote very little that was not inspired by external and practical considerations. This is partially due to the fact that he lived during a difficult and turbulent age, and was throughout his life forced to struggle more in deed than in word. Nevertheless, his literary heritage is considerable.

Dogmatic and Polemical Works

Most important are his dogmatic and polemical works. The work *Adversus Eunomium* [*Against Eunomius*], a refutation of an *Apologia* by Eunomius which has not survived, was composed in 363/365. The surviving copy of Basil's work contains five books, but the two concluding books are undoubtedly not the work of Basil. They are only a collection of observations on the con - troversy, not a coherent argument, and were apparently written by Didymus. Basil also wrote an extensive doctrinal epistle *De Spiritu Sancto* [*On the Holy Spirit*] to Amphilochius of Iconium in about 375. A book written against the Manichaeans, which is mentioned by Augustine, has not survived.

Other works by Basil have a homiletic character. In his *In Hex -aemeron* (a sermon on *Genesis* 1: 1-26), which was apparently delivered on fast days, Basil provides a literal and realistic exegesis of the Bible narration. He also composed thirteen homilies on individual psalms, and here he uses an allegorical method of exegesis. Twenty-one other homilies were written on various themes, including *On Intoxication, On Anger,* and *Against Money-Lenders.* A characteristic discussion titled *Ex -hortation to Youths as to How They Shall Best Profit by the Writings of Pagan Authors* can hardly be called a homily. A *Commentary on Isaiah I-XVI* has been attributed to Basil but probably does not belong to him, although it was written during his era. It seems that Basil compiled a commentary on *Job*, but this has been lost. Basil's writings on asceticism have already been discussed.

St. Basil's Epistles

Basil's epistles deserve particular attention. They were collected by Gregory the Theologian, and 365 letters have survived (some of which are letters to, not by, Basil). Most of them were written after Basil became bishop, and they provide extremely valuable material for the history of the epoch. Several letters form almost complete theological treatises, especially Basil's well-known letter to his brother Gregory of Nyssa on trinitarian theology. Three epistles to Amphilochius of Iconium deal with Church rules, and selections from them were included in various canonical collections. Eighty-five canons have been taken from these letters and supplemented by seven more canons from other letters and from chapters 27 and 29 ("On the Meaning of Tradition") from Basil's book *On the Holy Spirit.* This book was also originally an epistle to Amphilochius.

The collection of canons made sometime before 565 by John Scholasticus, patriarch of Constantinople, contains sixty-eight of Basil's canons. The so-called "Syntagma to the Fourteen Chap -ters," a document written in the seventh century, contains ninety-two canons from Basil. The Trullan Synod of 692 gave official approval to these canons and made their observance mandatory along with the other rules established by the council. The majority of these canons deal with penance. They are a record of Church custom and tradition, and contain Basil's own additions of "material similar to that which I have been taught by my elders."

III
THOUGHT

THE WORLD AND MAN

CREATION AND TIME

Basil the Great begins his commentary on the *Hexaemeron* by affirming the truth of the account it gives of the creation of the world. "The creation of heaven and earth did not take place by itself, as some people have imagined," he writes, "but it had its reason in God." The world had a source. The bodies in the heavens move in a circular motion, and "just because our senses do not see the source of this circling" does not give us reason to conclude that the nature of these rotating bodies is eternal. Circular motion begins from some point on a circumference; the point is simply unknown to us. That which had a beginning will end, and whatever will end had a beginning. The world exists in time and is composed of substances which are subject to genesis and destruction.

Basil asserts that time was created by God as an environment for the material world. Time is succession and replacement, and it is always flowing and moving forward. At the beginning of time God created the world. But, the beginning of time is not time itself. "Just as the beginning of a path is not yet a path, or as the beginning of a house is not yet a house, so also the beginning of time is not yet time, nor even the very smallest part of time." The beginning is simple and has no duration. The beginning of time can be approached by moving backwards from the present. If God created heaven and earth "at the beginning," this means that "the act of creation was instantaneous and not subject to time." God's creation of the world by His will did not take place in time, but He created suddenly and instantaneously, or, in the words of the "ancient commentators," "briefly" (Basil is referring to the translation of Akila). Time began with the world. "Time is continuation which is co-extensive with the existence of the world."

CREATION OF NATURES OUTSIDE TIME

According to Basil, God created the angels before He created the visible and material world. Therefore angels are created outside of time and without time, and angelic being does not presuppose time or require it. This enables Basil to assert that angels are immutable. "There was, before the beginning of the world, a certain state which was appropriate to powers that have existed before the world, which are superior to time, and which are eternal and everlasting. Within this condition the Creator of all things created the intellectual light which brings bliss to all who love the Lord, the intelligent and invisible natures, and all the other adornments of these creatures, which can only be con-templated by us. They exceed our understanding to such an extent that we cannot even give them a name."

Angels were brought into existence by the Word of God. They were not created in an immature form, or in such a way that they had to perfect themselves through gradual exercise in order to be worthy of the Spirit. "The angels are not subject to change. There are no children, youths, or elders among them, but their nature is always pure and immutable. Sanctification was infested in their original state, in their very substance." "Therefore," Basil says in conclusion, "they are never inclined to sin because they are immediately sanctified as part of their nature. By the gift of the Holy Spirit their virtue is constant." They have been living in sanctity and spiritual joy from before the beginning of the world.

CREATION OF THE VISIBLE WORLD AND DEVELOPMENT OR EVOLUTION

God created the visible world in a single instant, but the world did not immediately assume its complete form. Basil does not deal with the substance of heaven and earth because he feels that to do so would be pointless. He rejects the concept of an "unqualified substratum" as the foundation of the world. Any-thing that is without qualities does not exist, and qualification presupposes existence. The nature or substance of matter is incomprehensible to us.

The primordial world was without order, "the world was invisible and in chaos." This is not because matter and form were at one time separate. On the contrary, God created everything, "not just a half of everything, but the whole heaven and the whole earth, both their substance and their form." This primordial world had not yet fully developed into the state which it had the potential to attain. "Because of the forces with which the Creator had en-dowed it the earth was ready to give birth to every thing but it was waiting for the proper time when, at God's command, it would bring to light that which it had generated." The *Hexaemeron* is thus a description of the proper ordering of the world.

The first day of creation stands outside time and before devel-opment, and Basil is hesitant to call it the first in the series of other days. It "existed in a particular manner," and it is eternal and self-enclosed. It is "outside weekly time" just like the eighth day, "the beginning of days, which is contemporary with the light. It is the holy day of our Lord and it was glorified by His resurrection." On this day God through His word and command gave to the world the "grace of light."

The word or command of God which was responsible for cre-ation became a "unique law that has remained on earth for future time, giving the earth the strength to generate and bring forth fruit." Basil compares this to a top or gyroscope. After it is set in motion a gyroscope continues to turn, and in this same way "nature, after it originated by the first command, has been expanding, and it will continue to expand until the end of the universe." Material nature is like a sphere moving on an inclined surface. It has been set in motion by a single command and con-tinues to move in a regular way as created things are generated and destroyed. The world is a unified whole in spite of the variety of its components, for it has been bound together by God "into a single interconnected unit and into a single harmonious body through an indestructible union of love." The genera and the species of existence have been preserved because that which is generated is similar to whatever generates it. In every genus and species, whether animal or vegetable, there is a seminal force. "Every created thing in the whole of creation fulfills some particular law of its own."

The ordering of the world was achieved in a series of instan-taneous outbursts. This is how Basil depicts the generation of the vegetable world. "Let the earth bring forth fruit . . . And the earth, following the law of the Creator, began to sprout, and in one instant of time passed through all the stages of growth, and immediately gave forth vegetation which was perfect. There was nothing at that time to stop growth. There had been nothing before that on the earth, and everything came into being in one instant, with all the attributes proper to it. Every plant was clearly distinguished from the others and recognizable by its own properties. The voice which gave the command spoke only briefly, and it was more a movement of will than a true voice. However, the idea contained within the command was complex and diversified. When animal life was produced the earth did not bring forth something which had previously been hidden in it, but by God's command it received the strength to generate that which it had not had before. Consequently, Basil asserts that animal life originates through spontaneous generation.

THE HARMONIOUS DIVERSITY OF THE GREAT PAGEANT OF THE COSMOS

Basil spoke of the world's harmonious diversity with the en-thusiastic appreciation of an aesthete. "Everywhere we can see some ineffable wisdom." The artistic completeness and order of the universe, the great pageant of the cosmos, elevates the mind to the contemplation of the Creator and Artist of everything. "The temporal is like the eternal," Basil exclaims. "And if visible things are so beautiful, the same must be true of invisible things. For Basil, the whole world bears witness to God. "If you look at even a stone," he writes, "even that will indicate the might of the Creator. And you will find the same if you look at an ant or a gnat or a bee. The wisdom of the Creator can be seen in the very smallest things."

Basil apparently used the commentary of Poseidonius on Plato's *Timaeus*, which has not survived, in his own interpretation of the *Hexaemeron*. He has translated Biblical imagery into the language of Hellenistic cosmology.

MAN AS THE HIGHEST LEVEL OF CREATION

In the order of the universe there are various stages which lead to perfection, and man stands at the highest level. Man was created in a different way than the lower world. This is expressed in the Bible, which clearly reveals the "dogma of truth" about the Word, the "assistant" in creation. Man was made in the image of God. He is immortal and is made for spiritual life. In the words of Basil, man is the only form of earthly life which was created by God. In creating man God "put in him some of His own grace, so that man can recognize what is similar to him by its similarity." Man is made up of a physical body and a soul which is sheltered within it. By its nature the body is unstable and is in constant transform-ation. It is "ceaselessly flowing and dispersing itself."

The world was put together and therefore will come to an end. It is the dwelling place of mortal things. Since they participate in the essential nature of this totality, men repeatedly die, even be-fore death separates their souls from their bodies. A man is a soul. According to Basil man is "intellect united with flesh which has been adapted to him and is suitable for him." The body as a "proper abode for the soul" has been designed by God with great wisdom. "We are soul and intellect, since we are created in the image of the Creator. What is ours alone is the body and the sensations we experience through it." The body is often a prison

for the soul. "As we strive for heavenly life our corporeal ex -
istence is harder than any punishment or dungeon."

THE SOUL'S INTUITION

Basil repeats the words of Plato when he says that "anger,
desire, timidity and envy all confuse the soul's intuition. In the
same way that a dull eye does not perceive visible objects, it is
also impossible to attain a knowledge of truth with a troubled
heart. Therefore, we should withdraw from worldly affairs and not
introduce superfluous thoughts into our souls." Physical con -
tinence and strict fasting are very important, for only a pure and
peaceful mind can reach the knowledge and contemplation of
the truth. It is necessary to achieve "complete silence within the
innermost temple of the heart," for every passion "causes
confusion and hinders the vision of the soul." It is impossible to
know the truth unless the heart is at peace. Intellect pre -
dominates within the soul.

"Intellect is beautiful," writes Basil, "for in it we possess that
which makes us similar to the Creator." Basil follows Plato in dis -
tinguishing the faculties of the soul. Lower than reason are the
properties of irritability and desire $\theta\nu\mu\delta s$ and $\dot{\epsilon}\pi\iota\theta\nu\mu\dot{\iota}\alpha$ or $\tau\delta$
$\dot{\epsilon}\pi\iota\theta\nu\mu\eta\tau\iota\kappa\delta\nu$. Irritability, or the soul's capacity to will, must
subordinate to reason. If this is not the case, it can become
uncontrollable and can distort the soul by evolving into passion
or anger. The "internal storm of an agitated soul" darkens and
blinds the mind, making "knowledge" impossible. By itself,
however, "irritability is a spiritual nerve which gives the soul the
strength for great deeds." As long as it does not hinder thought,
irritability strengthens the soul and produces courage, patience
and restraint. "If the soul has become weak through volup -
tuousness, irritability will temper it as iron is tempered by
immersion in water, and will make a soft and feeble soul steadfast
and firm." Righteous irritation, guided by reason, expresses itself
in religious fervor. It is proper to love virtue and hate sin with
equal intensity. "There are times when it is good to show hatred,"
Basil writes, especially for the devil, the destroyer of men, the
father of lies and the cause of sin. "But be compassionate to your
brother. If he is sinful, he will be given to the eternal fire with the
devil."

Desire can also be useful to the soul if it is subordinate to
reason and is directed to the love of God and the longing for
eternal bliss. Basil considers that each faculty of the soul "can be
either good or bad, depending on the way it is used." Everything
depends on "concord" and proportionality, on the harmony or

"symmetry" of spiritual life. The source of this harmony is reason. Action in accordance with reason is virtue. It shows the integrity of the soul and it is crowned by loving communion with God. Sin is movement away from God, that is, from Life. It is the "loss of life" and the beginning of death. The first sin is the preference of the material and sensual to the spiritual. The righteous path leads from matter to the spirit, to life. "Whoever fixes his attention on the radiance and grace of this beauty," says Basil, "will take something from It and will be marked by It, as though by a dye, when he exposes his own face to its colored rays. In this way the face of Moses, who participated in this Beauty, was glorified during his communion with God." The path of virtue is the path of reason and spiritual contemplation, θεωρία.

KNOWLEDGE OF GOD AS ACCESSIBLE TO MAN

The knowledge of God is accessible to man. In the first place, the majestic panorama of the world displays harmony in each of its parts and as a whole, and man can and should conclude that this order must have a rational cause. There must exist an Artist of every thing. Aristotle had already demonstrated this in his cos - mology. According to Basil a man who fails to recognize God by contemplating the wonderful beauty and harmonious order of the world is like a man who can see nothing even at noon. In the second place, man can know God by knowing himself. Basil echoes the Bible when he says "heed yourself" (*Deuteronomy* 15: 9). "The careful observation of your own self will guide you to the knowledge of God. For if you 'heed yourself' you will not have to look for the evidence of the Creator in the universe."

"The incorporeal element within you that is your own soul will enable you to understand that God too is incorporeal. You will know that He is not limited to any one place, just as your mind has no previous existence in some other place, but comes into itself only when it is united with your body. You will believe that God is invisible when you have come to know your own soul, for it also is inaccessible to the eyes of the body. It has neither color nor outward appearance, and it has not outline by which it can be perceived, but you know it by its action. Therefore when you think about God do not rely on what you see with your eyes, but believe with your mind, so that your concept of God may be achieved through your intellect."

THE INADEQUACY OF NATURAL KNOWLEDGE OF GOD

Of course, the knowledge of God which can be attained by our natural faculties is inadequate and incomplete. It merely prepares us to receive Divine Revelation through Sacred Scripture. Scripture is the treasure house which contains our knowledge of God. According to Basil "there is not a single superfluous word in it." However, even Scripture does not enable us to completely understand God, for God must ultimately remain incompre - hensible to us. By the evidence of our senses we know that God exists. We can even comprehend *how* God exists. But what God *is*, and what His "essence" is, is not and can not be known by man or by any of the celestial intellectual powers. "I know that God is," says Basil, "but His essence is beyond my under - standing." The primary reason for this is that God is eternal and boundless, but the capacity of the created mind is always limited. Our knowledge of God is therefore never complete. It is at most an aspiration.

This does not invalidate the objectivity of religious cognition. Something which is incomplete is not necessarily untrue. "We have been given eyes so that we can know what is visible. However, this does not mean that everything that is visible is within our range of vision. The entire vault of heaven cannot be completely viewed at once. We observe as much as we can, but there is much that remains unperceived by us. However, we do not say that the sky is invisible simply because there is a part of it we do not see. On the contrary, it is just this limited perception we have of it that makes it visible and knowable to us. The same should be said of God."

Furthermore, since that which we perceive must be expressed by multivalent concepts, we can never penetrate beyond the properties and qualities of things. These qualities enable us to perceive and to express the nature of things, but never exactly or completely. In other words, the essence of things, even created things, is ultimately inaccessible to us. We cannot even compre - hend the essence of an ant. This idea was later developed in greater detail by Gregory of Nyssa.

The problems of the limitation of man's knowledge of God and the role that cognition plays in the formation of religious concepts became particularly important in Basil's continuing debate with Eunomius. The problematics of religious anthropology and of cognition became the focal points of this controversy, which was as much a matter of philosophy as it was of theology. The Ano - moean doctrine of Eunomius was based on Gnostic principles.

Basil responded to Eunomius by developing his theories of religious cognition and the creative character of human cognitive activity. These theories were not systematically elaborated, and Basil only indicated their basic premises. His work was later completed by his younger brother Gregory of Nyssa.

THE TEACHING OF EUNOMIUS AND BASIL'S CRITIQUE

Eunomius' Stress on Definition of Concepts and Dialectical Connections as Reflections of Ontological Interrelationships

The teaching of Eunomius is based on his examination of the objectiveness of human conception. He distinguishes two types of names, which for him means that there are two types of conception. In the first place there are names "which have been named by people," which are the result of human thought. These names are arrived at "by reflection," κατ᾽ ἐπίνοιαν. They are a sort of logical device or intellectual construct which designate things alone by referring to them in a way that is commonly agreed on. They are "proper names," the conventional signs of things. They do not contain any information about the inner structure or nature of the objects they refer to. These names are merely words and signs. According to Eunomius, "part of that which is achieved by reflection exists only as words without meaning, and another part of it exists only in the mind." It is impossible to derive any objective knowledge from this kind of name.

If all of our "names" or concepts were only our own constructs, the objective knowledge of things would be impossible. However, Eunomius also asserts the existence of other, superior names, which do give objective knowledge of the thing they represent. This idea is based on Platonic premises which have been modified by the Stoic theory of "seminal words." Things have names which signify their actual substance and which are immutably connected with them. These names reveal the "energy" or action of the essence of each thing. "The Wisdom of God is revealed in them, and these names are adapted to every created thing." These are the "names of wisdom," and they extend to concepts and ideas. These names are made accessible to man by God, Who has planted the "seeds of names" in human reason. By developing these seeds through purely logical analysis we are able to attain a knowledge of essences through such names. In this way we acquire indisputable and immutable knowledge of the thing. This is why Eunomius puts so much stress on dialectics and on the strict definition of concepts and ideas. Logical and dialectical connections are reflections of ob - jective and ontological interrelationships.

Eunomius derives his theology from Gnostic premises. He believes that our knowledge of God and Divine essence can be complete, and that this complete knowledge can be attained by analyzing the name of God. God is ἀγέννητος, ungenerated. The church historian Socrates quotes Eunomius as saying that "God knows no more about His own essence than we do. It cannot be said that God's essence is better known by God than by us. Whatever God knows about it we also know, without the slightest difference." This is because the nature of all reason is unified and unchanging.

Thus, in the words of Gregory of Nyssa and Theodoret, for Eu - nomius, theology became an "art of words," a logical and philo - sophical analysis of expressed concepts.

Basil's Stress on the Impossibility of Reducing Experience to Intellectual Concepts

In his critique of the teaching of Eunomius Basil first of all rejects the division of names into ontological names and meaningless names "which are the result of reflection." It is not true that "names which come from thought and reflection do not mean anything and are only sounds which fall from the tongue to no purpose." These would be delirium or idle talk, and not the product of reflection. Whatever is achieved by reflection pos - sesses some degree of mental reality. Even false concepts, which arise in dreams or in the aimless activity of the mind, have a certain stability. "Reflection" should be understood as the activity of the mind in its efforts to achieve comprehension. Reflection is thought. It is mental penetration or analysis. "When after close examination that which at first seems to be simple and a unit turns out to be diverse, this multiplicity which has been distinguished by thought is said to be differentiated by 'reflection'."

"The body, for example, at first glance appears to be simple, but with the help of reason we see that the body has great di - versity. By reflection we distinguish its color, outline, duration, size, etc. Similarly, everyone has a basic conception of a kernel of wheat, and this enables us to recognize one when we see it. On closer examination, however, it becomes clear that our consid - eration must take into account a number of phenomena, and different names are given to this single kernel to designate its multiplicity. We call the same kernel a fruit, a seed, or food. Each of these predicates occurs to us as we reflect, and these conceptions are assimilated by us as soon as we have conceived them. Thus, everything which can be perceived by the senses as an object at first appears to be simple, but when we contemplate it we see that it must be understood by means of many different concepts. This is perception through reflection."

Thus, Basil opposes the idea of the immediate and direct perception of the object as a whole, through which the object is revealed to the mind as being present and real, with his idea of the secondary intellectual analysis which consolidates perception by means of additional concepts and words. This secondary perception is formed or "invented" by the intellect, but this does not detract from its objectivity. For Basil, it is the mind's activity as it arrives at comprehension by penetrating the object it contemplates which is the basic feature of cognition.

The intellect defines objects primarily by their interrelationship. Through these it arrives at new concepts, which may be either negative or positive. Intellectual recognition is achieved by the perception of an object in its relation to other objects. This is why there are different kinds of names. Some names designate individual objects, such as man, horse, or ox. Other names express mutual relationships and "show the contiguity of one name to another," such as son, slave, or friend. Independent names "do not designate substances, but define the properties which characterize each thing." We distinguish things by their names and "we imprint within ourselves our own concept of the particular distinguishing features which we observe in things." Names and the concepts which are distinguished in them are the means by which we analyze things, and analysis is the main goal of cognition.

Analysis of an object presupposes contemplation, but at the same time it never exhausts it. There is always something "irrational" which cannot be isolated and expressed, and this means that the ultimate "essence" of things is incomprehensible to us. It is from this point of view that Basil approaches the possibility of knowing God. Every theological concept must be based on contemplation or perception, which are our means of knowing reality. By means of concepts we can break up and distinguish the information we receive through experience, but concepts can never express experience completely or exactly. Therefore they can never replace it. It is impossible to reduce experience to intellectual concepts, but concepts are possible and meaningful only through experience and within it. The mind is aware of only

that which it perceives, and can identify only that which it contemplates.

The Revelation of the Names of God – Knowledge of God's Energy, not God's Inaccessible Essence

This is particularly true in theology, where every attempt at
understanding God must be based on Revelation. According to
Basil, there is no single name which can encompass the nature of
God and which is able to completely express Him. "The individual
meaning of many different names forms a partial concept which is
unclear and poor in comparison with the whole, but this is suf–
ficient for us." Although these names are only relative definitions,
they are stable. Some of them express the nature of God by
rejecting "that which is not in Him," by "negating or prohibiting
concepts which are foreign to God." Other names indicate what
God is and how the mind should conceive Him. Both types of
names primarily express the relation of our minds to God. They
are a standard which guides us as we attempt to penetrate
Revelation and contemplate God. These names are only for our
benefit. They do not refer to the independent object itself, but
only to the object as we perceive it. They name the object of
perception for the perceiver. All of these names refer to God as
He has been revealed in the world through Revelation. The
names of God enable us to know Him in His actions, in His
"energy." According to Basil, "We believe that we know our God
by His actions, from His 'energy,' but this does not mean that we
approach His actual essence. His action or 'energy' descends to
us, but His essence remains inaccessible."

The names of the Trinity, which tell us about God by designating the relationships with Divine Being, are an exception. But
even they refer to God analogically, in such a way that He
becomes accessible to us. The Divine Fatherhood and Sonship
are incommensurate with human relationships, and when we
elucidate these concepts we should remember that the analogy
is only approximate.

There is no reason to accuse Basil of relativism. He does not
deny the objectivity of human cognition, but he places greater
stress on the mind's activeness. For Basil the process of cognition is valuable as a religious experience because in cognition
man achieves intellectual communication with God. There are
many names which tell man about God and express man's
participation in the various forms of Revelation, which is "manifold
in its activity, but simple in its essence." Basil's teaching on our
knowledge of God expresses his basic concept of man as a

dynamic being who is always in the process of becoming. The idea is common to all three Cappadocians, and Gregory of Nyssa and Gregory the Theologian develop it in greater detail.

TRINITARIAN THEOLOGY

Distinction between "Essence" and "Hypostasis"

Basil's main contribution to theology is his definition and explication of the Trinity. The Nicene teaching on the unity of the Divinity, which was expressed by the word "consubstantiality," was more clearly developed than the idea of the Divine Trinity, which had been given less emphasis. This was the reason that the Nicene fathers were accused, unjustly, of Sabellianism. Since the concepts "essence" and "hypostasis" were con-sidered to be identical, there was no word sufficient to express the nature of the "three" which had been left undefined. The concept of "person" had not been clearly elaborated at this time, and moreover it was tainted because of its use by the Sabellians. The only way to overcome the indefiniteness of Trinitarian termin-ology was by distinguishing and opposing the terms "*essence*" and "*hypostasis.*" It had to be logically demonstrated that these were not just different words, but distinct concepts.

The term "*hypostasis*" had been used in the past to distinguish the three in the Holy Trinity, especially by Origen and by Dion-ysius of Alexandria after him. For them, however, "*hypostasis*" designated almost the same as "essence," and they considered that as a definition it was too strong and that it compromised the unity of essence, honor, and glory. Bolotov has aptly remarked that "the teaching of three natures and three essences lies hid-den behind the radiant concept of three hypostases." Therefore, when the fathers at the synod of Ancyra began to talk about three hypostases they were immediately accused of "tritheism." The council of Alexandria of 362 under the direction of Athan-asius declared that both forms of expression had the same meaning. This, however, did not resolve the problem. Both terms had to be defined and established within an integral conceptual system. It was not possible to be satisfied with classical philo-sophical terminology because its vocabulary was insufficient for theology. Classical terms and concepts had to be reshaped. This task was undertaken by the Cappadocians, and first of all by Basil.

Four Sources for Basil's System of Theology and Metaphysics

There are four sources for Basil's system of theology and metaphysics. First, Basil's reasoning often shows the influence of the teaching of Origen, which was adopted by Gregory Thau - maturgus, and of Gregory's own creed.This influence is the source of Basil's basic antithesis of created to noncreated, of subordinate to superior.Basil is loyal to Gregory's tradition and frequently refers to the "words of the most blessed Gregory, which have been preserved in memory," to testify to his own faith.

A second source for Basil's theology are the definitions and premises of the "*homoiousians*," although he rejects their term, ὅμοιος, of like (essence), in favor of the Nicene ὁμοούσιος, of one essence. Basil takes from the *homoiousians* not only the term *hypostasis*, but also the distinction of the *hypostases* according to their "distinguishing properties," κατ' ἰδιότητα. In Basil's us - age the word ἴδιος, which had been a connecting term for Athan - asius ("own and proper Son," "own and proper Father"), is used to designate individuation and means "particular"– ἰδίωμα.

Neoplatonism is a third source for Basil, especially in his teaching on the Holy Spirit. Plotinus also uses the concept of "three hypostases" in developing the dialectic of the One. He re - fers to "three primary hypostases," and the One, the Intellect, and the Soul of the world from a "primary Trinity," ἡ ἀρχικὴ τριάς. Plotinus also speaks about the "consubstantiality" of the hypostases [ὁμοούσιόν ἔἰαι], since each one is constantly transformed into another and reflected in another. His "Trinity" is distinguished from the empirical world by its own distinctive features. However, Plotinus approaches Origen by stressing the hierarchic and subordinationist nature of his trinity.

Finally, Basil takes the basic outline of his trinitarian theology from the metaphysics of Aristotle. He was predisposed to this by the general tendency of Eastern theologians to base their doc - trine of the Divine Trinity on the concept of triunity, of "particular," "individual," and "concrete" features. The reason for this is that in Scripture the Trinity is described as Father, Son, and Spirit. It was left to theologians to demonstrate the substantial Unity of the Three, their "consubstantiality," both as numerical unity and as ontological equality, as "similarity in everything." This idea is con - tained in all baptismal creeds, including the Nicene, which confess "one God the Father, one Lord Jesus Christ the Son of God, and one Holy Spirit." Eastern theology did not begin with the concept of unity, but worked towards it. This is how it differs from Neoplatonic speculation, which had more in common with Western theology and especially with Augustine.

Essence — Basil and Aristotle

Basil speaks most frequently about the Three. What he calls "*hypostasis*" is really closer in meaning to "*essence*" or "first essence," Aristotle's πρώτη οὐσία. At the same time the term "*essence*" [οὐσία] becomes identical to the Aristotelian term "second essence," which is used to signify common or generic being. It designates the qualitative characteristics of an object "what it is" in distinction from its concrete mode of existence, "how it is." Basil refers to this as μορφαί. In this way the concept "essence" becomes similar to the concept "nature," φύσις. For Basil, however, "essence" does not designate only common fea - tures which are secondary or derived, or which are differentiated and distinguishable by quality. "Essence" primarily refers to the indivisible numeric unity of Divine Being and Life. "Essence is Being."

Basil was not a strict Aristotelian. He adopted only certain features of Aristotelianism and rejected the system as a whole, claiming that it could lead to false and heretical conclusions. He criticized Eunomius for "thinking like Aristotle and Chrysippus." Gregory of Nyssa also considered that Eunomius was an impious "defender of Aristotelian dogmas." Basil found in Aristotle the logical means for defining theological concepts and for expres - sing the ontological reality of the Three (not only in name, but in actuality) and the absolute identity of their properties.

Basil also found in Aristotle corroboration for his own ideas on the unknowableness of "essence." Aristotle is able to describe being only through its properties or concrete forms, because the ultimate foundations of being are unknown. For Aristotle, this "unknowableness" is determined by the formless and un - qualified substratum which is beneath all matter. For Basil, how - ever, the inexhaustibility and completeness of "essence" place it above qualification. This is connected with the ambiguity of the concept δύναμις, which can mean either undeveloped potential or power and strength.

The significance of the influence that these various schools of thought had on Basil should not be overstated. Basil was not inspired by an abstract interest in speculation and metaphysics, but his theology was developed from living experience and contemplation and from Church tradition. He was interested in philosophy only as a source for the logical constructs and systems by which he could clearly express and defend the truths of faith, and reject or prevent ambiguous or incorrect inter - pretation. This explains his eclectic approach to philosophy. He was trying to transform heterogeneous elements into a coherent system of theology, not metaphysics. He accomplished this task, and the Church recognized the truth of the Trinity in the form - ulation of "one essence" and "three hypostases" which he elaborated.

"Three Consubstantial Hypostases"

The formula "three consubstantial hypostases" was not entirely new. The innovation of the Cappadocians consisted in freeing familiar concepts from their previous ambiguity. Most importantly, a clear distinction was made between the concepts "essence" and "hypostasis." Basil sees these as opposites, "that which is general" in distinction to "that which is particular" and belongs to an individual. "If I must briefly state my views," he writes, "es - sence is related to hypostasis in the same way that the general is related to the particular."

Basil clearly explains himself in a letter to his brother Gregory. This letter's (38/43) authenticity has been questioned. It may still prove authentic and, even if not, the thought here is identical to Basil's. This letter is an important document in the history of theology because it sets forth Basil's dogmatic beliefs. Basil be - gins by pointing out that there are different kinds of names and definitions. "Some names, which are used about objects which are multiple and can be counted, have a meaning which is common to many objects. An example of such a name is man. Whoever says this word designates by this name a common nature. This name is not used to specify or designate some one man. Peter is not more 'man' than Andrew or John or James. The common nature of the object being designated extends to everything that can be signified by the same name. Therefore it must be subdivided so that we can recognize Peter or John, and not man in general. Other names have a particular or individual meaning. They refer not to the common nature of the object which they designate but to the object's distinguishing prop - erties, which are not shared by other objects which are similar to it. An example of such a name is Paul, or Timothy. Such words do not refer to a common nature, but name certain specific objects and separate them from their collective significance. Therefore we can say that a "hypostasis" is a proper name. The meaning of the word 'man' is not definite, and when we use this word we convey a general idea. Although this word indicates the nature of an object, it does not designate a real object by its proper name. In using the word Paul we point to the proper nature of the object we are naming. Thus, hypostasis is not a concept of indefinite essence, and it does not designate an object by the elements it has in common with other objects. Hypostasis is a concept which represents an object by its visual and distinctive properties, and gives form to that which is general and undefined in a given object."

In other words, the noun "essence" refers to a certain group of characteristics which are common or generic ("homogeneous"). Within this group of common elements the "hypostatic" names single out "that which is particular." They define something in - dividual ("a certain man") "by its particular features." By increasing the number of features they narrow the range of the concept. In doing this these names concentrate attention on that which actually exists.

"Hypostasis is the distinguishing sign of individual existence." Basil takes this grammatical and logical idea and "transfers it to divine dogma." In the first place, "every idea about the Being of the Father" must be identically and immutably true for the Son and the Spirit. This is necessary because of the "consub - stantiality," the unity of essence and Divinity, of the Godhead, because of the "very Being of God." This truth is contained "not only in some one individual thought," for "Divine Being is higher than any thought." It is also expressed in the many names of God, all of which are equally and identically applicable to the Three. In the second place, the Trinity is not only called "Three," but *is* Three. The names of the Trinity are "hypostatic," that is, they designate what is real and actual. Aristotle also opposed distinctions that are "hypostatic" to distinctions that are purely nominal. "Therefore," Basil says elsewhere, "we confess that the Divinity has one essence, and we do not express differing con - cepts of Divine Being. We also confess individual hypostases, so that our ideas about the Father, Son, and Holy Spirit are clear and unblurred. For if we do not recognize the distinguishing features of the Fatherhood, the Sonship, and the Sanctification, we confess only the general concept of Divine essence, and it is impossible for us to correctly set forth the teachings of our faith." (*Letter 236 to Amphilochius*).

According to Basil Scripture has revealed to us that One God has the names Father, Son, and Spirit. These names are dis- tinguished not by general features, nor by degrees of divinity, glory, honor, or cognoscibility (as was done by Arius and the subordinationists in general, and especially by Origen). These names are distinguished by incommensurable and "unmerged" ontological characteristics. They maintain the completeness of "substantial" definitions but also enrich them by adding new ontological features. Thus it is necessary to say "God the Father, God the Son, and God the Holy Spirit."

We not only recite the common attributes of the Divine Being but we also distinguish its particular names. We enumerate them and join them together with the conjunction "and." "In this way we teach that each name has its own designee because these names are the signs of the objects they name." "When it is necessary to form individualized conceptions according to the different features existing within the Trinity," writes Basil, "then we define that which is distinctive not by the features that are common to these concepts, such as 'uncreatedness' or 'in-accessibility'. We look for those single features by which the concept of Each is clearly and individually separated from that which is common to all." These are the particular and distinguishing features. In conclusion Basil says that "until we reach a particularized conception of the individual qualities of Each, it is impossible for us to properly glorify the Father and the Son and the Holy Spirit."

It should be emphasized that Basil insists on the confession of three hypostases, and is not satisfied by the acknowledgement of "three persons." The concept "person" lacks the definiteness which "hypostasis" has in its very etymology. *Hypostasis* is from ὑφίστημι (ὑπό and ἵστημι; see ὕπαρξισ; ὑποκείμενεν). Furthermore, the suffix σις adds the sense that the basic meaning is static, not dynamic (or processional). According to Basil whoever does not use the expression "three hypostases" "is confessing only a distinction of persons. He does not avoid the Sabellian heresy, for Sabellius tried to merge these concepts by distinguishing only persons and claiming that the same hypostasis is transformed according to whatever need arises." Basil tries to exclude the possibility of sequential transformation from the concept of hypostasis by insisting that Each of the Three has "its own Being."

The Impression of Ambiguity in Basil's Teaching

In spite of its logical structure Basil's teaching is not entirely free from ambiguity. It is not without reason that his contemporaries accused him of splitting up the Trinity, and even of tritheism. Basil's trinitarian theology can in fact produce such an impression if it is limited to his opposition of the general to the particular, and if this is considered to be self-sufficient and definitive. However, Basil never states that this opposition exhausts the mystery of the Divine Trinity and Unity. Instead, he uses it as the basis for a clear theological terminology which strengthens ideas by giving them form. For Basil, this opposition is only formal and logical. It is true that the examples he uses to elucidate his thought seem to entail division, and not merely distinction, and it is questionable that the three Divine hypostases can be strictly compared to three men, Paul, Silvanus, and Timothy.

The basis of the theological problem is not the fact that the three hypostases must be enumerated but the fact that these Three are united in one God. It is necessary not only to dem - onstrate the hypostatic nature and ontological stability of the distinctions within the Trinity, but first of all it must be shown that these are the forms of a single Divine Being. The concept "hypo - stasis" must be delimited not only from "mode" or "person" in the Sabellian sense, but also from "individual."

One God is knowable in a Trinity of hypostases, not of modes (as in the teaching of Sabellius) and not of individuals. Basil un - derstands that an "hypostasis" is not the same as an individuality, and he is not satisfied by general references to "distinguishing features." It is clear that not every distinguishing feature is "hypostatic" simply by virtue of its particular definiteness. While it is true that "hypostases" are differentiated by their distinguishing features, it is not easy to logically separate "hypostatic" features from other distinguishing features. There are no clear boundaries between distinctions that are "accidental", κατὰ συμβεβηκός, and "hypostatic." The fact that there can be nothing "accidental" in the Divine Being does not resolve the problem. These dis - tinguishing features have been devised by man, and many of them define God in terms of His activity in creation and salvation. In a certain sense these are "accidental" with respect to Divine Life. It is these features which have led men into the error of sub - ordinationism, in which the economic distinctions of the man - ifestations or actions of the hypostases are considered proof of their ontological inequality.

Revelation and the Hypostatic Distinctions

The hypostatic distinctions have been established not by logic but by experience and Revelation. A logical structure has only been superimposed on the testimony of Revelation in order to give it form. According to Basil, "It is enough for us to con - template the names which we have received from sacred Scripture and to avoid innovations. Salvation is not in devising names, but in truly confessing the Divine Being in which we believe." Therefore, the task of theology is to explain the names of the Trinity as revealed in the Word of God. Logical systems are a means for achieving this.

Basil's conception of number in relation to God is vital for an understanding of his Trinitarian theology. He emphasizes that enumeration in the proper sense of the word is impossible here because the nature of the plurality of Divine Being is not such that it is merely countable. In theology number is transformed from quantity to a quality. The truth of the Triunity is not an arithmetic truth, and its mystery is not a mystery of the numbers three and one. "Let it be said to those who accuse us of tritheism that we confess that God is single not in number, but in nature. Everything that is called single in number in reality is not single and is not simple in nature. Everyone confesses that God is single and not complex. Consequently, it is not in number that God is single, for number is a property of quantity, and quantity is a feature of corporeal nature. Every number designates some - thing which has a material and limited nature, and singleness and unity are the features of essence that is simple and boundless." For this reason Basil concludes that "we must completely exclude any material and limited number from our concept of God."

In God there is no divisibility of finiteness to make possible numerical boundaries or distinctions. It is impossible to compare or differentiate that which is equal, greater, or less. When we think about God, we must overcome the material nature of number and the tendency of our limited reason to division. We must attain an understanding of a completeness which is un - interrupted and continuous. Only then will we see that the dis - tinguishable elements are not separate. With this in mind, the concepts of the general and the particular lose their sharp logical oppositeness. They are understood to designate a single and abstract moment within an integral whole. This uninterrupted completeness of being is the form of Divine unity.

Unity as the Foundation of Essence is Proper Only to God

God is single by nature and "unity is present in the very foundation of His essence." Such unity, wholeness, and con - centration of Being and Life, such complete "simplicity," is proper only to God. Therefore it is necessary to enumerate the Divine hypostases in an orthodox way, "not by addition, not by going from one to many by saying one, two, and three, or first, second, and third." When the Lord taught us about the Father, Son, and Spirit "He did not name them by counting, for He did not say 'I baptize you in the name of the first, second, and third, or in one, two, and three.' Instead, He gave us the knowledge of the truth in the Holy Names." The abstract form of the number three does not account for the concrete truth of the Tri-unity which is con - tained in the Names. In order to form a created unity many things are put together. A created unity is a derivative and a sum. It is not simple, and can be divided into many things. The components of this kind of "unity" and "plurality" are ontologically distinct and in - dependent. This is connected with the logical abstractness of "limited number" as a formal device.

In theology this problem is not a matter of the formal inter - relationship of numbers. The Divine Unity is realized fully and integrally as an immutable and indivisible Trinity. The Trinity is a perfect unity of essence and being. It is not an abstract formula of triunity but a specific Triunity which is revealed to us in the doc - trine of the Father, Son, and Holy Spirit. Therefore Basil opposes "enumeration" (be it subordinate or consecutive) with the Names. The knowledge of these Names, which designate onto - logical relations or states, leads us to a knowledge of the perfect Unity.

"There is much which separates Christianity from the errors of paganism and Judaism," writes Basil, "but in the good news of our salvation there is no doctrine more important than faith in the Father and the Son." This faith is sealed in us by the grace we receive at baptism, when the highest truth of God, which is incommensurate with our natural knowledge of Him, is revealed to us. In Christianity God is revealed not only as a creator but also as a Father. He is not only the Builder of creation but also the Father of the Only-Begotten Son. The name Father reveals the Divine generation and Sonship, and also reveals the Spirit, who proceeds from the Father. Thus, the name Father reveals the mystery of the Trinity, which is not a formal Triunity but is three separate hypostases: the Father, Son, and Spirit.

Basil always designates the hypostatic features within the Di - vine Life by the names which have been received in Revelation: the Fatherhood, the Sonship, and the Sanctification. In this he differs from Gregory the Theologian, who defines the hypostatic attributes more formally as Ungeneratedness, Generation, and Procession, and from his brother Gregory, who uses the terms Ungeneratedness, Only-Begottenness, and Being through the Son.

The names of the Trinity reveal the mystery of Divine unity. According to Basil, "Unity is present in the very idea of their essence. Although there is a difference in the number and properties of each, unity is contained in the very idea of the

Divinity. This is because a single "principle," a single "source," a "single cause of Divine Being" is inherent in God. The Father is the principle and cause of the Son who is generated and the Spirit who proceeds. He is the central point of Divine Being and Life. The causality contained within Divine Life is eternal, for everything in the Divinity is unchanging and immutable. The opposition of "that which causes" to "that which is cause" and the distinction of "first" and "second" are meaningful only in the con - text of our process of reasoning. They designate the order in which we are able to comprehend the Divinity.

In the Divine hypostases "there is nothing which has been added, nothing which is independent from or differs from the Divine nature. This nature cannot be separated from itself by the insertion of something extraneous. There is no empty or unoc - cupied space to interrupt the unity of Divine essence or to split it apart with empty intervals." On the contrary, between the Divine hypostases there is "a certain incomprehensible and ineffable relationship," "an uninterrupted and indissoluble relationship," "a relationship of essence," and "a relationship of nature." The wholeness of Divine nature reveals the unity and identity of Divine Being. Basil expresses the relationship of the hypostases by saying that "by His essence God is consubstantial with God by His essence."

Divine Life and the Generation of the Son

Therefore our conceptions about God must also be integral and unbroken. "Whoever conceives of the Father at the same time conceives of the Son. Whoever thinks about the Son does not separate the Son from the Spirit." It is impossible to imagine a separation or division by which the Son could be considered without the Father, or the Spirit could be separated from the Son. Every division which occurs in life is caused by time, and it is impossible to consider that time has a relation to God. "What will there be after the end of the Immortal? What was there before the generation of the Eternal?" Our contemplation must "extend beyond the generation of the Lord," and comprehend the con - tinuity of the Divinity "as it exists at a distance from the present." Eternal Being is an attribute of all the Divine hypostases in an equal degree. There is no development, no becoming, and no duration in the Holy Trinity because it has no interruptions and no plurality. The idea of inequality is inapplicable here. In conclusion Basil writes that "no matter how much we contemplate the past, we cannot escape from the fact that 'God was.' No matter how greatly we strive to see what came before the Son, we cannot go beyond the Beginning." "In the beginning was the Word."

The Father and the Son are one by their Divinity. "Everything which belongs to the Father can also be contemplated in the Son, and everything which belongs to the Son belongs also to the Father. This is because the Son completely abides in the Father and contains the Father completely in Himself, so that the hypostasis of the Son is an image by which we can know the Father." The Son is the living image of the Father. The Son is not a "reflection" which has been cast in time, but a reflection which is eternal. He is a coeternal radiance. "The eternal light shone forth from the ungenerated light, the life-creating Source proceeded from the true Strength, the Strength of God appeared from the absolute Strength."

All the Father's strength is directed towards the generation of the Son, and all the strength of the Only-Begotten is directed towards the Spirit. Thus the Spirit contains the Strength and essence of the Only-Begotten, who in turn contains the essence and strength of the Father. All of their strength is involved in this, for there is no complexity in the Divinity and there can be no division. It is impossible to conceive of any distinction between light and light. "The radiance of glory is like the radiance of a flame. This radiance does not follow after the flame, but as soon as the flame blazes up the light shines forth from it. According to the apostles, we should recognize that the Son comes from the Father in the same manner." The Spirit can be contemplated in the Son and the Father in a similar way. "With the help of the strength that enlightens us we turn our gaze to the beauty of the image (that is, the Word) of God who is invisible, and through this beauty we arrive at a conception of the Archetype (the Father), whose beauty is greater than any other. In this the Spirit of knowledge is inseparably present. To those who seek the truth the Spirit gives in Himself the mystical ability to contemplate the Image. He does not show this Image outside of Himself, but leads the way to knowledge within Himself."

Basil expresses the unbroken and undiminishing unity of Divine Life with the word "consubstantiality." For him this Nicene term signifies not only complete coincidence, not only the identity of the divine properties and attributes of the Three Hypostases, and not only "similarity in everything" or "similarity in essence." Most importantly it designates the "mutual re-lationship" of the Three and the ineffable unity of the Trinity. This was later referred to as "interpenetration" (John of Damascus calls this περιχώρησις [perichoresis]). Basil considers that the rainbow is the best image of the Divine Trinity which can be found among created things. In a rainbow "one and the same light is unbroken, and yet has many colors." These colors are part of a single phenomenon. There is no center or transition among the colors, and the rays have no visible boundary. We clearly see the distinctions and yet we cannot measure their distance. Together the many colored rays form a single white whole, and a single essence is manifested in the diverse colors of the radiance. This is the way we should conceive of the unity of the Trinity.

The unity of Divine activity, the unity of Dominion, Power, and Glory, testifies to the unity and consubstantiality of the Godhead. Basil always stresses that Divine activity is united and indivisible. "The Father, Son, and Spirit sanctify, give life, illuminate, and comfort. Let no one ascribe the power of sanctification to the activity of the Spirit alone. Everything else which is achieved among those who are worthy is the work of the Father, Son, and Spirit in an equal degree: every grace and strength, direction, life, comfort, immortality, freedom, and every other good which descends to us." Basil concludes by saying that "the identity of the activity of the Father, Son, and Spirit clearly proves the unity of their nature." This means that the Divinity is one and that its activity is unified.

Within this unified activity we can distinguish three components. The Father is the originating and commanding cause. The Son is the cause which creates, and the Spirit is the cause which perfects. "The Father commands, the Son creates, and the Spirit perfects." This distinction in activity does not imply divisibility, "for there is one single Origin of Being, which creates through the Son and perfects in the Spirit." "If the Father creates through the Spirit," Basil says elsewhere, "this does not mean that the creative power of the Father is imperfect, or that the Son has no power to act. Instead, this demonstrates their singleness of will." Every Divine action is a unified action on the part of the whole Trinity. The Three Hypostases and their ineffable order are reflected in Divine activity, which is always from the Father through the Son in the Spirit. "When we receive our gifts, we first of all turn our thoughts to the Bestower, and next to the Sender, and then we raise our minds to the Source and Cause of all good."

Divine Life and the Holy Spirit

According to Basil, in every action the Spirit is united with and indivisible from the Father and the Son. The Spirit "perfects" or "completes." He is the ineffable third of the Trinity. "He is recognized after the Son and with the Son, and has His Being from the Father." Scripture teaches us that the Only-Begotten is the "Source and Cause of all good things which are revealed in us by the activity of the Spirit," for everything comes to be through Him" and "everything exists in Him." Therefore, "every - thing has an irrepressible desire to return to Him, and strives towards the Source and Provider of life with boundless love." The Only-Begotten brings everything from nonbeing into being "not without another source," but through Him we receive grace from God, from the Father.

The mystery of the Trinity is reflected in the movement of Divine actions from the Father through the Son in the Spirit to creation. We know and contemplate the Father in the Spirit through the Son. The Spirit proceeds and is sent from the Father, the single eternal source, through the Son. The Spirit contains the glory of the Only-Begotten within Himself, and within Himself He communicates the knowledge of God the Father to those who truly worship. Therefore, the "path to the knowledge of God is from the one Spirit, through the Only-Begotten Son, to the one Father. Conversely, natural grace and sanctification and the worthiness of the kingdom extend from the Father through the Only-Begotten to the Spirit.

Basil developed and defended his doctrine of the Holy Spirit in his polemic against Eunomius and the Pneumatomachi. Ac - cording to the evidence that Gregory the Theologian has left about this controversy, Basil "turned aside from the direct path" and avoided openly confessing the Spirit of God. He testified to the Divinity of the Spirit descriptively, by means of quotations from Scripture. Many people condemned him for this, but his silence was only a temporary device which enabled him to maintain his pastorate. It was Basil who first developed an integral doctrine of the Spirit. In doing this he followed Athanasius, who had set forth the Divinity of the Spirit in his *Letters to Serapion.*

Athanasius bases his dogma on soteriological premises. His doctrine of the Son is developed from the image of Christ as the God-man and as the manifestation of the Word, and his doctrine of the Spirit is founded on the Spirit's manifestation in His sanctifying activity. Only the Father's consubstantial Word can give life and save creation and unite it with God. The reality of the salvation which God has sent to us enables us to reach the conclusion that the Savior and Comforter are Divine. Because Basil reasons in this way, his treatise on the Holy Spirit is primarily concerned with sanctification.

Basil had to prove and defend the Divinity of the Spirit. At this time the opinion of theologians was divided on this question, and Gregory the Theologian has described this era by saying that "some have conceived of the Spirit as an activity, some as a creature, some as God, and some cannot decide on anything. Even many of those who consider Him God are orthodox in mind only, while others have decided to honor Him with their lips as well." In order to resolve these contradictions and arguments Basil relied on Scripture and tradition, especially the tradition of prayer.

Basil's teaching is based on the baptismal invocation. The Lord Himself taught us about baptism and "united the Spirit with the Father as a necessary dogma for our salvation." In the baptismal invocation the Spirit is named with the Father and the Son. "He is not added to these two, but He is perceived within the Trinity." Although the Spirit is named in the third place and "is Third by order and dignity," He is not third by nature. "The Holy Spirit is one and He is proclaimed separately," says Basil. "He is not one out of many, but simply one. In the same way that the Father is one and the Son is one, the Spirit is also one. Therefore He is as far from created nature as any integral whole is not similar to that which is composed from many things. He is united with the Father and the Son because all things that are one are related." The Spirit is holy by nature, and this is the cause of His natural unity with the Father and the Son. "He is called holy just as the Father is holy and the Son is holy, and the Spirit's nature is filled with sanctity." Thus the "natural Sanctifier can be recognized and contemplated in the Three Hypostases." The same must be said about the other properties of the Divinity. "The Spirit's names are common to the Father and the Son, and He has these names because of His natural unity with Them." To diminish the dignity of the Spirit is to destroy the Trinity and to negate the truth of the Trinitarian dogma.

The first day of Christian life, the day of salvation and re-surrection through baptism, is sanctified by the invocation and confession of the Spirit with the Father and the Son. In baptism we die so that we may have new life, and "the pledge of life is given by the Spirit." In the Holy Spirit we are united with God, and "God lives in us through the Spirit." Basil asks, "How can that which makes others into gods not be Divine itself?" Furthermore, "there is no gift which descends to creation without the Spirit."

The Spirit is the "source and principle of sanctification," and creation "partakes of salvation" in Him. He is a source which never runs dry, is never divided, and is "never exhausted by those who come to it." His essence is simple but his powers are many. He is entirely present everywhere and in each of us. He is never di-vided, and when we join Him we do not cease to be whole. His action is like the rays of the sun. It seems to everyone who enjoys the sun's warmth that he is the only one receiving it, but the sun's radiance lights up the whole earth and sea and dissolves to - gether with the sky. In the same way the Spirit seems to be unique to everyone in whom He abides, but all of His grace pours down on everyone. Everyone enjoys this grace to the greatest degree he is capable of, and not to the greatest degree which is possible for the Spirit.

This indivisible wholeness is proof that the Spirit is divine. Basil says that "the Spirit is the Sovereign of sanctification." He is an "intellectual being, endless in His strength and boundless in His greatness. He cannot be measured by time or by all the ages." The Holy Spirit is sought by "everything which needs sanc - tification. Everything which lives virtuously desires Him, is nourished by His inspiration, and is enabled to achieve its proper and natural end. He perfects others and Himself needs nothing. He lives without renewal and is the giver of life. He does not grow by addition but has always been whole. He is complete in Himself and He is everywhere."

"The Spirit has existed before the ages together with the Father and the son. You will find that anything which may stand beyond the boundary of the ages came into existence only after the Spirit. At creation the heavenly powers were established by the Spirit. The Spirit gives to these powers communion with God, the ability to resist sin, and eternal blessedness." They are holy because they participate in the Spirit. "If we in our speculations try to remove the Spirit, we upset the assembly of angels, des - troy the authority of the archangels, throw everything into confusion and make their life disordered, indefinite, and outside of any law." The wisdom and the harmony of the host of angels is from the Spirit, and "it can only be preserved through the di - rection of the Spirit." The Spirit works in a similar way among visible creatures. It seems that Basil, possibly under the influence of Origen, limits the action of the Spirit to the sphere of intel - lectual creatures." In any event this is all he has written about.

The activity of the Spirit is evident in the Old Testament in the blessing of the patriarchs, the law, the miracles, the prophecies, and the heroic deeds. The Spirit is even more active in the New Testament. "The coming of Christ was preceded by the Spirit. Christ appeared in the flesh and the Spirit was also there. His powers of healing were from the Holy Spirit. Demons were driven out by the Spirit of God, and the Devil was rendered helpless in the presence of the Spirit. Sins were forgiven by the grace of the Spirit. The Spirit was present at Christ's temptation, and He was present when Christ performed miracles. The Spirit did not leave Christ even after He rose from the dead."

Even the Church's administration is achieved through the Spirit because its "order" has been "established by the distribution of the gifts of the Spirit." The Spirit is especially active in spiritual life. "Although the Spirit fills everything with His strength, He is communicated only to those who are worthy. The Spirit is as - similated by the soul only when passions are cast out, since passions attain mastery over the soul because of its attachment to the body and separate it from God. He who has cleansed himself from the shamefulness that evil has produced in him returns to his natural beauty, and by his purity he restores the original aspect of the regal image. Only such a man can approach the Comforter. And He, like the sun when it meets a clear eye, will show you the Image of the Invisible One in Himself. In the blissful contemplation of the Image, one will see the ineffable beauty of its Archetype. Through the Spirit our hearts are uplifted, the weak are guided, and we are made perfect. When a ray of light falls on shining and transparent bodies, those bodies also become radiant and return a new light from themselves. In this same way souls which are illuminated by the Spirit become spiritual and pour their grace on others. From the Spirit we re - ceive foreknowledge of the future, understanding of the mysteries, apprehension of what is hidden, distribution of gifts, life in heaven, a place in the chorus of angels, unending joy, eternal life in God, similarity to God, and the highest of all our desires: we are deified." Basil's ascetic ideal is charismatic. The Spirit purifies and gives knowledge. He is the "intellectual light which gives to every reasoning creature who desires it the power to see." By the grace of the Spirit the mind becomes capable of perceiving the Divinity. We know God with the help of the Spirit, and "our knowledge of God is possible only in the light of the Spirit."

Finally, the grace of the Spirit will be revealed at the last resurrection, when "that which has been destroyed will be given new life." Even now the Spirit resurrects and renews, "restoring our souls for spiritual life." The "crown of the righteous" is the grace of the Spirit and the "cutting off" of the impious (*Luke* 12: 46) is their final estrangement from the Spirit. Thus the activity of the life-giving Spirit is manifest in everything, from the beginning to the end, from eternity and creation to the last judgment. Life is God, and the Spirit, as the source of life, must also be God. Outside the Spirit there is darkness, death, and hell. Basil's doctrine of the Spirit is based on the experience of spiritual life, on the mystery of baptism, and on the mystical concepts of similarity to God and deification. It represents his personal religious ideal. Gregory has recorded his answer to the ruler who demanded that he obey the orders of the Arian Valens: "I cannot bow to a creature since I have been created by God and have been commanded to become a god."

CONCLUDING REFLECTION ON BASIL'S THOUGHT

Basil's confession of faith gives us evidence about Church traditions and especially about the liturgy. His book on the Spirit was written to explain and defend the glorification of the Trinity. He draws his faith from Scripture but at the same time describes the sanctifying and life-giving activity of the Spirit in the language of Neoplatonism. This "Neoplatonism" is most clearly evident in his teaching about the Spirit. In dealing with the Spirit he repeats much of what Plotinus said about the world soul. More exactly, he applies the vague and confused insights of Plotinus to the con - templation of a definite object, and he demonstrates the strength of the Spirit and the activity of the Trinity in the "divinity" which Plotinus had tried to elucidate. He did not so much adapt Neo - platonism as overcome it.

CHAPTER FIVE

ST. GREGORY THE THEOLOGIAN

I
LIFE

Gregory has left many autobiographical writings, and his descriptions of his life are filled with lyricism and drama. He was by nature inclined to silence and retirement, and he constantly sought isolation so that he could devote himself to prayer. However, he was called by the will of God and the wills of others to words, deeds, and pastoral work during a period of extreme confusion and turmoil. Throughout his life, which was full of both sorrow and accomplishments, he was constantly forced to overcome his natural desires and wishes.

Gregory was born about 330 at Arianzum, his father's estate near Nazianzus, "the smallest of cities" in southwestern Cap - padocia. His father, who in his youth had belonged to the sect of Hypsistarians, was the bishop of Nazianzus. Gregory's mother was the dominant personality in the family. She had been the "teacher of piety" to her husband and "imposed this golden chain" on her children. Both his heritage and his education de - veloped Gregory's emotionalism, excitability, and impression - ability, as well as his stubbornness and his strength of will. He always maintained warm and close relations with his family and frequently reminisced about them.

From his earliest youth Gregory cherished a "flaming love for study." "I tried to make the impure sciences serve the true ones," he said. In accordance with the customs of those times Gregory's years of study were years of wandering. He received a thorough education in rhetoric and philosophy in his native Nazianzus, in both Cappadocian Caesarea and Palestinian Caesarea, in Alexandria, and finally in Athens. He deferred his baptism until his maturity.

In Alexandria Gregory was probably taught by Didymus. In Athens he became very close to Basil, whom he had earlier met in Caesarea in Cappadocia and who was his exact contemporary. Gregory always looked back on his years in Athens with pleasure: "Athens and learning." As he later described it, it was in Athens that he, like Saul, "sought knowledge and found happiness." This happiness was his friendship with Basil, who caused him more joy and more pain than anyone else. "We became every -

thing for each other. We were comrades, table companions, and brothers. Our love of learning was our only goal, and our warm affection for each other grew constantly. We had all things in common, and a single soul bound together that which our two bodies separated." Theirs was a union of trust and friendship. The temptations of "ruinous Athens" did not distract them. They knew only two paths, one leading to the church and their religious instructors, and the other leading to the teachers of the secular sciences. They valued their calling as Christians more highly than anything. "We both had only one exercise, which was virtue, and only one goal, which was to renounce the world for as long as we had to live in it, and to live for the future." During this period of ascetic discipline they studied both philosophy and religion.

Gregory always remained a "lover of learning." "I am the first of the lovers of wisdom," he said. "I never prefer anything over my studies, and I do not want Wisdom to call me a poor teacher." He referred to philosophy as the "struggle to win and possess that which is more precious than anything." In this he included secular learning as well: "We derive something useful for our orthodoxy even from the worldly sciences. From that which is inferior we learn about that which is superior, and we transform that frailty into the strength of our teaching." Gregory continued to defend erudition later in his career. "Everyone who has a mind will recognize that learning is our highest good. I mean not only our most noble form of learning, which despises embellishment and verbal prolixity and concerns itself only with our salvation and the contemplation of beauty, but also worldly learning, which many Christians incorrectly abhor as false, dangerous, and distant from God. But we will not set up creation against its Creator. Learning should not be scorned, as some people think. On the contrary, we should recognize that those who hold such an opinion are stupid and ignorant. They want everyone to be just like themselves, so that the general failing will hide their own imperfections, and their ignorance will not be exposed." These words were spoken by Gregory at Basil's funeral. He never wanted to forget the lessons of Athens, and he later denounced Julian the Apostate for prohibiting Christians from teaching rhetoric and the secular sciences.

In Athens Gregory was taught by Himerius and Prohaeresius, who was probably a Christian. Most likely he was not a pupil of Libanius. He studied ancient literature, oratory, history, and especially philosophy. In 358 or 359 he returned home. Basil had already left Athens, and the city had become empty and depressing. Gregory was baptized, and decided to renounce the career of a rhetor. He was attracted by the ideal of silence and dreamed of retiring to the mountains or desert. He wanted to "hold pure communion with God and be fully illuminated by the rays of the Spirit, without anything earthly or clouded to bar the Divine light, and to reach the Source of our effulgence and to stay all desires and aspirations. In doing this our mirrors are superseded by the truth." The images of Elijah and John the Baptist attracted him. But at the same time he was overpowered by his "love for Divine books and the light of the Spirit, which is acquired by studying the word of God. Such studies are im‑possible in the silence of the desert." This was not all that kept Gregory in the world, because he loved his parents and con‑sidered that it was his duty to help them with their affairs. "This love was a heavy load and dragged me down to earth."

Gregory continued to lead a severe and ascetic life even amid the worldly distractions of his parents' home. He tried to combine a life of detached contemplation with a life of service to society and spent his time in fasting, studying the Word of God, prayer, repentance, and vigil. He was ever more strongly drawn to the desert in Pontus where Basil was practicing extreme asceticism. In his closeness to God Basil seemed to be "covered with clouds, like the wise men of the Old Testament." Basil summoned Gregory to share his silent labors, but Gregory was not immed‑iately able to satisfy his own longing. Even then his withdrawal was only temporary. He later recalled with joy and light-hearted humor the time that he spent in Pontus, a time of deprivation, vigilance, psalmody, and study. The friends read Scripture and the works of Origen as their years of learning continued.

Gregory's studies ended when he returned from Pontus. His father, Gregory the Elder, was managing to fulfill his duties as bishop but with difficulty. He had neither the intellectual back‑ground nor the strength of will necessary to make his way through the arguments and controversies that raged around him. He needed someone to assist him and his choice fell on his son. This was a "terrible storm" for the younger Gregory. Gregory the Elder had authority over him both as his father and as his bishop, and he now bound his son even more firmly to himself with spiritual ties. Gregory was forcibly and "against his will" ordained by his father. "I was so grieved by this act of tyranny," Gregory wrote, "that I forgot everything: friends, parents, my native land and people. Like an ox stung by a gadfly, I returned to Pontus, hoping to find a cure for my grief in my devout friend." His feelings of bitterness were mitigated by time.

Gregory's ordination took place at Christmas of 361 but he re‑turned to Nazianzus only at Easter of 362. He began his duties as presbyter by reading his famous sermon which starts with the words: "It is the day of the resurrection . . . Let us be illuminated by this celebration." In this sermon he described his high ideal of the priesthood. Gregory felt that contemporary prelates were far from achieving this ideal, since most of them saw their offices as a "means of subsistence." It seemed that less was expected from the shepherds of souls than from the shepherds of animals. It is this consciousness of the high demands of the priest's calling which caused Gregory to flee from the duties he felt unworthy and incapable of fulfilling.

Gregory remained in Nazianzus as his father's assistant for almost ten years, hoping that he would manage to avoid being called to a higher office. His hopes were in vain. In 372, once again against his will, Gregory was assigned to the bishopric of Sasima, "a place without water or vegetation, without any civilized conveniences, a tiresome and cramped little village. There is dust everywhere, the noise of wagons, tears, laments, tax collectors, instruments of torture, and chains. The inhabitants are passing foreigners and vagrants."

The bitterness which Gregory felt at this new act of tyranny against his desire to live in retirement was magnified by the fact that it was authorized by his closest friend, Basil. Gregory was indignant that Basil showed no understanding for his longing for silence and peace, and that he had forced him to become involved in his struggle to maintain his episcopal jurisdiction. Basil had instituted the bishopric in Sasima in order to strengthen his own position against Anthimus of Tyana. "You accuse me of lethargy and sloth," Gregory wrote to Basil in irritation, "because I have not taken possession of your Sasima, because I do not act like a bishop, and because I do not arm myself to fight by your side the way dogs will fight when you throw them a bone." Gregory accepted his office sadly and unwillingly. "I have ceded to force, not to my own convictions." "Once again I have been consecrated and the Spirit has been poured out upon me, and again I weep and lament."

Gregory's joy in this friendship was never restored. Much later at the funeral of his father he complained in Basil's presence that "in making me a priest you handed me over to the turbulent and perfidious marketplace of souls, to suffer the misfortunes of life." He reproached Basil further: "This is the outcome of Athens, our study together, our life under one roof, our companionship at one table, a single mind between the two of us, the marvels of Greece, and our mutual vow to set aside the world. Everything has shattered! Everything is cast to the ground! Let the law of friendship vanish from the world, since it respects friendship so little." Gregory ultimately went to Sasima, but, by his own admission, "I did not visit the church which had been given to me, I did not perform service there, I did not pray with the people, and I did not consecrate a single cleric."

Gregory returned to his native city at the request of his father to assist him in his duties as bishop. After his father died Gregory temporarily took over the administration of the orphaned church. When it finally became possible for him to escape from his pastoral work, he "went like a fugitive" to Seleucia in Isauria. He stayed at the church of St. Thecla and devoted himself to prayer and contemplation. But once again his withdrawal was only tem - porary. In Seleucia he received the news of Basil's death, and this peaceful interlude was ended when he was summoned to Constantinople to take part in the struggle against the Arians.

When Gregory went to Constantinople as a defender of the Word, it was once again "not by my own will, but by the coercion of others." His work in Constantinople was difficult. "The Church is without pastors, good is perishing and evil is everywhere. It is necessary to sail at night and there are no fires to show the way. Christ is sleeping." The see of Constantinople had been in the hands of the Arians for some time. Gregory wrote that what he found there was "not a flock, but only small traces and pieces of a flock, without order or supervision."

Gregory began his ministry in a private house which was later made into a church and given the name Anastasis to signify the "resurrection of orthodoxy." Here he delivered his famous *Five Theological Orations*. His struggle with the Arians was often violent. He was attacked by murderers, his church was stormed by mobs, he was pelted with stones, and his opponents accused him of brawling and disturbing the peace. His preaching, however, was not without effect. "At first the city rebelled," he wrote. "They rose against me and claimed that I was preaching many gods and not one God, for they did not know the orthodox teaching in which the Unity is contemplated as three, and the Trinity as one." Gregory was victorious through the strength of his oratory, and towards the end of 380 the new emperor Theo - dosius entered the city and returned all the churches to the orthodox believers.

Gregory was forced to struggle not only against the Arians, but he also had to oppose the supporters of Apollinarius. He en - countered further resistance from orthodox prelates, especially Peter of Alexandria and the Egyptian bishops. These at first ac - cepted him, but then illegitimately consecrated Maximus the Cynic as bishop of Constantinople. Gregory later recalled the "Egyptian storm cloud" and Peter's duplicity with bitterness.

Maximus was driven out but found a temporary shelter in Rome with Pope Damasus, who had a poor understanding of Eastern affairs. Acceding to popular demand, Gregory temporarily as-sumed the direction of the administration of the Church of Constantinople until a Church council could be convoked. He wanted to withdraw but the people held him back: "You will take the Trinity away with you."

At the Second Ecumenical Council, which opened in May of 381 under the direction of Meletius of Antioch, Gregory was appointed bishop of Constantinople. He both rejoiced at and regretted his confirmation to the see, "which was not entirely legal." Meletius died while the council was still in session and Gregory replaced him as president. Gregory disagreed with the majority of prelates on the question of the so-called "Antiochene Schism," and sided with Paulinus. The dissatisfaction which had long been building up against him suddenly burst out. Some churchmen were dissatisfied with leniency, since he had not requested the aid of the civil authorities against the Arians. Gregory had always been guided by the rule that "the mystery of salvation is for those who desire it, and not those who are coerced." Other prelates were disturbed by the inflexibility of his doctrinal beliefs, and especially his uncompromising confession of the divinity of the Holy Spirit. Still others thought that his con-duct was unbecoming to the dignity of his rank. "I did not know," Gregory said ironically, "that I would be expected to ride fine horses or to make a brilliant appearance perched on a carriage, or that those who met me would treat me with servility, or that everyone would make way for me as though I were a wild beast." The question of the legality of Gregory's transfer from Sasima to Constantinople was also raised at the council. It was obvious that this was a pretext for intrigue against him. In great chagrin Gregory decided to give up his see and to abandon the council. He was bitter about leaving the "place of our victory" and his flock, which he had won to the truth by his actions and words. This bitterness never left him.

On leaving Constantinople Gregory wrote to Bosporius, bishop of Caesarea, "I will withdraw myself to God, who alone is pure and without deceit. I will retire into myself. The proverb says that only fools stumble twice on the same stone." He returned home ex-hausted both physically and morally and filled with bitter memories: "Twice I have fallen into your snares and twice I have been deceived." Gregory sought rest and isolation, but once again he was forced to take over the administration of the widowed church in Nazianzus, "forced by circumstances and fearing the attack of enemies." He had to struggle against the

Apollinarians [also referred to as Apollinarists in English] who had illegitimately established their own bishop in Nazianzus, and intrigues and quarrels began again.

In desperation Gregory asked Theodore, the metropolitan of Tyana, to replace him with a new bishop and to remove this burden which was beyond his strength. He refused to attend any councils. "It is my intention to avoid all gatherings of bishops because I have never yet seen a productive outcome of any synod, or any synod which resulted in deliverance from evils rather than addition to them." He wrote to Theodore, "I salute councils and conventions, but only from a distance because I have experienced much evil from them." Gregory did not attain his freedom immediately. He was overjoyed when his cousin Eulalius was finally invested as bishop of Nazianzus, and he retired from the world to devote the rest of his life to writing. He traveled to desert monasteries in Lamis and other places. He became weaker and frequently sought relief by bathing in warm water springs. The lyrics he wrote as an old man were filled with sadness. Gregory died in 389 or 390.

II
WORKS

Orations

Gregory was an outstanding stylist. He was a brilliant philologist and had a great gift for language. It is true that his style oc-casionally seems overly refined and mannered, or excessively agitated, but the strength of his thoughts and emotions more than compensates for this. Gregory was primarily an orator, and his homilies and sermons compose the greatest part of his relatively small literary heritage. Forty-five of his sermons have been preserved, most of them written during his years in Con-stantinople. The most important of these are *The Five Theol-ogical Orations* (27-31) on the doctrine of the Trinity. These are among the most outstanding examples of Christian eloquence. They can hardly be considered improvisations.

Many of Gregory's orations were intended for delivery on feast days. Among them is the thirty-eighth oration on the Theophany or Birth of Christ. This is the oldest known Christmas oration in the East and dates from 379 or 380. The forty-fifth oration on Easter explains the saving work of Christ and was written in Arian-zum some time after 383. Gregory also composed several funeral orations which are important for the historical material they contain. These include the *Panegyric on St. Basil*. The oration *In Defense of His Flight to Pontus* is especially interesting, and was later elaborated into an independent treatise on the respon-sibilities of the clergy. It served John Chrysostom as the model for his own tract on the priesthood. Gregory also composed an in-vective against Julian the Apostate some time after the emperor's death. Most of Gregory's orations were written for particular occasions.

Poetry

Gregory also wrote poetry. Later editors have collected his verse into two volumes of historical poems and theological poems. These are more exercises in rhetoric than true poetry, with the exception of the personal lyrics, which display genuine emotion. Gregory was a master of poetic style, even though he occasionally abused his talents. His verse autobiography *On His Life* also contains much important material. Gregory never hid the didactic intention behind his poems. He hoped that his verses would serve as an alternative to pagan poetry, since the study of that could be dangerous, and he also wanted to counteract the harmful influence of Apollinarius, who expounded his theology in verse. Gregory's poetry was a great comfort to him in his old age.

Letters

Gregory wrote a large number of letters of which 245 have survived. Most of these were written during the last years of his life and deal with personal matters. The letters were collected by Gregory himself at the request of his young great-nephew Nicobulus. Gregory's letters display his mastery of rhetoric and one of them, *Letter 51*, is a treatise on the rules of composition. This is the reason that they can be considered as literature. With the exception of the epistles to Basil few of the letters contain much historical material. Gregory also wrote dogmatic epistles, two to Cledonius and one to Nectarius of Constantinople. The authenticity of the *Epistle to the Monk Evagrius on the Divinity* is doubtful.

The Influence and Authority of Gregory's Works

The works of Gregory the Theologian were widely known, and until the end of the Byzantine empire they were considered authoritative. There were more commentaries and exegesis written about him than about any of the other fathers, with the exception of the Areopagite. Maximus the Confessor was one of the first to write a commentary on Gregory and the Areopagite, his so-called *Ambigua*. Later exegeses were written by Elias of Crete, Basil the New (archbishop of Caesarea; tenth century), Nicetas of Heraclea (end of the eleventh century), Nicephorus Callistus Xanthopoulus (fourteenth century), and many others, including some anonymous writers. John Zonaras and Nicholas Doxopatros also wrote commentaries on Gregory's verse. All of this demonstrates the great popularity of Gregory's works. He was one of the main sources of authority for John of Damascus, and Michael Psellus called him the Christian Demosthenes.

III
THOUGHT

WAYS TO A KNOWLEDGE OF GOD

The Importance of the Knowledge of God in Gregory's Thought

Gregory's doctrine on the ways of attaining a knowledge of God is one of the most important aspects of his system of theology. This doctrine is not merely an introduction to his thought. For Gregory man's basic task in life is to know God, and through this man can achieve salvation and "deification." The created mind recognizes God and through intellectual contemplation is united, or reunited, with Him. In this way God is united with man when He assumes human nature through the human intellect, which is similar to His own. In his writings against Apollinarius Gregory states that "mind is united with mind, since this is what is closest to it."

Gregory emphasizes the importance of striving to know God in both his lyrical prayers and in his theological instructions. As a theologian he develops an orthodox teaching on the knowledge of God in order to oppose the extreme positions held by certain groups of heretics, especially the rationalistic Eunomian Ano - moeans and the overly fastidious Apollinarians, who consider the human intellect hopelessly sinful and beyond purification. "It is impossible for human reason to be without sin" is the way Gregory of Nyssa summarizes their thought. To oppose the Eu - nomians Gregory sets forth a doctrine of the limits of man's knowledge of God, which can be achieved only through ascetic discipline. To counteract the teaching of the Apollinarians he stresses that the human mind is created in the image of God and is therefore radiant.

The Usefulness of Platonic and Neoplatonic Terminology for Approaching Biblical Truths

Gregory frequently uses Platonic and Neoplatonic terminology. Part of the reason for this is that his studies had shown him that some of the philosophers who were secular or "alien," as he once described them in a reference to Plato, had nevertheless managed to approach the truths contained in the Bible. There - fore their terminology could be useful. Gregory was also mot - ivated by the need to argue effectively against certain heretical sects whose doctrines were based on secular philosophy. Furthermore, the use of Platonic comparisons and imagery had long been established by the practice of the school at Alex - andria. Gregory had read Plato and probably Plotinus as well. He also knew that the Christian teachers Clement and Origen had taken some of their material from Plato.

At the same time Gregory always uses the Bible to defend his arguments. He supports his teaching on the ways of gaining a knowledge of God with Scriptural texts, which in fact are its primary source. In his application and interpretation of the Bible he follows the Alexandrian tradition of exegesis, which was always predominant in the patristic doctrine of the knowledge of God.

The Intellect and the Knowledge of God

God is intellect. Gregory states that the Great Intellect "or any other perfect essence is comprehensible only by intellectual effort." The intellectual powers, the angels, are created in the image of God. For centuries the Mind of the World, "reigning in the emptiness of the ages," saw within itself the archetypes of the world that would later arise. God "invents" the "images" of the intellectual and heavenly world first, and then He designs the material and earthly world. His "thought becomes action," which is completed by the Word and perfected by the Spirit. The world of angels is the first creation to come into being. They are like God through their intellectual and spiritual nature. They are not only immutable but actually cannot be inclined to sin. Then God creates the world of visible things, and harmoniously combines the heavens and the earth. The unrefined and sensual nature of earthly things is foreign to God, but their beauty and proportion reflect His Wisdom and Strength. Within the material world God creates man, "the form of creation which is intermediate between mortality and immortality." This is a new world, and "this small world contains the great world."

Man, who "beholds visible creation and also mysteriously participates in intellectual creation," is placed on the boundary of the two worlds and at the very center of existence. It is in man that God "by His great wisdom has mingled creation." Man is created from dust and yet he bears the image of Divinity, "the image of the Immortal One, because intellect rules in them both." The Word of God "took part of the newly created world and fashioned my image with His immortal hands. He imparted to me His own Life when he gave me a soul, which is the spirit of the invisible Divinity." Gregory elsewhere refers to the soul as the "breath of God" or a "small part of the Divinity."

This is the reason that the goal of human life lies beyond the earth and beyond the senses. Man is a "new angel" who has been put on earth, and he must rise to the heavens and the radiant realm of the elect. He has been called to become a god through adoption and to fill himself with the supreme light. "This is a magnificent goal, but it can be achieved only with difficulty," Gregory writes. Man has been created in the image of God and is therefore expected to "become similar" to God. According to Gregory, the nobility of lofty souls consists only in "preserving the image within themselves, and making themselves similar to the Archetype" to the greatest degree that is possible for prisoners of the flesh. Men are able to do this because of the natural relationship which exists between the human soul and the Divine.

God as the Ultimate and Inaccessible Light

God is the ultimate and inaccessible light, "the purest radiance of the Trinity." The second light is the order of angels, who are "rays or participants in the first light." The third light is man. Even the pagans called man a light "by virtue of the intellect within him." God is the "lamp of the intellect," and when the human intellect is illuminated by the Archetypal light it also becomes radiant. "God is to the intellect what the sun is to material nature," Gregory writes. "One illuminates the visible world, and the other enlightens the invisible world. One gives light to corporeal vision, and the other makes intellectual natures like God."

Gregory is here using the Platonic comparison of the Greatest Good and the sun, a comparison which the Neoplatonist had developed into an integral doctrine of metaphysical light. Gregory uses Platonic imagery and, like the Platonists, stresses the corrupting influence of the senses and the body in general. However, the idea which he expresses in Platonic language is not itself Platonic. According to Gregory, "similarity" to God is pri - marily achieved through the sacraments. The goal of the sacra - ments, he writes, is to "give wings to the soul, steal it from the world and return it to God, to preserve the image of God if it is whole, to support it if it is in danger, to renew it if it is harmed, and to instill Christ in our hearts by means of the Spirit. Everyone who belongs to the celestial ranks is transformed into a god by the sacraments and made a participant in heavenly bliss." It is not fortuitous that baptism is called "illumination," since it is the beginning of man's path towards the light. At the end of this path the sons of light will be completely similar to God and God will be fully contained within them.

Christ, the Word Incarnate, and Deification

All of this is achieved through Christ, the Word Incarnate. He comes to make us gods. He assumes our flesh to redeem the image and to make the flesh immortal. The Word of the Father is an "unchanging Image" who "comes to its own image." He "unites himself with an intellectual soul for the sake of our souls, to purify that which is similar to Himself through His own similarity." The reason that Gregory objects so strongly to the doctrine of the Apollinarians is that he considers the intellect to be the highest of man's attributes. "The most important things in human nature are the image of God and the strength of the intellect." It is only through his intellect, which is formed in the image of God, that man can approach the Divinity.

Gregory supports the bold formulation of Basil: man is a creature but has been commanded to become a god. The path of "deification" is a path of purification and the elevation of the intellect, κάθαρσις. This is achieved through renouncing the material world of the senses, because the senses darken the mind. It is also necessary to concentrate on the self, to fight against the passions, and to attain a state of impassivity or "apathy." In Gregory's conception an ascetic is a wise man and a philosopher, and he has much in common with Clement of Alexandria's "gnostic." As a youth in Alexandria Gregory had studied with Didymus, who shared many of Clement's ideas. Gregory's image also shows the influence of Hellenism and can be compared to the ideals of the Stoics and Platonists. It is especially similar to the ideal of Plotinus. To a certain extent the whole system of Plotinus is a doctrine of "purification" as the way to God, a goal to which the spirit is drawn by desire, love, and the aspiration to completeness and perfection. Man yearns for full consciousness. To reach this end, it is necessary to renounce the body and to "go into oneself" in order to attain simplification and ecstasy.

Death in Platonism and in Gregory's System

Plotinus also summons man to silence and isolation, to retirement and hesychia. Like Plato, he conceives of philosophy as an exercise in preparation for death. Gregory frequently paraphrases, and once directly quotes, the maxim from Plato's *Phaedo* that "the task of a philosopher is to release the soul from the body." For him true life is contained in the process of dying because in this world it is impossible to attain full similarity to God or complete communion with Him. Only infrequent and scattered rays from the realm of Light can reach us here. Gregory often approaches Plato by calling the body a prison.

It seems that Gregory consciously incorporates many elements of Platonism in his own philosophy. He sees nothing surprising or misleading in the fact that Hellenic philosophers were able to develop the technique of ascetic discipline or that they were aware of the natural processes of thought and the natural laws of the soul. By using the imagery of the Hellenic philosophers in his religious writings Gregory is simply speaking in the language of his time. Essentially, however, his ideals do not coincide with theirs. Plato and his followers were seeking knowledge but had no key, whereas Gregory's striving is guided by the image of Christ and the doctrine of the consubstantiality of the Trinity. His yearning for death and the liberation of the soul from the body ("a ruinous bond," he cries in a moment of despair) have nothing in common with the spiritualism of the classical philosophers. For Gregory the body, like the intellect, is deified when the Word of God assumes flesh. "If you have a poor opinion of mankind, let me remind you that you are the creation of Christ, and the breath of Christ, and a true part of Christ. You are both heavenly and earthly. You are a creation worthy of eternity. You have been created a god and through Christ's suffering you are going forward to unending glory."

Although it is necessary to renounce earthly things in this life and "not to have excessive love for our present state," there will come a time when the flesh will be resurrected. At the funeral of his brother Gregory said: "The words of wise men have convinced me that every good soul which is loved by God will, as soon as it is set free from the bonds of the body, depart from here, and it will immediately be able to perceive and contemplate the blessings that await it. As soon as that which has darkened it is purified or laid aside (I do not know how else to describe it), the soul feels a wonderful pleasure, rejoices, and gladly goes to meet its Lord. This is because it has escaped life on earth, which is an unbearable prison, and has thrown off the fetters which restrained it, keeping the mind on material things and holding down the wings of the intellect. Then the soul will see and reap the blessings that have been prepared for it."

"Later the soul will receive the flesh that has been made suit - able for it, with which it once shared its pursuit of wisdom here on earth. This it receives from the earth, which originally gave it flesh and then preserved the flesh. Then in a way which is incom - prehensible to us and known only to God, who joined them together and then separated them, the soul will take the flesh with it to receive its inheritance of coming glory. In the same way that the soul through its close union with the flesh shared in its hardships, so now the soul gives to the flesh its joys, gathering it up completely within itself and, after the mortal and mutable part of it is swallowed up by life, becoming one with it in spirit, in mind, and in God."

This hope is the reason for renouncing material things here in this life. "Why should I cling to things that are temporal?' Gregory exclaims. "I await the voice of the Archangel, the final trumpet, the transformation of heaven and earth, the liberation of the elements and the renewal of the entire world." The goal of Gregory's ascetic discipline is the purification of the flesh, not liberation from it. "I love it as one who serves me, and I do not turn from it as though it were an enemy. I flee from it as I would from a prison, but I respect it as my coheir."

The Resurrection and the End of the Body As the Prison of the Mind

As a Hellenist Gregory doubts that the intellect is bound to the body. However, he knows what the Hellenes did not know: he knows that the body is created by God and that it becomes a prison for the mind only through the Fall. It ceases to be a prison by virtue of the resurrection of Christ. The mixture was leavened and became new.

The Knowledge of God and Ascetic Discipline

We approach deification by striving to know God. This can only be accomplished through ascetic discipline. "Not everyone can achieve an understanding of God," Gregory states in his writings against the Eunomians. "No, not everyone. It is not easy to attain and is impossible for those who are bound to material things." Not everyone should dare to speak freely about God. In order to do so it is necessary to have a pure or at least a purified soul. Just as the sun's radiance can be harmful to weak vision, it is dangerous for that which is corrupt to approach that which is pure. One must be free of external mire and enjoy a state of inner quietude and peace.

Man should constantly think about God, and this is the only thing that is absolutely necessary for life. The study of theology, however, should not be constant, nor should it be undertaken prematurely. It must be approached gradually and with restraint. In this way Gregory not only hopes to avoid futile and blasphemous argumentation, but he also tries to indicate that without adequate preparation the proper aim of theology will not be recognized, and thus its study will be fruitless. A troubled soul cannot truly reflect the image of the sun, and philosophy should be approached "only when we have quiet within ourselves and we are not distracted by the material objects around us." The concepts being dealt with must be clearly defined. "For if the mind is not enlightened, or if terms are carelessly used, or if the ear has not been purified and does not retain what it hears, then for any one of these reasons, as surely as from all of them together, the truth will unavoidably be lame and unsatisfactory."

The Gradual Stages of the Knowledge of God

Knowledge of God is attained in gradual stages. Not everyone can immediately ascend the mountain, go into the cloud, and speak with God. Those who are impure do better to remain at the foot of the mountain and listen to the voice and trumpet of the orthodox instruction of others. They themselves should not try to study theology before they are ready, but should look on the mountain covered by storm clouds and lightening and accept the miracle to the greatest degree of their ability. This is not an echo of the elitism of the Alexandrian school, which divided men into "gnostics" who could attain knowledge and simple men who could not. This is instead a doctrine of degrees, each of which can be achieved through asceticism and discipline. "If you ultimately wish to be worthy of a correct understanding of the Divinity, follow the commands and do not fail to do as you are ordered, for deeds are the steps which lead to contemplation." This ladder is open to all, but not everyone ascends together. Men are not equal and neither are the gifts of the Spirit, which are given to each according to his capacity. This, however, does not destroy the unity of the Church.

Gregory states that "speaking about God is a great under-taking, but it is an even greater undertaking to purify oneself for God." For only in this way will God be revealed. "There are many paths to salvation and many paths leading to communion with God. It is necessary to follow them, and not only by means of words. It is enough to learn the simple faith, since through this God will give salvation. There is no need to philosophize. If faith were only accessible to philosophers, our God would be ex-tremely poor."

Gregory's Position on "Philosophizing"

Gregory is objecting not to true philosophy, but to argumentation for its own sake. He took this firm stand against excessive loquaciousness and imprecision during the period of the Arian controversies. He was opposed to idle curiosity about theological problems and insisted on a reasonable and well-defined system for acquiring knowledge. He wanted to avoid exciting the random curiosity of the crowd, which was easily stirred up by theological argument. At this point those who were imitating the sophistic tricks of Pyrrho and Chrysippus were benefiting from the general atmosphere of mistrust and confusion. Gregory therefore tried to set forth his philosophy "according to dogma, and not as an independent system; by following the example of the fishermen, not Aristotle; in a spiritual way, and not by clever tricks; and according to the rules of the Church, not the rules of the marketplace." Gregory hoped to direct the attention of those who were unprepared to things which were more accessible to them than the mystery of the three suns of the Divinity. "Think about the world or worlds, about matter, about the soul, about the intellectual powers, about good and evil, about the resurrection and final judgment, about the ultimate reward, and about the sufferings of Christ."

During the era of the activity of the Cappadocian fathers, the arguments of the Arians often degenerated into sophistry and a "science of blasphemy." Gregory tried to fight against this tendency, but he was never hostile to true theology or philosophy. "Speak when your words are more valuable than silence, but love silence when it is better than words." Gregory loved and respected wisdom and for exactly this reason he frequently chose to be silent. He considered that theology was a way of striving toward God, and therefore he was restrained in his use of words and much preferred quiet reflection.

Gregory's Opposition to Eunomian Confidence in Rationalism – Contemplation of God

Gregory's quarrel with the Eunomians was not only about their methods of teaching. Their loquaciousness was fed by their optimistic confidence in their own rationalism, which Gregory did not accept. He opposed it with his doctrine of the limitation of man's ability to know God. Once again he turned to Hellenistic terminology and imagery in order to convey the teaching of the Bible. God is the ultimate desire of all speculation. The greatest good is the knowledge of God, and this can be attained through contemplation, θεωρία. "What seems to me to be best of all," Gregory writes, "is to shut off my senses, escape from my flesh and the world, maintain no communication with human affairs that is not absolutely necessary, and to speak to myself and God, to live superior to visible things, to always carry the divine image within myself, pure and unmixed with the deceptive impressions of the lower world, and to be and to constantly become more and more a clear mirror of God and divine things, to add light to light and greater radiance to that which is less clear, until I ascend to the source of that illumination and achieve the bliss of my ultimate goal. This truth will make mirrors unnecessary."

In contemplation we do not only passively reflect the Divinity, and the soul is not simply a mirror. Contemplation means union with God and it must be achieved through practice, through πρᾶξις. This is the only way to establish contact with God. Man is united with God and God is united with people, with "gods." As man strives to ascend, he is renewed. "I am transformed and I am improved. From being one man I become another, and I ex‑ perience a divine change." Even at these heights, however, God is hidden from man. "But what has happened to me, my friends, you who share the mystery and, like me, love the truth?" Gregory exclaims. "I went forward to attain God. With this in mind I freed myself from the material world, gathered myself into myself as much as I could, and started to ascend the mountain, but when I looked around myself I hardly saw the back of God (cf. *Exodus* 33: 11-23) or the spiritual Rock (*I Corinthians* 10:4), the Word who became incarnate for our sakes. Looking more closely, I saw that I contemplated not the first and pure nature of the Trinity, which is known to Its own self. I contemplated not that which abides behind the first curtain and is veiled by the cherubim, but I saw that which is further outside and stretches itself towards us. What I saw is the grandeur which is visible in the creatures made and ruled by God." In other words, even in the highest stages of contemplation it is not God Himself which is revealed, but only His glory and magnificence; not the light, but the radiance of the light. Gregory insists that the nature of the Divinity is unknowable. "To claim a knowledge of what God is is to be deluded."

Gregory writes that the Godhead is the "Holy of Holies, hidden even from the seraphim." God is infinite and impossible to behold, and it is only the fact that He is infinite which is accessible to us. God is "like a sea of being, unlimited and infinite, extending beyond the boundaries of all conception of time and nature, and it is only by His intellect that we have an indication of His truth. This image, however, is lost before we can catch it, and it slips away before we can grasp it. It illuminates that which holds dominion in us, if that is pure, in the same way that flashes of lightning illuminate our vision." God is known "not by considering what is in Him, but what is around Him." Even at the highest point of its striving the human mind can contemplate only an "image of the truth." This image is similar to the sun's reflection on the water, which is the only means for weak eyes to know the sun. This has clearly been drawn from a passage in Plato's *Politicus*: "All this is shadows and images on the water." Gregory may have taken the comparison of the contemplation of God to the observation of a reflection in a mirror from either St. Paul (*I Corinthians* 13: 12) or Plato (through Plotinus).

The Vision of God

Gregory is trying to say something more than that we know God only incompletely and through reflection. In this partial con - templation we possess the truth because we truly behold Him, even though His inaccessible essence remains unknown to us. The "enlightenment" which comes from God and His "des - cending" action (or "energy"), which was also described by Basil, are the true rays of the Divinity which penetrate all creation. That we know God "through a mirror" does not mean that this knowledge is only symbolic. It is a true vision of God and provides us with a genuine participation in the Godhead.What God is by His essence and nature has never been known and will never be known by man. However, God is accessible to us not only through contemplation and not only by analogy with the works and creations which express His perfection. God has been seen. He appeared to Moses and Paul, not in His own nature, it is true, but also not just as an image. God can be known through Revelation.

The Experience of Faith as Knowledge

Thus the Cappadocians adopt the ideas of Plotinus and Philo and distinguish between "what is transcendental" and "what is immanent" within the Divinity. They make this system of philos - ophy more complete by introducing the doctrine of grace, which they know as a result of the Christian experience.

Gregory writes that Plato, "one of the Greek theologians," once said that "it is difficult to understand God but impossible to ex - press Him." Gregory corrects this: "It is impossible to express God, but to understand Him is even more impossible." The experience of faith cannot be fully conceptualized and therefore God cannot be named. He is a nameless God. "O, You who are higher than anything, how else am I to express You? How can words give You praise? There are no words to express You. How can the mind gaze upon You? You are inaccessible to every mind. You are one and everything. You are not one, not single, and not everything. O, You of all names! How can I name You, who cannot be called one thing?" Theology can only describe God apophatically, by prohibition and negation. Of all the positive names only the name "He who exists" truly expresses something about God and belongs properly to Him and only to Him, just as independent being belongs only to Him. God is above essence, category, and definition, and the name God is purely relative and designates Him only in His relation to creation.

Apophatic Theology

It is probable that Gregory was influenced by Clement of Alexandria in his use of apophatic theology. The two theologians are similar not only in their terminology, but also in their use of Biblical texts. Gregory greatly modifies the agnostic tone which is sometimes evident in Clement's writings.

Gregory seems to consider that apophatic theology, definition by negation, is more effective than cataphatic definition, which provides knowledge through analogy. This is because all ana - logies are imperfect and misleading. "Even when a small similarity is found, much more is lost, and I am left unenlightened and only with that which has been chosen for comparison." In apophatic theology a more exact description of the ineffable mysteries which are revealed in contemplation is given through negation.

The Gradual Stages of Revelation

Knowledge of God is attained in degrees, and there are also degrees in revelation. There is a path leading upwards and a path which comes down from above. "In the course of the ages," Gregory writes, "there have been two great transformations in human life, which are called the two Testaments. They are described in Scripture as two upheavals (*Haggai* 2: 7: "I will shake heaven and earth, sea and land, and all nations, and the treasure of all nations will come hither"). One transformation led from idols to the Law, and the other from the Law to grace. I bring the good news of the third upheaval. This world will pass away in favor of another world, which is permanent and cannot be shaken." Both Testaments came into being gradually, not all at once. "We had to know that we were not being forced, but that we were being convinced." The truth was revealed in "gradual changes." In this same way knowledge of God is achieved only through gradual addition. "The Old Testament clearly revealed the Father, but the Son was present with less clarity. The New Testament revealed the Son and the Divinity of the Spirit. Now the Spirit abides with us and gives us a clearer knowledge of Himself. It is fitting for the triple light to illuminate us gradually."

Revelation has been accomplished and the mystery of the Trinity is manifest. However, it has still not been fully absorbed by man. Man must penetrate the mystery until "that which has been desired for us is completely revealed." Gregory predicts that "when we go inside, the Bridegroom will know what to teach and what to say to the souls which have entered. He will communicate with us and give us the most absolute and perfect knowledge." Only the pure in heart will see the Pure One and the triple radiance of the Divinity. "They will inherit the perfect light and will contemplate the holy and majestic Trinity, which will enlighten them more fully and more purely and will ultimately unite them with the absolute mind. This is how I conceive of the Kingdom of Heaven." They will receive "absolute knowledge" of the Trinity and they will know "what It is." Similar ideas were expressed by Origen.

TRINITARIAN THEOLOGY

St. Gregory, the "Theologian of the Trinity"

The Church has given Gregory the title "Theologian of the Trinity." This is appropriate for him not only because he spent his whole life defending the orthodox doctrine of the Trinity against false and heretical teachings, but also because for him the contemplation of the Trinity is the ultimate goal of all spiritual life. "Ever since I first freed myself from the material world," Gregory writes, "I have devoted myself to radiant thoughts of heaven, and the great intellect, which has taken me away from here, has separated me from the flesh and hidden me in the heavens. Since then the light of the Trinity has illuminated me and I can imagine nothing more radiant than It. From the highest throne in heaven the Trinity pours an ineffable light down on everyone, and the Trinity is a Source for everything which is separated from the highest things by time. Since then, I say, I am dead to the world and the world is dead to me." All of Gregory's religious verses are dedicated to the Trinity. "The Trinity is my adornment and the goal of my thought," he cries. At the end of his life he prays to join "my Trinity and Its compound light, my Trinity, since even Its dimmest shadow leads me to ecstasy."

Much of Gregory's doctrine of the Trinity is developed from the teaching of Basil the Great, whom he recognized as his "teacher of dogma." Gregory uses Basil's terminology in his own theology, but in a more exact and structured way. He does not hesitate to "devise new names" when this is necessary for him to be clear and orthodox. Gregory is also influenced by Athanasius, especially in his doctrine on the divinity of the Holy Spirit, even more than Basil is. About Athanasius Gregory writes: "A great number of Fathers were first given the ability to know the doctrine of the Son, and Athanasius was later inspired to teach about the Holy Spirit."

The full strength of Gregory's personal experience and vision is evident in his doctrine of the Trinity. His basic premise is that "the Trinity is in truth a Trinity." "In truth" means in reality. The name of the Trinity, he writes, "does not enumerate several unequal things, but designates a totality of things which are equal to each other," united by and in nature. Gregory constantly emphasizes the complete unity of the Divinity. "The perfect Trinity is composed of three perfect elements." "As soon as I think about One," he writes, "I am enlightened by Three. As soon as I distinguish Three, my mind is elevated to One. When I conceive of One of the Three, I still consider It as a whole . . . Whenever I contemplate the Three as a totality, I see a single effulgence, and I cannot separate or measure this compound light." The Trinity is a Unity and the Unity is a Trinity. "There is an eternal sharing of nature among the eternal Three." Each of the Three contem - plated by Itself is God, and all Three contemplated together are also a single God. "One God is revealed in three lights, and this is the ultimate nature of the Trinity."

Gregory tries to describe the mystery of this nature. The separate elements in God's nature can be distinguished but not divided. It is a combination of separate elements. The Divinity is a single whole in Three, and this whole is Three which contain the Divinity or, rather, which are the Divinity." It is as though three suns are contained in each other and their light is blended together. There is no division within the Trinity and It has no independent sections, just as there is no division or gap between the orb of the sun and its light. "There is a single Divinity and a single Strength which abides in the Three as a whole and in each individually, without distinction of essence or nature, without growing or shrinking, without addition or subtraction, everywhere equal and everywhere the same, just as the heavens have a single beauty and grandeur."

Trinity and Analogies to the Created World

Gregory avoids trying to explain the mystery of the Trinity by drawing analogies to the created world. The source of the spring, the spring itself, and the flow of the spring are not separate in time, and even when these three properties are distinguished it is clear that they are all a single phenomenon. However, Gregory writes: "I do not want to propose that the Divinity is a spring which never ceases (this is in distinction to Plotinus), because this comparison involves a numerical unity." The distinction among the waters of a stream exists "only in our way of thinking about it." The sun, its rays, and its light form a complex whole. There is the sun and there is that which is from the sun. This analogy, however, can give rise to the idea that the essence belongs to the Father and the other persons are only the "powers of God," just as the rays and the light are to the sun. Therefore analogies with creation are not helpful. They always contain the "idea of motion" or deal with "imperfect and fluctuating natures," and their triunity is really only a becoming and a changing of form. That which is temporal is not God.

Gregory's Elucidation of His Mystical Vision

The contemplation of the Trinity in its perfectly consubstantial and yet unmerged state is part of Gregory's spiritual experience, and, even though he has no confidence that he can succeed, he tries to describe the object of his meditation. He does this through a series of images, comparisons, and antitheses. His writings seem to be a description of what he has actually seen, and not only an exposition of his reasoning. Gregory expresses his own mystical experience in the formulas of contemplative theology and tries to elucidate it by using the devices of Neoplatonic philosophy. "We have one God because the Divinity is One. Everything that exists through God strives to raise itself to the One, even while believing in Three. Neither One nor the Other is more or less God. One is not first and the Other behind it. They are not separated by desire or divided by strength, and anything which is proper to divisible things has no place in them. On the contrary, that which is separable within the Divinity is not divisible. Because of the identity of their essence and powers each of them is a unity independently, and also when they are all unified. This is our conception of this unity, as much as we are able to understand it. If this conception is trustworthy, then we thank God for this knowledge."

Gregory's Qualification of Plotinus' "Overflowing Effusion"

Triunity is an interpenetration or motion within the Divinity. Gregory echoes Plotinus by stating: "The Divinity goes beyond singleness because of its richness, and has overcome doubleness because it is beyond matter and form. It is defined by triunity because it is perfect. The Trinity is overflowing, and yet it does not pour itself out into eternity. In the first case there would be no communion, and in the second case there would be disorder." This idea is directly drawn from Plotinus, and Gregory identifies with it: "This is the same for us." But he is careful to qualify himself: "We do not dare to call this process an excessive effusion of good, as did one of the Hellenistic philosophers who, when speaking about the first and second causes, referred to an 'overflowing cup'." Gregory rejects this interpretation of Divine Being on the ground that it involves uncaused, independent motion.

For Gregory the Triunity is a manifestation of Divine Love. God is love and the Triunity is a perfect example of "unity of thought and internal peace."

The Existence of Trinity as Outside of Time

The complete unity of the Trinity is primarily expressed by the fact that Its existence is unconditionally outside of time. God is eternal by nature and is beyond sequence and divisibility. It is not enough to say that God has always been, is, and will be. It is better to say that He is because He "contains within Himself the whole of being, which has no beginning and will never end." "If there has been One from the beginning, there have also been Three." The Divinity "is in agreement with itself. It is always iden - tical, without quantity, outside of time, uncreated, indescribable, and has never been and will never be insufficient for Itself."

It is impossible to conceive of any change or "division in time" within the Divinity. "For," Gregory writes, "to put together a Trinity from that which is great, greater, and greatest (that is, the Spirit, Son, and Father), as if it were the radiance, rays, and sun, would be to make a graduated ladder of Divinity. This would not lead the way to heaven but would lead down from it." This is because the mutual relationship of the hypostases of the Trinity is entirely superior to time.

God the Father as the Source

"There should be no one so zealous in his love for the Father that he would deny Him the attribute of being a Father. For whose Father can He be if we consider that He is separated not only from creation, but also from the nature of His own Son! One should not detract from His dignity as a Source, since this belongs to Him as a Father and Generator." "When I call Him a Source, do not imagine that I am referring to a source in time, or that I am presuming an interval between the Begettor and the Begotten. Do not separate their natures or falsely assume that there is something existing to separate these two coeternities abiding within each other. If time is older than the Son, this is because the Father caused time before the Son."

Thus, the being of the Father and the generation of the Only-Begotten coincide exactly, but also without confusion. The generation of the Son and procession of the Spirit should be considered to have taken place "before there was time." The Father never began to be a Father in time since His very being had no beginning. He "did not take being from anyone, not even from Himself." He is properly the Father "because He is not also the Son." Gregory draws this idea from Athanasius.

Although the hypostases are coeternal and superior to time, they are not independent of each other. The Son and the Spirit "have no beginning in relation to time" but They are "not without an ultimate Source." The Father, however, does not exist before them because neither He nor They are subject to time. The Son and the Spirit are coeternal but, unlike the Father, they are not without a source, for they are "from the Father, although not after Him." This mysterious causality does not entail succession or origination. Nothing within the Trinity ever comes into being or originates because the Divinity is completion, "an endless sea of being." Gregory is aware that this distinction is not easy to comprehend and that it can be confusing to "simple people." "It is true that that which has no beginning is eternal, but that which is eternal is not necessarily without a source, if this source is the Father."

Gregory demonstrates that to overemphasize the dignity of the Second and Third Hypostases is in effect to detract from the First: "It would be extremely inappropriate for the Divinity to achieve complete perfection only after changing something about Itself." "To cut off or eliminate anything at all from the Three is equal to cutting off everything. It is a rebellion against the whole Divinity." Gregory asks: "What father did not begin to be a father?" And he answers: "Only a Father whose being had no beginning." In this same manner the Son's generation is coincident with His being.

The Divine Unity and Identity of Essence

The complete and immutable unity of the Divinity determines the consubstantiality, the "identity of essence," of the hypo-stases of the Trinity. But the distinctions of each hypostasis do not disappear within the Divine unity. For Gregory, as well as for Basil the Great, the unity of the Divinity means an identity of essence and a monarchy that is from the Father and to the Father. The influence of Platonism is evident in the description of this "dynamic" unity. In Gregory's theology this dynamic aspect is dominant, and in this respect he is closer to Athanasius than to Basil.

Although Gregory conceives of the basic difference between "essence" and "hypostasis" as the difference between the general and the particular, he makes relatively little use of this concept. "What we hold in honor is monarchy," Gregory writes. "Not a monarchy which is limited to one person (this is in dis-tinction to Sabellius), but one which is composed of an equality of nature, a unity of will, an identity of motion, and a convergence to a one, single Whole of those elements which are from this One. This is impossible in a created nature," that is, a nature which is complex, derived, or originated. Everything which the Father has belongs also to the Son, and everything which belongs to the Son belongs to the Father, so that "nothing is particular because everything is held in common. Their very being is common and equal, although the being of the Son is from the Father." But this should not be "given more attention than is proper."

Differences between Gregory and Basil

The individual properties of the Three are immutable. These "properties" [ἰδιότητες] "do not distinguish essence, but are distinguished within one essence." In Gregory's understanding the concepts "hypostasis" and "property" are nearly the same. He also uses the expression "three Persons" τρία πρόσωπα, which Basil avoids. Gregory is responsible for developing a theological terminology which is close to Western usage through his identity of hypostasis and person, τπεῖς ὑποστάσεις ἤ τρία πρόσωπα.

Gregory also differs from Basil in his definition of the individual properties within the Trinity. He avoids the terms "fatherhood" and "sonship" and does not describe the personal attribute of the Spirit as "sanctity." He usually defines the properties of the hypostases as ungeneratedness, generation, and procession, ἀγεννησία, γέννησις, ἐκπόρευσις. Possibly he uses the term procession, ἐπόρευσις, to designate an individual property of the Father in order to put an end to the speculation of the Eu - nomians that "ungeneratedness" defines the essence of the Divinity. He takes this word from Scripture ("who proceeds from the Father." *John* 15: 26) in the hope of avoiding pointless arguments on the "fraternity of the Son and the Spirit." Gregory also attempts to forestall possible efforts to explain the exact meaning of these terms through analogies with the created world. Only the Trinity Itself knows "the order It has within Itself." How is the Son generated? How does the Spirit proceed? Divine generation is not the same as human generation. It is impossible to equate things which cannot be compared. "You have heard about generation. Do not attempt to determine how it occurs. You have heard that the Spirit proceeds from the Father. Do not try to find out how." "How? This is known by the Father who generates and the Son who is generated, but it is veiled by a cloud and inaccessible to you in your shortsightedness."

The Hypostatic Names and Mutual Relationship of Persons

The hypostatic names express the mutual relationship of the persons, σχέσεις. The three persons are three modes of being, inseparable and yet not confused, each "existing independently." They cannot be compared in such a way that one can be said to be greater or less than the others. Neither is one before or after the others. "The Sonship is not an imperfection" in comparison with the Fatherhood, and "procession" is not less than "generation." The Holy Trinity exists in complete equality. "All are worthy of worship, all have dominion, they all share a single throne and their glory is equal."

The Trinitarian Common Name

The confession of the Trinity expresses a complete knowledge of God. Gregory refers to the baptismal creed and asks, "In whose name are you baptized? In the name of the Father? Good! However, the Jews also do this. In the name of the Son? Good! This is no longer according to Jewish tradition, but it is not yet complete. In the name of the Holy Spirit? Wonderful! This is perfectly complete. But are you baptized simply in their individual names, or in their common name? Yes, in their common name. And what is this name? There is no doubt that this name is God. Believe in this name and you will flourish and reign."

The Divinity of the Holy Spirit

Much of Gregory's writing is devoted to defending the divinity of the Spirit. This issue was still being debated in 370 and also later at the Second Ecumenical Council. "Now they ask," he writes, "what do you say about the Holy Spirit? Why do you introduce something which is not known from Scripture? This is said even by those who have an orthodox understanding of the Son." "Some consider the Spirit the energy of God, some a creature, and some believe that He is God. Others have not made up their minds on anything. They say that this is because of their respect for Scripture, as if nothing about this were clearly set forth in it. Therefore they do not honor the Spirit, but also do not deny His dignity, and take no definite position on Him, which is pitiful. Even among those who recognize His divinity some are orthodox only in their hearts, whereas others dare to confess Him with their lips." Amidst this confusion Gregory's teaching is clear. "Listen well: the Spirit has been confessed by God. I say further,

'You are my God'. And for the third time I cry out, 'The Spirit is God'." "Nothing has yet caused such commotion in the uni - verse," Gregory writes, "as the boldness with which we proclaim that the Spirit is God."

Gregory follows the example of Athanasius by citing the baptismal creed in defense of his doctrine of the consubstantial divinity of the Holy Spirit. Baptism is accomplished in the name of the Holy Trinity, the unchanging, indivisible Trinity whose members are completely equal. "If the Holy Spirit is a creature, you have been baptized to no purpose." "If the Spirit is not worthy of veneration, how does He make me a god in baptism?" Gregory asks. "And if He is to be venerated, is He not also to be adored? And if He is to be adored, how can He not be God? Each of these things implies the next, and this is the true golden chain of our salvation. Through the Spirit we are reborn, and in being reborn we are given new life, and through this we know the dignity of the One who has given us new life." Therefore, "to separate One from the Three is to dishonor our rebirth, and the Divinity, and our deification, and our hope." "You see," Gregory writes in conclusion, "what the Spirit, who has been confessed by God, gives to us, and what we are deprived of if He is cast out." The Spirit is the Sanctifier and the source of enlightenment, "the light of our intellect, who comes to those who are pure and makes man a god." "By Him I know God, for He Himself is God and makes me a god in this life." "I could not bear to be deprived of the possibility of becoming perfect. Can we be spiritual without the Spirit? Can one who does not honor the Spirit participate in the Spirit? And can one who has been baptized in the name of a fellow creature honor the Spirit?" Athanasius reasons in a similar way.

Scripture bears witness to the Spirit, but its evidence is not entirely clear and we must "penetrate the surface to know what is contained within it." Gregory explains that Scripture should not be understood only literally. "Some things which are contained in Scripture do not exist, and other things exist but are not found in Scripture. Some things do not exist and Scripture says nothing about them, but other things exist and are also described in Scripture." Scripture says that God sleeps and becomes awake. This is a metaphor, not a description of reality. Conversely, the words "ungenerated," "immortal," "eternal," and others have not been taken from Scripture, but it is obvious that "although these words are not found in Scripture, nevertheless they have meaning." We should not lose sight of things for the sake of words.

The Spirit was active among the fathers and the prophets, for He enlightened their minds and showed them the future. He was proclaimed by the prophets who foretold the great day when the Spirit would be poured out on all mankind (*Joel* 20: 28). The Spirit also bore witness to Christ. "Christ was born as the Spirit foretold. Christ was baptized and the Spirit was present. Christ was tempted and the Spirit raised Him up. Christ's strength was perfected and the Spirit was with Him. Christ ascended and the Spirit succeeded Him." The Savior revealed the Spirit in stages, and the Spirit gradually descended to the disciples, sometimes in the breath of Christ, sometimes working miracles through them, and finally appearing in tongues of fire. The whole New Test - ament is filled with evidence of the Spirit and His powers and gifts. "I tremble when I consider the richness of His names," Gregory cries. "Spirit of God, Spirit of Christ, Mind of Christ; He gives new life in baptism and resurrection. He breathes where He wills. He is the Source of light and life. He makes me a shrine (*I Corinthians* 6: 19) and makes me a god. He perfects me. He is present at baptism and He is conferred on me through baptism. He does everything that God does. Through tongues of fire He bestows His gifts and makes us Bearers of the good news, Apostles, Prophets, Pastors, and Teachers." He is "another Comforter" and "another God." Although the divinity of the Spirit is not explicitly proclaimed in Scripture, there is much solemn evidence of this. Gregory explains the reticence of Scripture on the doctrine of the Spirit by showing that revelation takes place in economic stages.

The spiritual experience of the Church is also a form of revelation, and through this experience the Spirit makes clear His own dignity. It further seems to Gregory that "even the best pagan theologians had a conception of the Spirit, but did not agree on a name for Him and called Him the Intellect of the world, the external Intellect, and so forth." Gregory is here referring to Plotinus and the Neoplatonic conception of the World Soul. Basil the Great also applied many of Plotinus' definitions to the Holy Spirit in his treatise to Amphilochius.

Gregory develops his doctrine of the Spirit analytically. He reaches the conclusion that the Spirit is divine from the fact that the Gifts He gives are divine. However, for Gregory, this remains at best a pedagogical device to be used in argumentation. In his personal experience the divinity of the Spirit is revealed through the contemplation of the Trinity, and the truth of the Triunity reveals the immediate consubstantiality of the Spirit. Therefore Gregory does not designate the individual property of the Spirit as "sanctity," which would have an economic meaning. He does, however, speak about "procession" [ἐκπόρευσις; ἐκπέμψις] in order to indicate the place of the Spirit in the indivisible triunity of the Divinity.

THE MYSTERY OF SALVATION

Human Life and Union with God through the Single Person of the God-Man

Gregory sees the meaning and goal of human life in "deification," in actual union with the Divinity. This is possible because "that which is dominant" in man has been made in the image of God. More importantly, it is possible through the "humanity of God." From this point of view a clear dogma of the completeness of the two natures united in the Hypostasis and Person of the God-man is vitally important for Gregory's doctrine of salvation. Gregory's teaching is similar to that of Athanasius, but while Athanasius opposes the heresies of the Arians by stressing the absoluteness of the Divinity within the God-man, Gregory in writing against Apollinarius emphasizes Christ's humanity. The basic principle of his soteriology is that if human nature has not been fully assumed by Christ, it can be neither healed nor saved by Him. As part of his polemic against the Apollinarians he advances the doctrine of the "substantial" union "of two natures" within the single person of the God-man.

Christ was born, the laws of nature were breached, and the lower world became full. "I proclaim the glory of this day. He Who is incorporeal has become incarnate, the Word has been firmly fixed, the Invisible has become visible, the Impalpable can now be touched, Timelessness has begun, and the Son of God has become the Son of man." The birth of Christ is a theophany and "God is made manifest in being born." God has not only become manifest, for the incarnation is a true "assumption" of human nature. "He assumes my flesh in order to save His image and to make the flesh immortal," Gregory writes. "Each mystery of Christ causes me great rejoicing, and the greatest joy is my perfection, that I am made perfect, given new life, and that I return to the First Adam." This is a "new and wonderful commingling."

"When man failed to become god, God made Himself a man to do me honor," Gregory writes. "God was uncompound from the beginning. He became united with human nature, and then He was nailed to the cross by the hands of His murderers. This is our teaching about God, Who has become one with us." Christ is God incarnate, and not a deified man. In Christ "human nature is completely joined with the whole Divinity, not in the way that a prophet, divinely inspired, is in communion with God Himself, with something divine, but in essence, so that God has humanity in the way that the sun has rays." In Christ humanity is "anointed" not merely by an action of God but by His presence. At the same time God has completely assumed human nature. "In brief," Gregory says in conclusion, "our Savior is both one and the other." He then qualifies himself: "But He is not only one plus the other , for both of them are commingled so that God has become man and man has been deified." Gregory chooses words which emphasize the intimacy and completeness of this union in which the components nevertheless retain their individuality.

The Two Natures of Christ, the God-Man

In the eclectic language of Hellenism κρᾶσις, σύγκρασισ, and μῖξισ, all of which designate "commingling," stand in opposition to σύγχυσις, which implies absorption, and παραθέσις, which indicates a mechanical union or juxtaposition. According to Alexander Aphrodisias, the author of a well-known commentary on Aristotle, κρᾶσις signifies the "complete and mutual union of two or more bodies in such a way that each retains its own essence and substantial properties." He uses the image of fire and iron as an example, and this image was adopted by the patristic writers as a symbol of the unity of natures in the God-man. Later the use of this term was altered. "Commingling" was also the most exact term from the vocabulary of philosophy to express the orthodox conception of the unconfused unity of the two, at least until it was tainted by the heretical usage of the Monophysites. In "commingling" the doubleness is maintained and the unity is also recognized. It signifies "one" and "two" at the same time, and this is precisely the mystery of the Person of Christ. He is not two, but "one from two."

Gregory clearly distinguishes the "two natures" of Christ. One nature is "subject to suffering" and the other is "immutable and above suffering." This is the main thrust of his exegetical polemic against the Arians. "There was a time when He who is now des - pised by you was superior to you. Now He is a man, but once His nature was not compound. He remains that which He has always been, and He has assumed that which He previously did not have." Gregory examines the evidence of this double nature contained in the Gospel by considering the "mystery of the names," the mystery of the double names and the double symbols, the manger and the star. All names and all symbols, however, refer to one and the same, " "One God from both."

"He was a mortal, but also God; He was from the tribe of David, but He was also the Creator of Adam; He had a body, but was incorporeal; He was borne by the Virgin, but could not be contained; the cradle held Him, but the Magi were led to Him by the star. As a man He struggled, but He cannot be overcome and He defeated the tempter three times. As a mortal He was subject to sleep, but as God He tamed the seas. He was tired by His journeys, but He gave strength to the weak. He prayed, but who is it who hears the prayers of those who are perishing? He was a Victim, but also the High Priest. He is a Priest, but He is God." He is One Person, One God-man, One Christ, One Son, and "not two sons," which is the false teaching of Apollinarius. His two natures have been joined in essence and have penetrated each other. Gregory is the first to use the word κρᾶσις to express the unity of the two natures in the God-man. "His natures and His names have been commingled and therefore they each are transformed into the other."

The Divinity remains immortal and humanity is "deified." The unity of the two natures in the person of Christ is based on the principle that "that which is strongest is victorious." By "dei - fication" Gregory does not imply that human nature is trans - formed or that it undergoes transsubstantiation. What he means is that it is in complete communion and interpenetration with the Divinity. In the God-man human nature has been deified at its very source, for God Himself has become human. By virtue of this "commingling" each name is now applicable to the other.

Gregory devotes a great deal of attention to the suffering and death of God, since through this he confesses the unity of natures in the Person of the God-man. For this reason he insists on the name "Bearer of God": "Anyone who does not recognize that Mary is the Bearer of God is estranged from the Divinity." The reason for this is that deification is possible for us only through the humanity of the Word and its consubstantiality with us. In the Word humanity is deified through commingling with God.

The Apollinarian Problem

Apollinarius does not understand how "two complete com - ponents" can commingle and form a new and complete whole. It seems to him that if God is "completely" united with human nature in Christ, then Christ has two natures, and the person of the God-man is a unity only externally. Such a union cannot bring salvation. Apollinarius' reasoning rests on the premise that everything which is real and "complete" is also hypostatic, so that each nature can be fully realized only in an individual person. Therefore, if the human nature of Christ is complete, He must contain a human person or hypostasis, but the unity of the person of the God-man presupposes a unity of nature, μίαν φύσιν. In order to defend the unity of the person of the God-man Apollinarius is forced to deny the full "completeness" of Christ's human nature. "An incomplete component united with a complete component does not result in a double nature." The other possibility is to deny the completeness of the Divinity in Christ. This Apollinarius does not accept because it invalidates the truth of salvation. It seems to him, and not without reason, that this extreme position was the doctrine of the Antiochene fathers.

Apollinarius also considers that two intellects cannot be united since two sources of thought and two wills must always be in conflict. For him this is especially true because of the inclination of the human will to sin, and therefore he denies that Christ has a free and mutable human intellect. Christ assumes animate flesh only, only a body and a soul, and not a human "spirit" or "mind." He becomes flesh, not man. Apollinarius is a trichotomist. He holds that the flesh and the soul of Christ are human but that His "spirit" (νοῦς) is the Divine Word. Thus the humanity of Christ is only similar to ours, and not consubstantial with it. Furthermore, Christ's animate body necessarily "coexists" with the Divinity. It is an abstraction which has no independent existence apart from the Word which assumes it. In effect Apollinarius denies any independence of action to the human nature in Christ, which is merely a tool of the Word. His explanation of the union of that which is moved and its mover shows the influence of Aristotle.

Gregory does not try to deny the premises of Apollinarius' reasoning, nor does he argue with his identification of nature and person, φύσις and ὑπόστασις. Instead, he attacks his doctrine of salvation. Gregory tries to show that salvation is impossible in the terms which Apollinarius proposes because according to his conception no true union of the two natures takes place. "If Christ has flesh but no intellect," he exclaims, "then I am deceived. His body is mine, but whose soul does He have?" Gregory demonstrates that human nature is a unity and cannot be divided into parts.

Essentially the Apollinarians deny the human nature in Christ. "They deny His human nature and internal similarity to us by introducing this new idea of a likeness that is merely visible. This would purify only the visible part of us . . . When they say that His flesh is only a semblance and not real, this means that His flesh does not experience any of the things that are proper to us, and that His flesh is free of sin." Gregory concludes that "with such flesh the Divinity is not human." "Assuming flesh" without "as - suming human nature" cannot bring redemption. "That which has not been assumed has not been healed, but that which is truly united with God is saved. If only a part of Adam fell, then that part which is assumed is saved, but if all of Adam fell, then he is completely saved only by complete union with Him who has been born man in completeness." "Do not believe that our Savior has only the bones and sinews of human form," Gregory writes, "be - hold a whole man and recognize his Divinity."

To the objection of Apollinarius that "two complete com - ponents cannot both be contained in one body" Gregory answers that this "co-presence" must not be understood only in the physical sense. It is true that bodies are impenetrable and that "a vessel with one capacity cannot hold two such measures." However, this is not true for things that are "intellectual and incorporeal." "I contain in myself a soul, and an intellect, and the gift of speech, and the Holy Spirit. Even before I existed the Father contained in Himself this world, this totality of visible and invisible things, and also the Son and the Holy Spirit. This is the nature of everything that is conceptual, since such things are not corporeal and can be indivisibly united to things which are similar to them, and also to bodies. Our hearing can encompass many sounds and our sight perceives a multitude of features in visible objects, and this is also true of our sense of smell. Our senses do not limit each other or crowd each other out, and a tangible object is not made less by the great number of other objects."

The union of God and man is a mystery. We can approach an understanding of it only by means of our intellectual perception, which is what Apollinarius had attacked. Man's intellect has been formed in the image of God, and it is through this intellect that he can be united with God, the Highest Intellect, since that is what is "nearest to it and most like it." When two intellects are united, they do not lose their individuality, but neither are they nec - essarily in conflict. The type of combination which the Apol - linarians suggest would result in a purely external unity. "Their likeness resembles a mask worn at a theatrical performance," and in their conception God is not the God-man but merely wears a "curtain of flesh." Their argument that the intellect is inclined to sin is also invalid because the flesh too is sinful. Is it not to heal these weaknesses that God takes on human nature? "If the worse element is assumed so that it is sanctified by Christ's as - sumption of the flesh, why is not the better element also assumed so that it may be sanctified through Christ's assumption of human nature? If the old mixture is leavened and becomes new, why cannot we also be leavened and be commingled with God, so that we may be deified through the Divinity?" It seems to Gregory that the reasoning of the Apollinarians implies that the intellect is the only property of man which is condemned and beyond salvation. He therefore accuses them of granting too much dignity to man's physical nature. "You worship the flesh, for the man you propose has no intellect." For Gregory, on the contrary, even if the intellect is in need of healing, it is the property of man which is most open to salvation because it has been created in the image of God. "The renewal of the image" is the goal of redemption and the Word comes to man as an Archetype to its image.

Gregory's Christology is in accord with his religious ideal. The argument he presents against Apollinarius is not so much a system of theology as a confession of faith. He is able to express his faith in very precise language and anticipates the formulas later used in the fifth century, "two natures" and "one person."

The Crucifixion and Salvation

Humanity is saved through union with God. However, the Incarnation alone does not accomplish salvation. Gregory stresses that the Crucifixion is vital for redemption. The death on the cross is a manifestation of the greatest good and the greatest gift of God, "the suffering of God, the Lamb, who is slaughtered for our sins." The Crucifixion is a sacrifice, "the purification not of a small part of the universe and not for a short time, but of the whole world forever." Gregory emphasizes that the Savior's death is a sacrifice, and he compares this sacrifice to the sacrifice in the Old Testament through which it was foretold. The Crucifixion is a sacrificial offering and Christ is the true Lamb, the High Priest, and the Conciliator. His death is a sacrifice and a ransom, λύτρόν.

Christ takes upon Himself all the sins of humanity, and it is for this reason that He suffers. "He has made Himself one of us," and "He is the Head of our body." He is not merely a substitute for us. Gregory tries to express the intimacy of the Savior's assumption of our sins through such neologisms as αὐτοαμαρτία, the "very principle of sin." He who is without sin is not defiled by assuming sin. The God-man ascends the cross of His own will. He carries our sins with Him so that they are crucified too. Gregory glorifies "the cross and nails, by which I am released from sin."

Gregory and the Notion of "Ransom"

For Gregory the full significance of the Crucifixion is not ex-pressed by the concepts of sacrifice and retribution alone. "There is one more question and dogma, neglected by many other people, but in my opinion worth examining," he declares in his *Oration on Easter.* "To whom has this blood which is shed for us been offered, and why? I mean the blood of our great and glorious God, the High Priest and Sacrifice. We were in the power of the evil one, sold under sin, and buying ourselves injury with our wickedness. Since a ransom is paid only to him who holds in bondage, I ask to whom this ransom was offered and for what cause? If it is to the evil one, then this is an outrage! If the robber receives a ransom not only from God, but a ransom that is God Himself, then he has such an immense payment for his tormenting that it would have been right for him to have left us alone. But if it is paid to the Father, then in the first place I ask how? And next, why was the blood of His Only-Begotten Son pleasing to the Father, who would not accept even Isaac when he was offered by his father, but changed the sacrifice and put a ram in the place of the human victim? Is it therefore not evident that the Father accepts this sacrifice not because He asks for it or demands it, but because man must be sanctified by the humanity of God, and so that He might deliver us Himself, and overcome the tormentor, and draw us to Himself through the mediation of the son, who arranges this to honor His Father, whom He obeys in all things." It may seem that Gregory gives no direct answer to this question, but he does in fact respond, although only briefly: "Let the rest be respected in silence."

The Cross as Rebirth and Purification

The Cross is victorious over Satan and hell but it is not a ransom. The Cross is a gracious sacrifice and it is not a payment to God. The Cross is made necessary by human nature, not by the Divinity. The root of this necessity is man's sin and the degeneration of the body. Through Adam's fall the flesh was weighted down and became a corpse which burdened the soul, but the flesh is purified and relieved of its burden through the blood shed on the Cross. In one passage Gregory refers to the Crucifixion as a baptism "by blood and suffering." Elsewhere he speaks about the two kinds of purification which are Christ's gift to us: "We are purified by the eternal Spirit who purges the earlier damage in us which we received from the flesh, and we are also purified by our blood (for I call the blood which Christ my God has shed our own), which expiates our original weaknesses and redeems the world." The Crucifixion is a rebirth, and therefore baptism has a part in it. We die with Christ and are buried with Him, and we arise from the grave and through the grave. "It is necessary for me to suffer this redeeming change, so that just as good can lead to grief, so from grief our good arises."

At the Crucifixion the original purity of human nature was restored. "We needed God to become flesh and die in order to give us life. There were many miracles at that time. God was crucified and the sun darkened and again shone forth, for it was fitting for creatures to suffer with their Creator. The veil was torn, and blood and water were shed from His side: one because He was a man; the other because He was above man. The earth trembled and rocks were sundered for the sake of the Rock. The dead arose as a pledge of the final resurrection of all men, and there were miracles at the sepulcher. But not one of these is equal to the miracle of my salvation. A few drops of blood renewed the whole world and did for all men what rennet does for milk by drawing us together and binding us into a unity."

Death as Resurrection

Christ accepted everything proper to man, "everything which is filled with death," and by dying He destroyed death. Death is Resurrection, and this is the mystery of the Cross. Therefore, on Easter Gregory speaks about the suffering of God. "On this day Christ was summoned from the dead. He turned aside the sting of death, destroyed the dark chambers of hell, and gave freedom to all souls. On this day He arose from the tomb and showed Himself to the people for whose sakes He was born, died, and arose, so that we, renewed and redeemed from death, could rejoice with You in the Resurrection."

For the whole of humanity Christ as a man is a "leaven for the mixture." The salvation and "deification" given in Christ are given to everyone who is united with Him in the holy sacraments and through the effort of striving towards Him. For Gregory, all the ages of history have foretold the coming of Christ. He sees the Old Testament and the Passover under the law as an "indistinct prototype of a prototype." "This is what I dare to say." But the Easter we celebrate now is also incomplete. it also is only a prototype. "Soon our participation will be more absolute and more complete, and the Word will drink new wine with us in the Kingdom of the Father, teaching us and revealing to us what He now shows us only partially. What is this drink and this food? For us it is to learn and for Him it is to teach and to communicate His word to His pupils, for teaching is also food for him who gives nourishment." First of all He will teach us about the Trinity. In the Father's Kingdom we will hear the voice of rejoicing and we will see the "vision of glory," the "most complete and most perfect radiance of the Trinity, which will no longer hide itself from intellects which are bound and distracted by the senses. There the intellect will be able to perceive and contemplate the Trinity completely, and It will illuminate our souls with the light of the Divinity." This is similar to Origen's conception of the afterlife, although Origen considers that the just will learn the secrets of the cosmos, not that they will contemplate the Trinity.

The Fate of the Unrepentant

Gregory has written little that deals with eschatology. He frequently speaks of man's call to "deification," and preaches the necessity of ascetic discipline. He summons sinners to repentance but mentions the fate of the unrepentant only in passing. Their greatest punishment will be rejection by God, and this will be a torment and a "shame to the conscience" that will have no end. For just men God is light but for the unjust He is fire, and "this most terrible fire is eternal for the wicked." Possibly Gregory admits that purification can be achieved after death because he writes that sinners "may there be baptized by fire. This is the last baptism, the most difficult and prolonged, which eats up matter as if it were hay and consumes the weight of each sin." It is probable that he had in mind only the fate of unrepentant Christians because he also writes: "I know a fire which is not purifying, but avenging. The Lord sends it down like rain on every sinner, adding to it brimstone and storms. It was prepared for the devil and his angels and for everyone who does not submit to the Lord, and it burns up the enemies around Him." However, Gregory adds that "some may prefer to think that this fire is more merciful and worthy of Him who punishes." Gregory does not agree with the extreme position of the Origenists.

CHAPTER SIX

ST. GREGORY OF NYSSA

I
LIFE

Gregory of Nyssa was a younger brother of Basil the Great. He was born sometime around 335 and almost nothing is known about his youth. He probably studied at home in Caesarea. Gregory later said that his brother Basil was his teacher and he always spoke of him with reverence, describing him as the equal of the apostles who came after them only in time. He admitted that "I lived with my brother for only a short period, and only received as much instruction from his divine tongue as was necessary for me to understand the ignorance of those un- initiated in the secrets of eloquence." In other words, Basil taught him only rhetoric. Gregory names his sister Macrina as the other important teacher of his youth, and his reminiscences of her are full of gratitude. Gregory grew up in an atmosphere of culture and asceticism, but little else is known about the details of his education.

In his youth Gregory was greatly attracted by the study of philosophy. Even after he had entered the clergy as a reader he became a teacher of rhetoric and devoted himself to the study of pagan literature. This displeased his family and friends. Gregory the Theologian wrote to him in friendly reproof: "What has happened to you, O wisest of men? Others do not praise you for this ignoble glory or for your gradual descent to the lower life, or for your ambition, which, in the words of Euripides, is the worst of all demons . . . Why have you become angry with yourself that you should throw away the sacred books, filled with sweet waters, which you once used to read to the people . . . and take up with books filled with salt water that are impossible to drink? Why do you prefer to be called a rhetorician than Christian?" Gregory admonished him to come to his senses and to vindicate himself before God and the faithful, before the altars and the sacraments from which he had distanced himself.

During the period of his distraction by secular philosophy Gregory also studied Origen, who had an enormous influence on him. He read Philo and Theognostus as well. Gregory's Ori- genism was later modified under the influence of Basil, who purposefully directed his epistle on trinitarian terminology to

Gregory in the fear that Gregory was straying from orthodoxy. Gregory's enthusiasm for secular learning was only temporary, and he later condemned the worldly sciences as fruitless: "They constantly suffer pains of labor which never culminate in new life." However, he always remained a Hellenist through the influence of Origen.

Gregory acceded to the influence of his family and returned to the ministry. He married but continued to live a chaste and ascetic life. It seems that he temporarily retired to his brother Basil's monastery on the shores of the Iris in Pontus. Gregory did not have a strong character and his experience with life was limited. During the controversy which followed Basil's election to the see of Caesarea, Gregory unsuccessfully tried to make peace between Basil and their uncle by forging letters. Basil told him that the earth should open up beneath him for such actions but he later accepted his brother's repentance and was completely reconciled with him. After this incident it is easy to see why Basil considered Gregory unfit for serious responsibility and objected when Gregory was nominated as an envoy to Rome: "He is inexperienced in the affairs of the Church." However, in 371 he consecrated Gregory bishop of the town of Nyssa.

Gregory helped his brother in the struggle against heresy not by his activity in Church administration but as a writer and theologian. He was persecuted for his orthodoxy and brought to trial in Galatia. In 375 Demosthenes, the governor of Cappadocia whom Basil described as a "friend of the heretics," ordered him to be taken into custody. In 376 he was condemned in absentia and was deposed for misappropriation of funds and for his "illegal" consecration. Gregory spent three years in exile and returned to his see only in 379 after the death of Valens. He was greeted by popular rejoicing. His return to Nyssa was shortly followed by the deaths of Basil and then Macrina. This was a heavy blow for Gregory. One of his letters to the monk Olympius contains a moving account of the last days of his sister, who was herself an outstanding Christian and ascetic.

Gregory considered himself the heir to his brother's labors and immediately began to work on the writings which Basil had left unfinished, including the commentary on the *Hexaemeron* and the polemic against Eunomius. Friends recognized him as a worthy successor to his brother. At the Antiochene council of the 146 fathers in 379 he was sent on a mission to report on the condition of the Church in Arabia, which was rumored to be corrupt and heretical. Possibly he visited the Holy Land at this time, but some scholars consider that this journey took place later. The Palestinian Church had been without spiritual lead -

ership for some time (St. Cyril spent altogether thirteen years in exile), and corruption was widespread. Gregory was greeted with suspicion and immediately became involved in controversy with the Apollinarians.

The abuses in the Holy Land made a painful impression on Gregory, and for this reason he disapproved of the custom of pilgrimages. They could be especially harmful for women, whose purity and chastity were often endangered in the course of such voyages. Palestine was overflowing with vice and every kind of impiety. Furthermore, Gregory wrote: "Why should you try to do that which is not done by the saints or others who are close to the Kingdom of Heaven?" The Lord did not command us to go to Jerusalem as a good deed. "What advantage is gained by those who visit these places? It is not as if the Lord has been living there in the body until the present day, but has gone away from those of us who live in other lands; or as if the Spirit is flourishing in Jerusalem, but is unable to come to us here . . . A change of place does not bring God closer to you. No matter where you may be, the Lord will come to you if your soul is such that He can dwell and walk in you. But if the inner man in you is full of deceit, then even if you stand on Golgotha, or on the Mount of Olives, or under the memorial of the Resurrection, you are as far from receiving Christ into yourself as one who has not even begun to confess faith in Him." On the contrary, "the true Bethlehem, and Golgotha, and Mount of Olives, and Resurrection, are all found in the heart of the man who has God." What will we find in Jerusalem that is new? "We will find that the Christ who was manifest there was the true God, but we confessed this before we came to Jerusalem, and after our journey our faith has neither diminished nor increased. We also knew that He became man through the Virgin before we were in Bethlehem. We believed in the Re - surrection of the dead before we saw His tomb. We confessed the reality of the Assumption before we saw the Mount of Olives." It is more important to "travel forth from the body to our Lord than to travel from Cappadocia to Palestine."

In 381 Gregory took part in the Second Ecumenical Council. By this time he was a well-known and influential figure. Through an edict of the emperor on July 30, 381, Gregory was included among the bishops who were to be regarded by orthodox believers as the central authorities of the Church Communion. Prelates were nominated from each province, and Gregory shared the nomination from Pontus with Helladius of Caesarea and Otreius of Melitane. His later relations with Helladius caused him much difficulty.

In 382 and 383 Gregory was again present at the councils in Constantinople and continued his struggle against the Arians. He made the acquaintance of the nun Olympiada, who was greatly respected for her piety by John Chrysostom. In 394 Gregory participated in a council on the affairs of the Church in Arabia. This is the last event in his life of which we have definite knowledge. He probably died in 394. Even during the life of John Chrysostom he disappeared from public notice. A few fragments of information have been preserved about the last years of his life and seem to indicate that his authority was widely respected and that he continued to be influential in Church affairs, although he probably spent little time in Nyssa.

Gregory's contemporaries considered him the great defender of orthodoxy against the Arians and Apollinarians, the "pillar of orthodoxy" and "the father of the fathers." This reputation was later questioned during the era of Origenist controversy. At one point Gregory's name was not included in a list of the "selected fathers," and his immediate influence diminished. However, later at the Seventh Ecumenical Council he was again named "the father of the fathers." Critical discussion of Gregory's theology began as early as the fourth century, and Barsanuphius has given the reason for this reevaluation. "Many saints who became teachers surpassed their own instructors by receiving approval from above to set forth a new teaching. At the same time, however, they preserved what they had received from their former instructors, even when this teaching was false. After these men became spiritual teachers they did not pray to God to reveal to them whether that which their earlier instructors had taught them had truly been inspired by the Holy Spirit. Since they respected the wisdom of their instructors, they did not examine their words. They did not ask God if these words were true." Gregory's theology had been developed under the influence of Origen, and thus it contained elements of school tradition along with orthodox Church doctrine. Gregory's system was never condemned as a whole but it was later purged of its Origenism.

II
WORKS

Gregory did not elaborate a complete system of theology, even though he had perhaps the most strictly logical mind of all the fathers. His theology was influenced by Origen and also by the thought of the Neoplatonists. Gregory wrote on all aspects of theology. Some of his works are polemic and topical, and others reflect his own personal interests.

Exegetical Works

As an exegete Gregory continued the work of Basil, but some of his writings follow the Origenist tradition of commentary. The first group includes two supplementary treatises to the *Hex - aemeron*: *De opificio hominis* [*On the Making of Man*] and *Ex - plicatio apologetica in Hexaemeron* [*An Apologetic Explication on the Hexaemeron*], which were composed soon after Basil's death. Here, as in other works, Gregory follows the example of Basil, and his exegesis also shows the influence of classical philosophy, especially the commentaries of Posidonius and others on Plato's *Timaeus*.

Gregory's other exegetical works were written later in his life, and in these his method of interpretation is strictly allegorical. They are united by the common theme of the necessity of a moral and ascetic life as a way of knowing God. The most im - portant of these are *De vita Moysis* [*On the Life of Moses*] which clearly shows the influence of Philo, and a commentary of *Fifteen Homilies on the Song of Songs* which Gregory interprets in the Origenist tradition. Gregory defends the allegorical method of exegesis in the introduction to this commentary, which is dedicated to Olympiada. In his consideration the *Song of Songs* presages the spiritual wedding of the human soul and the Church with Christ, the most greatly desired heavenly Bride - groom. In his *Accurate Exposition of Ecclesiastes* Gregory deals with the necessity of freeing the mind from passions so that it can ascend to that which is above the senses. He describes the stages leading to moral perfection in a homily *In psalmorum inscriptiones* [*On the Titles of the Psalms*], paying particular at - tention to the sixth psalm. Apparently he also wrote an explanation on *Proverbs*. Most of Gregory's exegesis is devoted to the Old Testament, and from the New Testament he has written only on the Beatitudes and the Lord's Prayer. His ex - egetical works also include a homily *De pythonissa* [*On the Ventriloquist*], a topic which had attracted the attention of Origen. In opposition to Origen Gregory supports the position of Me - thodius of Olympus and Eustathius of Antioch by asserting that it was a demon and not the spirit of Samuel which appeared to Saul. Gregory's dogmatic and polemical writings also contain interpretative commentary.

Polemical Works

Gregory's polemical writings include twelve (or in some opinions four to thirteen tracts, depending on what one con - siders under this rubric) tracts against Eunomius, which examine the heretic's arguments against Basil's theology. These "words of objection" were written mainly in 380 and 381, and they were later supplemented by a commentary on the creed which Eu - nomius presented to the emperor Theodosius in 383. Gregory attacks the doctrine of the Anomoeans and sets forth Basil's orthodox teaching on the Trinity. The epistle to Ablabius *Against Those Who Falsely Accuse Us of Saying That There Are Three Gods* [*Ad Ablabium quod non sint tres dii*] is also devoted to the defense of Basil's dogma. In the last years of his life Gregory wrote two treatises against Apollinarius which provide a detailed exposition of Apollinarius' doctrine on the heavenly flesh of Christ and the absence in Christ of a human intellect. Gregory attacks not only Apollinarius himself but also his doctrines as they were reinterpreted and debased by his disciples. He briefly deals with the same theme in the epistle To Theophilus of Alexandria [*Adversus Apollinaristas ad Theophilum episcopum Alexan - drinum*]. Gregory also composed a homily on the Holy Spirit in op - position to the Macedonian Pneumatomachi [*De Spiritu Sancto adversus Pneumatomachos Macedonianos*]. A homily against Arius and Sabellius has been ascribed to Gregory but was not written by him (it may be the work of Basil the Great).

Dogmatic Works

The fundamentals of Gregory's doctrines are contained in his *Great Catechism* [*Oratio catechetica magna*] which he composed no later than 385. This work contains arguments against certain heresies but is not strictly polemical. It was primarily written as instruction for catechumens. By means of Scripture and his own reasoning Gregory sets forth the orthodox doctrines of Faith, the Holy Trinity, the Incarnation, Redemption, the Sacraments, Bap - tism, the Eucharist, and the Last Judgment. His other dogmatic works include a short treatise on the Holy Spirit written to Eustathius of Sebaste [*Ad Eustathium de sancta Trinitate*]; an epistle to Simplicius on faith [*Ad Simplicium de fide sancta*], which explains the dogma of the Divinity of the Word and Spirit; and *Ad Graecos ex communibus notionibus* [*To the Greeks, On the Basis of Universal Ideas*]. A dialogue on the soul and resurrection [*Dialogus de anima et resurrectione qui inscribitur*

Macrinia], which is presented as being conducted by Gregory's sister Macrina, was written under the influence of Plato's *Phaedo*. It is one of his most personal works. Gregory deals with similar problems in the treatise *On the Premature Death of Infants*. A dialogue *On Fate* [*Contra Fatum*] between a bishop and a pagan philosopher is a defense of free will against astrology and fatalism.

Ascetic and Moral Works

Among Gregory's ascetic and moral works are a long tract *On Virginity or Perfection* [*De virginitate*], which he wrote in his youth, and several shorter treatises: *What is the Christian Name and Profession* [*Quid nomen professione Christianorum sibi velit*]; *On Pefection and What a Christian Should Be* [*De perfectione et qualem oporteat esse Christianum*]; and *On the Goal of Godly Life, to the Monk Olympius* [*Ad Olympium*]. Gregory's ascetic ideal is expressed with particular clarity in his epistle *On the Life of Macrina* [*Vita Macrinae*], which was written soon after her death.

Sermons

Few of Gregory's sermons have survived. The most significant are the orations on the great feasts: on Christmas, Epiphany, Easter, and Pentecost. He also composed orations of St. Stephen, Theodoret the Martyr, the Forty Martyrs of Sebaste, Ephraem the Syrian, and Gregory Thaumaturgus. His funeral orations are devoted to Basil and Meletius of Antioch, among others. Gregory's homiletic works are not outstanding and his style is heavy and artificial. He is at best in dealing with ascetic themes, which always had great personal interest for him.

Letters

Gregory has left at least 26 to 30 letters, most of which provide information on his personality and biography. His letter on pilgrimages to Jerusalem is especially significant. The canonical epistle to Letoius contains eight rules and was included in the Nomocanon and other collections. His rules for penitential discipline were determined according to his knowledge of psychology, and were probably formed on the basis of Church tradition and his own experience as a clergyman. Gregory also wrote an epistle on Easter, the "universal feast of creation," which celebrates the resurrection of humanity, which had fallen through sin. His epistle 25 to Amphilochius is very interesting for the history of Christian art and architecture, for he describes in detail a *martyrion* in construction.

III
THEOLOGICAL THOUGHT

THE LIMITATION OF OUR KNOWLEDGE OF GOD

The Inner Power of the Soul

The human soul naturally "moves towards beauty which is invisible." Man has an "inner immaterial power" which enables him to perceive the spiritual. "Whoever purifies his soul even a little will see God's love for us in all its purity, and he will see the intent God had in creating our souls. He will find that humanity by its very essence has been joined to a desire for goodness and perfection, and that man's nature has been united to an impassive and holy love for the blessed Image of which man is the likeness." This love and attraction cause man to experience an endless longing for God, Who is the ultimate goal of all desire and of all contemplation.

The Eternity of the Divinity and the Dynamic and Potentially Infinite Nature of Man's Struggle

This goal, however, is inaccessible and can never be achieved. "Let us learn about virtue from the Gospels," Gregory writes. "We know that the greatest goal of perfect virtue is for virtue to have no limitation or final goal. There is only one limit to virtue: it must strive to be endless. Possibly the perfection of our human nature consists in our having a vision of beauty within ourselves which is such that we always desire an even greater beauty." Furthermore, "it is dangerous to stop in this forward movement, for every good thing is limited only by that which stands in opposition to it . . . In the same way that the end of life is the beginning of death, a halt on the path to virtue is the beginning of the road to vice." This striving is endless. It must be uninterrupted because its goal is eternity. The eternity of the Divinity determines the dynamic and potentially infinite nature of man's struggle to perfect himself, in which every action is always the source of further actions which will extend beyond earthly life and time. Gregory describes it as a "completeness that will never be limited by satiation."

The Bridegroom is constantly telling the soul to arise and come to Him. "For the man who has truly arisen the continual need to arise will never end, and for the man who has set out to find the Lord the path leading to the Divine continuity will never be ex - hausted." We must arise without ceasing, and even as we approach the goal we must never stop moving forward. The Lord has said, "Let the man who thirsts come to me and drink" (*John* 7: 37). Gregory explains: "The Lord did not set a limit to this thirst, nor to the effort needed to reach Him, nor to the enjoyment we will have when we drink. On the contrary, He has not set a precise time, but advises us to constantly thirst and drink, and to always be striving towards Him." A true knowledge of God is reached by a path of thirst, effort, and vigorous striving. It is the result of a desire which is as strong as the passion of love, ἔρως. In Scripture the *Song of Songs* uses the image of a marriage to represent "the incorporeal, spiritual, and immaterial union of the soul with God." God is love and "He sends to those who are to be saved the chosen arrow of His Only-Begotten Son, having first dipped the triple prong of the arrow into the Spirit of life." This arrow is faith. As the soul moves upward in its ascent to the Divinity, it "sees in itself this sweet arrow," "an arrow of fiery love," "and the sweet torment of passion is multiplied." This passion is our love for God and longing to be united with Him.

God is inaccessible, yet man by nature longs for a knowledge of the Divinity as his greatest good. Man's path to God is defined by this contradiction. God is higher than cognition, but He can be recognized in everything around us. He is outside and above the world and higher than every essence, but He is also the Creator and Artist of the world, and therefore He can be seen and known through it. "By means of visible things the wisdom and Word of the artist are proclaimed in our hearts," Gregory writes, "and by the Wisdom which is visible in the universe we can guess about the Wisdom which created everything."

The Creator is revealed and visible to the human soul, which bears the image of God even though it has been defiled and has become impure. "The measure of God has been placed within you," Gregory writes. "He has sealed you with the image of the good things of His own nature in the same way that a design is imprinted on wax." Man must be able to see God in his own soul, which for this reason must be kept as pure as a mirror. The soul should be free from anything foreign to it, such as sensual inclinations and violent passions, which mar its surface and make a true reflection impossible. The body should lie dormant and inactive. Man must "leave everything that is visible," "stand outside of the material world," "free himself from the shelter of the flesh," "grind away from himself everything superfluous and corporeal," "in order to completely transform himself into an intellectual and immaterial being and make himself the clear re - flection of the beauty of his Archetype." A purified soul "should contain nothing except God, and should pay attention to nothing else." In this way man becomes similar to God, and the soul which has been cleansed through constant effort and vigil will reflect the Divinity.

The Soul and the Image of God

"Whoever then looks at himself will see within himself that which he has desired because in looking at his own purity he will see the image of his Archetype. If you look at the sun in a mirror, even though you have not turned your eyes to heaven you still see its radiance no less than those who look at its actual orb. In this same way the Lord tells you that, although you do not have the power to look directly at the light, by returning to the original state of grace in which your image was given to you at the beginning you will have what you seek within yourself. Purity, impassivity, and avoidance of all evil are Divine, and if all of these are present in you then there is no doubt that God is also in you. When your thoughts are purged of vice, free from passion, and far removed from profanity, you will be blessed with keen sight because in purifying yourself you have seen what is invisible for the impure and when you have removed the mists of the material world from the eyes of your spirit, you will clearly see bliss in the pure heaven of your heart. What will you see? Purity, sanctity, simplicity, and all the other radiant reflections of the Divinity, and in these you will see God." This is not only a vision of God, but true communion with Him. "It is not like some spectacle that God is offered to the purified soul."

The Platonic and Plotinian Influence

Gregory's ideas show the influence of Plotinus, who taught that man can know God only through knowing himself. The soul must gather itself up, concentrate on itself, and come to a knowledge of itself, and through this it will come to a knowledge of God. The mind must be purified in order to become similar to God and return to its original likeness to Him. This likeness is the means by which the mind knows God because, as Plato has written in *Meno* (80 E), "that which is similar is recognized by that which is like it."

Moses and the Mystical Ascent to God

Gregory sees an example of the mystical ascent to God in the figure of Moses the Lawgiver and in the appearance of God on Mount Sinai. The people were ordered to purify themselves, and the mountain was covered with a cloud and illuminated by fire. "By the power of God alone and without any other implement the air formed itself into individual words. These words were not only distinct, but they proclaimed the divine commandments." The people were afraid to ascend the mountain to listen, and only Moses entered the cloud. He himself became invisible when he penetrated the ineffable mystery of the Divinity and was in com - munion with the Invisible One." The appearance of God begins with light, and Moses had once seen God in His radiance in the Burning Bush. Now, having become closer to perfection, he saw God in a cloud and, sheltered by a cloud, he participated in eternal life. In Gregory's interpretation the first steps away from the path of error are light. A closer examination of that which is hidden leads into a cloud, which replaces visible things. Finally the soul enters the innermost sanctuary of the knowledge of God "which is enveloped on all sides by the divine cloud. Everything that can be seen and comprehended remains outside, and all that is left for the vision of the soul is that which is invisible and incomprehensible. In this cloud is God." The Divinity is "beyond the reach of the understanding."

As man ascends, the "inaccessible nature of Divinity" gradually becomes revealed to him and reason sees God in "the invisible and incomprehensible," in "a radiant cloud." Even when it reaches this cloud the soul realizes that it is as far from perfection as if it had never set out. According to Gregory, it is exactly this that is the highest truth of all. Our true knowledge is that we do not and cannot know because that which we seek is beyond our cognition. By its very nature the Divinity is higher than knowledge and comprehension. The first principle of theology must be that God is inaccessible. That which can be contemplated cannot be conceptually expressed. Whoever claims that God can be known merely shows that he has abandoned the One Who truly exists in favor of something which exists only in the imagination and which does not contain true life, for this life cannot be expressed by concepts.

Moses was led into the sanctuary not made by man and this is the ultimate extent of contemplation. He later reconstructed a material image of this divine temple at the command of God so that this miracle would not be forgotten and would be transmitted by the people of the lower world. In Gregory's interpretation this immaterial sanctuary is Christ, the Strength and Wisdom of God. Within the sanctuary Moses saw the intellectual powers which support the universe. Gregory follows the example of Philo in interpreting the symbolism of the priestly robes.

Moses descended to his people with the ten commandments of God, Who was the author of their essence and of their physical being. The people, however, had sinned and had made them - selves unworthy of this gift. Moses broke the tablets and was commanded to inscribe new ones, and on these, which were made from an earthly substance, God again set forth His law. Gregory interprets this as an allegory of mankind. Men were once indestructible and immortal. They were fashioned by the hand of God and His law was imprinted on them as their adornment. They were shattered by their fall to earth but were restored by Christ, the true Lawgiver, who cut their stone again with His own flesh. For Gregory the highest stages of contemplation reveal Christ, the Word Incarnate, the "manifestation of God in the flesh which was achieved for our sakes." It is He who was seen by the prophetic mystics of the Old Testament, and the *Song of Songs* was written about Him.

Gregory sees Moses as a great mystic. Moses was purified and ascended the mountain where he was initiated into the mysteries of God. He is an example for every soul. Each soul should have the faith to draw nearer to God in His impenetrable cloud, and should become its own stonecutter so that the commandments of God are carved on it as they were on the tablets of Moses. Then the soul will be embraced by the "divine night," and the Bridegroom will come to it. The Bridegroom will not reveal Him - self, however, for how can anything be revealed at night? He will stand at the door and beckon. He will give a sign of His presence, but He will not enter, for He has come to call. Even as it reaches its highest point the path must begin again. "That which is incomprehensible is infinitely greater than that which we can understand. The Bridegroom appears to the soul many times but by His voice He reveals to His bride that she has not yet seen Him." A man who stands on the shore of a river will always be at the starting point of his observation because the waters flow continuously and their streaming is only beginning.

Gregory also comments on God's appearance to Moses in the crevice of the rock (*Exodus* 33: 18-23). Moses asked God to show him His glory and to reveal the path to Him. "A voice from above," Gregory writes, "agreed to this request and did not re - fuse to grant this grace, but it only caused Moses to despair, for it revealed that what he desired is not possible for man." Moses only saw the "back of God."

All of this has a greater significance. It is the very effort of knowing God that is man's true knowledge of Him. "He who strives for God sees only His back." "Moses was impatient for God but all he learned was how to see Him. This is accomplished by following behind God and walking in the path He has left us." This is the only way for the one who is led to see the One who leads. "Whoever is following this path and then steps aside, or tries to see the face of the One who is leading him, sets for himself a path that has not been lain by his true Leader." God told Moses that He could not see His face. In Gregory's interpretation this signifies that "you will never stand face to face with the One who leads you because, if you do, your journey will be from the direction opposite Him. That which is good never looks directly at goodness but follows after it." For this reason God reveals that man cannot see His face and remain alive. To see the face of God one must be coming towards Him. Man should follow after God and not try to approach Him from the opposite direction. The path which leads from the direction opposite the path of virtue is the path of sin.

Gregory comments on other aspects of the Biblical narrative. God told Moses to stand on a rock. This rock is Christ, Who is absolute goodness. God placed Moses on this rock not so that he could rest, but so that he would be free to move forward. "Whoever ascends does not stand still and whoever stands still does not ascend." The man who ascends must be firm and he must not be distracted from the path of virtue. God showed compassion for Moses because "his desire to perfect himself could never be satisfied, and he was always striving for greater virtue." God appeared to Moses but this did not satisfy Moses' longing for Him. "God would not have shown Himself if this vision could have satisfied the yearning of His servant."

The Unceasing Growth of Participation
in Divinity

Man's continual struggle, his knowledge that his longing will have no end, and his resolution to accept this, all make him similar to the Divinity because It too is infinite. Everything which can be truly conceived of God must be boundless, and this is why our longing is also unending. "By leaving that in which we abide, we ascend to the greatest good." This striving is not futile but is a continual process of discovery. "When the soul participates in things that are superior to it, it becomes superior to itself. Once it begins to grow this growth never stops." "The good things in which it participates abide in it, and by its constant participation the soul receives good things in abundance." For this reason the longing of love is stronger at the highest stages of contemplation than at the beginning. "Participation in the Divinity is such that whoever partakes of it grows and becomes more receptive. This participation develops the capacities of the participant. Whoever receives this nourishment grows and never ceases to grow." Even when it is united with its desired object the soul longs for more. "And even when it achieves this it begins to yearn again. This bliss has become absolutely necessary for it, and it is pained and grieved when it does not receive the object of its desire." That which is desired continually slips away from the "embrace of the mind" and the soul's attempts to contain it are in vain. "They looked for Him but did not find Him, for He was beyond imagination and conception and ran away at the approach of reason."

"The soul stretches its hands out to its source, seeks that which cannot be grasped, and calls to that which cannot be overtaken . . . It looks for that which cannot be found and calls on the One who is ineffable, in spite of all His names. Thus the soul learns from its vigil that it loves One who is inaccessible and desires One who cannot be embraced. The soul suffers from the hopelessness of its longing until it realizes that its true desire is a bliss which is infinite and inexhaustible. The uppermost robe of grief and doubt is removed by the recognition that yearning, striving, and continual ascent are in themselves the true enjoyment of that which is desired. The fulfillment of one desire always leads to the desire of something greater. Therefore, as soon as the outer robe of hopelessness is removed, the soul sees that the indescribable beauty of its desired object, which exceeds its expectations, becomes ever more beautiful. The soul thus reaches the ultimate extent of desire. It reveals itself to its Beloved through the daughters of Jerusalem and admits that it has received the chosen arrow of God. It has been deeply struck by the arrow of faith and been fatally wounded by love." In the words of John, "God is love." In Gregory's interpretation the *Song of Songs* describes the love and longing experienced by the true believer.

Ecstasy as the Highest Stage of Ascent

The culmination of the ascent to God is a "divine and solemn intoxication" and a "frenzy of the mind." This ecstasy is the highest stage of contemplation and it cannot be comprehended in concepts or images. Gregory's descriptions of the ecstatic con-dition are influenced by Philo's theory of the knowledge of God, but he does not merely borrow or imitate the Greek philosopher's thought. Gregory uses Philo's terminology to describe his per-sonal mystical experience, which is similar to the experience of Basil the Great and other ascetics of the fourth century and later. Their mystical vision reveals Christ and not the Logos, as was the case for Clement of Alexandria and Origen. Gregory interprets the *Song of Songs* as a revelation of Christ. His commentary is not only an essay on mysticism but is an intimate diary of mystical experience which is conveyed in the form of an exegetical treatise.

The Wedding of the Soul with God

In the highest stages of contemplation the soul is united with God, becomes similar to Him, and lives in Him. "It becomes similar to His inaccessible nature when it is pure and impassive." This is the mysterious wedding of the soul, its "incorporeal, spiritual, immaterial union with God," which is man's greatest good and bliss. Once this union is achieved a mutual interpenetration takes place. God abides in the soul and the soul makes its home in God. This life in God is beyond expression and the great mystics have never been able to describe their contemplation and the mysteries of paradise that they have seen. "Although you may hear words about this," Gregory writes, "the knowledge of God will remain ineffable." Ideas and concepts are inadequate to God and "what He is by nature." Words are incommensurate with the Divinity because It surpasses cognition and reasoning and is "higher than the highest things." "The truth of existence is the true Life, and this is not accessible to our knowledge."

The Incapability of Human Reason and Knowledge of Conceiving of Uncreated Being

Human cognition is static and for this reason it is inadequate to the "mysteries of God." Gregory goes as far to say that every conception of God is an idol and a deceptive image, ἔιδολού. "Every idea which is developed through natural reasoning and supposition or which is comprehensible to the mind forms a divine idol and has no relation to God himself." The conceptions of the human mind are formed on the basis of contemplation and the observation of the visible, created world and when the mind is elevated beyond the bounds of created nature it recognizes the inadequacy of human reason. "The distance which separates uncreated being from every created substance is great and cannot be traversed."

God is beyond names. He does not have a proper name because "His being is above definition and cannot be encompassed by a word or a name." All names and all concepts entail limitation and definition but the Divinity is infinite and boundless and cannot be defined. "We know that this Being exists, but there is no name which can completely comprehend Its ineffable and infinite nature. If there is such a name we do not know it."

We cannot understand the Divinity by trying to separate Its properties and attributes because Its nature is uncompound and infinite. It had no source and there is nothing specific which defines Its essence except for the very fact that this essence is beyond conceptualization. In contemplating the Divinity there is no one thing on which the human mind can concentrate its attention. "It is like a vast sea and gives no sign by which we can discover its source." This is because man's ability to form concepts is limited. "In contemplating God we must not be restricted by any definition: not by time, nor place, nor color, nor outline, nor aspect, nor volume, nor quantity, nor extent, nor any name, thing or concept." Contemplative thought must be in constant motion. Gregory writes: "Our most basic dogma is that God cannot be comprehended by a name or a concept or any cognitive faculty of the mind. He is beyond the comprehension of men and the angels and the heavenly powers. He is ineffable and cannot be designated by words. There is only one definition which helps us to know His proper nature and this is that He alone is greater than definition."

Contemplation of God must be infinite and words are inadequate to Him. "There is only one name capable of signifying the Divinity and this is the ineffable wonder which arises in the soul at the thought of God." The soul becomes quiet, "for it is time to be silent and to cherish the unutterable marvel of this inexpressible force." Curiosity about the proper name of the ineffable nature of God can only lead to delusion. "Your name is myrrh which has been poured forth." We know the Divine myrrh by its fragrance but the nature of this mysterious essence cannot be named. Gregory writes in conclusion, "We know the extent of the glory of the One we venerate by the very fact that we cannot comprehend His incomparable majesty."

The Distinction between Contemplation of God and Knowledge of God

The soul's contemplation of God must be distinguished from knowledge of God. "The Lord has told us that bliss is not in knowing about God but in having Him in our hearts," Gregory writes. At the height of spiritual contemplation man is close to God and the Divine features he has within himself are revealed to him. Even then, however, true knowledge of God is impossible. "No matter how great its range of vision may be, no creature can ever completely get out from itself, and no matter what it looks at it sees only itself, even when it thinks it is seeing something higher. By nature it does not have the ability to look outside itself." This is especially true when we try to know God.

God as He is known to man is only an image which the mind has intuited and outlined in its striving toward Him. In the con-templation of intellectual being the mind goes beyond the knowledge provided by the senses and "by guessing" it at-tempts to grasp that which eludes the senses. Each man approaches that which he seeks in a different way and then "tries to express the concept he has formed of his object by attempting to make the meaning of his words correspond as closely as possible to that which he has understood." Thus language and cognition are only symbolic. When we speak about God the names we use do not serve to reinforce some reliable con-ception we have of Him but they are only symbols or analogies which "indicate" Him or point to Him. Therefore these words have no meaning outside the actual experience in which their sig-nificance or symbolism is revealed and realized.

"The human mind struggles to comprehend the inaccessible supreme Nature and to achieve contact with it. It is not perceptive enough to clearly see the invisible, but at the same time it is not incapable of approaching it and of guessing about that which it seeks. The mind is able to guess at part of its object through deduction and conclusion, and it discerns another aspect by the very impossibility of true perception. The understanding that this object is beyond its comprehension is true knowledge of it. The mind can understand that which is not a part of God's nature, but does not understand what should truly be conceived of Him." This is the reason that God has many names, and it is only in the totality of these names that the human mind can attempt to express the knowledge of God which it can gain through con-templation. These names are "like flashing sparks which cannot make completely visible the meaning they contain." "But when you take these into yourself, through your faith you will put yourself under the yoke of One who will enter you and become incarnate in you. For you are His throne, and you can make yourself His home."

The Two Types of Divine Names and Their Inability to Define God

Gregory follows the reasoning of Basil the Great and distinguishes two types of Divine names. Some names are negative
and attempt to express the Divinity by indicating that Its properties are the opposite of the attributes of creation. "The
meaning of each of these names indicates only God's otherness
from the things which we understand, but they do not explain His
proper nature." This group includes not only names that are
apophatic or negating but also positive names which indicate
absence or oppositeness. Gregory considers that even the
name "the One Who is Good" expresses no more than that God
is not evil and that He is its antithesis. When we call God a
"Source" we indicate that He has no source and is eternal.
"These names are a list of the weak and evil things that God is
not." They reflect the progress of the mind as it purifies itself and
becomes increasingly abstract in its ascent to the ineffable
knowledge of God.

Another type of name is derived from the actions and energy of
the Divinity because "He who is invisible by nature becomes
visible through His activity and He can be discerned in the things
around Him." These names are also inadequate to God's being.
"He who is above names receives many different names from us
because His grace to us is manifold." These names designate no
more than God's activity "as it relates to us." They also help to reinforce our orthodoxy. "We express everything we conceive
about the Divinity in the form of a name, and no name has been
predicated about God which does not represent a particular
conception. However, actions provide us with no single concept
of their author. "If I want to know something about the mind and
you show me a hill of wind-blown sand or the dust that the wind
has stirred up, you have not given me an answer to my question."
All we can know by observing the results of God's activity is that
He is their source.

"The miracles which can be observed in the universe are the
basis for the conceptions of theology according to which the
Divinity is named wise, omnipotent, good, holy, blessed, eternal,
the Judge, the Savior, and so forth." Miracles reveal to creation
the glory and greatness of God but not in its entirety because the
Divine energy revealed in them is only partial. "The miracles
which take place in the world do not provide clear evidence as to
that strength which is the source of their energy. I say nothing
about the nature which is the source of this strength. God's

works exceed the capabilities of human perception." The created world is too small to contain God's infinite Wisdom, Strength, and Glory, or to be a full and true image of the Divinity.

"From the testimony of Scripture," Gregory writes, "we know that the Divinity is ineffable and cannot be named and we assert that every name, whether it is known to us by means of some - thing proper to our human nature or through Scripture, is only an interpretation of a conception of the Divinity." God's names are all the invention of the human mind, which has tried to express its knowledge of God by describing that which it has intuited or con - templated. In this respect these names have a certain use - fulness. They can be false idols, however, when the mind ex - aggerates their limited worth by considering that they are adequate to God. In dealing with the Eunomians Gregory writes that their heretical teacher "has blatantly made an idol of his own opinion." He has deified the meaning of the word 'unoriginate'. In [Eunomius'] consideration it is not a quality which can be rel - atively ascribed to the Divinity, but he holds that 'unori - ginatedness' itself is God or the Divinity."

In his polemic against Eunomius Gregory carefully examines the names of God and shows that not one of them truly or adequately designates His essence. He points out that Scripture "has not declared the essence of the Divinity or made it known because it is impossible to comprehend and it cannot bring any advantage to the curious." The writers of Scripture "did not concern themselves with giving the Divinity a name because It is superior to all names." Even the mysterious names of "He Who Is," which is known through revelation, is not satisfactory. It is exactly this name, which is unqualified and predicates nothing about its subject, which testifies to the truth that God has no name and cannot be named. "Some names attempt to express a conception of God's being and others attempt to express the mode of His being. But until this very day God is ineffable and has not been explained by what has been said about Him." Gregory writes in conclusion: "We can know nothing about God except that He is, for this has been revealed by the words 'I am the One'."

Gregory's Doctrine of Conceptualization

Gregory's doctrine of the names of God evolves from his theory of conceptualization and nomenclature in general. This doctrine was developed to oppose the teachings of Eunomius but there is no reason to assume that polemical considerations forced Gregory to express his views only incompletely. There are also no grounds for considering Gregory a sceptic or a nominalist, or for asserting that his theory of names differs in its basic premises from his religious and metaphysical systems. What appears to be "nominalism" in Gregory's theory is really only the logical consequence of his use of negative attribution to designate the Divinity. Basically Gregory's theory of names is an elaboration of Plato's ideas on the same subject. The views of Eunomius are comparable to those expressed by Cratylus in Plato's dialogue of the same name.

Gregory considers that words are the "inventions of the human intellect." For this reason there are many languages. "If the law of nature had ordered names to come forth to us from the objects themselves, in the way that plants grow from seeds and roots," Gregory writes, "then all people would speak one language." The Tower of Babel does not imply that many languages were created by God. He simply allowed the nations to distinguish themselves by developing different languages. Gregory sees language as a product of man's creativity. The "invention" of language by man was not arbitrary or capricious but was accomplished through the natural faculty of reason. God gave man the gift of language as an intellectual capacity. "He gave us this faculty and then we ourselves create house, stool, sword, plow, and whatever else we need in life."

"Man's faculty or potential for language is the work of our Creator." Man can realize this potential in a free and creative way. God does not direct the physical movement of His creatures nor does He sit like a teacher of grammar to direct our use of language. Language, sounds, and the conceptions they express are all created by men through the Divinely bestowed faculty of "invention," ἐπίνοια. Gregory follows Basil the Great in defining invention as "the intellect's ability to discover the unknown by seeking to know the things removed from it with the help of deductions drawn from the things which are most immediate to the object of inquiry." Invention is the creative power of thought, a "more exhaustive analysis of the object of thought." Instead of ἐπίνοια, invention, Gregory occasionally uses the term διάνοια, judgment.

Invention is not merely fabrication, fantasy, or caprice. Nomenclature presupposes an object to be named and things are named so that we can point them out and so that our cognition and knowledge of them can be consolidated. Therefore names are not arbitrary because if they were they would not be names or signs. They would be devoid of sense and meaning. Naming things entails intention and premeditation. "The intellectual faculty of the soul has been given to us from God. Then it begins to move and look at things by itself and, to keep its knowledge from being blurred or imprecise, it puts an individual stamp on every thing, indicating this stamp by means of sound."

Gregory distinguishes the perception of objects from knowl-edge of them. "It is impossible for us to always have everything that exists in front of our eyes. There are some things that we know because they are always before us but we know other things because we have imprinted them on our memories. Nothing can be preserved by memory unless we have a name to designate the object we want to remember so that we can distinguish it from other objects."

We give names because we need to distinguish the con-ceptions we form from our experience, which is constantly changing. Names are unnecessary and even impossible for God because "His Wisdom and Strength have no difficulty in encompassing everything that exists in its individuality." God contemplates the entirety of the world and instantly com-prehends it without the help of names. The nature of human faculty for conception and nomenclature is such that the ultimate essence of things, even created things, cannot be known and named by man. The reason is that things are recognized in their relationships, in their activity, and in the effect they have on other things. When we talk about them we do not designate their true nature but only the properties and qualities we can discern in them. We do not know the essence of things because their foundation is known only to God. "Scripture does not examine the essence of creation because this is superfluous and brings no advantage. The human intellect cannot know the nature and source of creation because such knowledge would have to be radiant with the full majesty, power, and glory of the Creator." Therefore, "We know by means of our senses only as much of the elements of the world as is useful for us. We do not know what their essence is and this ignorance brings us no harm."

A name is a sign or a mark of a thing σημεῖον. It has a con-nection with its object. "Words which are invented have some-thing in common with their objects." In attempting to define the common element between the name and its object, Gregory proposes that this connection is established by the free and creative faculty of the intellect. Names are invented for things and united to them but they do not arise from things. A name is not the thing itself, but neither is it completely independent of it. A name is not an hypostasis. "Every name is the mark or sign of an object or idea but it does not exist and cannot be conceived of independently and by itself."

The Influence of Plato on Gregory's Doctrine

Gregory's theories were influenced by Plato, who expressed similar ideas in *Cratylus* in the second speech of Socrates. Things have a definite nature and their names should cor - respond to it. Names are θέσει, not φύσει. The lawgiver who cre - ates them is their artist. In creating them he gives form to the universal idea behind the name by means of sound. Names are the instruments of the intellect. Plato adds that there are different kinds of artists and that not everything created by them is equally valuable. Not all names are adequate and names can be unsuccessful in the same way that a painting can be a failure. A name is the likeness of a thing. In *Cratylus* Plato tries to respond to the question of whether or not names give us any information about their object, and his answer is negative. A thing can be known only by observation and contemplation, not by its name. Aristotle develops Plato's idea and states that names are established by men and that there are no names which arise from nature.

Gregory follows Plato in his reasoning. He turns his attention from the name to the thing itself because things represent inexhaustible experience. Things have a definite being which has been established by God, their Creator, and not by their names. We can discern their definite nature and to a certain extent express it but we can never create an exact replica of the world within our own intellects. This would be a pointless un - dertaking because such a replica would hide reality from us. Cognition and language are a means for overcoming our limitations. They are not a sign of our strength. We need words and concepts so that we can remember our experiences and describe them to other people who have not shared them. "It is necessary for us to put signs on things so that we can explain to each other the activity of our minds. If there were another way for us to express our thoughts, we would not use words as inter - mediaries. We would communicate with each other more clearly and more purely because our intellects alone would express the very nature of the things they observed." As the mind becomes purified in its ascent to God, the tongue falls silent. "Every means of expression is inadequate before the truth." Contemplation of the truth is beyond words, which are unnecessary to the intellect when it beholds true being. Contemplation is superior to lan - guage, for language is the instrument of human reason.

Gregory insists that certain experiences cannot be fully con - ceptualized. However, the ineffability and incomprehensibility of the Divinity do not mean that It is unapproachable. On the con -

trary, Gregory's belief in the possibility of "deification" is one of the outstanding features of his theology. What he wants to make clear is that human reason is limited and that conceptualization should not be respected to the extent that experience is ignored. Gregory does not deny that language is a valuable means of cognition, and he cites Scripture to prove his point. This is the reason for his rejection of the terminology of Eunomius. Gregory emphasizes the independence of the names of the Trinity, the Father, Son, and Spirit, which have been revealed to us by God.

Scripture as a Symbol of Spiritual Truth

For Gregory Scripture is a symbol of spiritual truth and therefore the literal Hebraic interpretation of the Bible is inadequate. "What seems at first to be a commentary on that which has been written will, if it is not understood in the proper sense, turn out to be something quite different from the truth which is revealed by the Spirit." The "body of Scripture" is a veil which covers the "glory contained in Scripture." The law and the prophets were a small window in the wall of our understanding and the rays of the truth penetrated through this window. "Behind this wall stood the truth, which was closely connected with the Archetype." Now the light of the Gospel pours forth on us in abundance.

Scripture is a record of Revelation, a "testimony of the truth which has been revealed to us." "We say that all Scripture has been inspired by God because it is the teaching of Divine inspiration. When you remove the word, which is its corporeal cover, what remains for you is the Lord, Life, and the Spirit." Scripture should be observed to the letter, as should all the precepts and traditions of faith. "Even great blasphemy and impiety have caused no change in the words which have been transmitted to us." "Because this faith was given to the Apostles by God, we will not abridge it, nor change it, nor add to it." All tradition must be respected as our "most ancient law of faith" and our "inheritance from the fathers." "The proof of our words is the tradition which has come down to us from the fathers. It has been transmitted to us as an inheritance from the Apostles through the saints who followed them," Gregory writes. We must "revere those whose authority has been witnessed by the Holy Spirit, abide within the bounds of their teaching and knowledge, and never dare to strive for that which was not accessible to the saints and holy men."

THE MYSTERY OF THEOLOGY

God as True and Complete Being

In Gregory's contemplation God is the full completeness of true and Sovereign Being. His being is the only Being, and Being is His very nature. "There is nothing which properly exists apart from and except for God's Being. It is above all essence and is the cause of everything," Gregory writes. The Divinity is bound - less and infinite, eternal and simple. "The nature of the Divinity is simple, unified, and uncompound." The Divinity is one, unin - terrupted within Itself, boundless, infinite, and there is nothing to hinder it or contain it. God has the motion of life within Himself, for "He is Life, and life is active within Him. This life never grows or diminishes through any addition or subtraction." Nothing can be added to that which is eternal and nothing can be removed from an impassive nature.

The eternity of the Divinity can be expressed by the symbol of a circle. A circle never begins; it has no first or last point; it is unified, and it is contained within itself. The eternity of God is also like this. "If we extend our thoughts from the central point of the present moment into the eternity of Divine Life, we see that this life is like a circle and is constantly overtaking itself. Everywhere we see the Divinity, which cannot be encompassed, never ends, and has no interruptions. We cannot recognize in It any individual part or boundary."

The Unending and Eternal Bliss of Divine Life

Gregory attempts to express the "unending and eternal bliss of Divine Life" through a series of definitions and images. "God is the One Who is beyond the boundary of everything, and Who has nothing beyond Himself. He has no end to His Being and He always exists from everywhere. The infinity of His being tran - scends the concepts of a final goal or an ultimate source. Every name of God expresses His eternity." Gregory's doctrine of the eternity of the Divinity is similar to the teaching of Origen, as is also his identification of unconditional being with goodness and bliss. All good is true being. God by His nature is every good that the mind can conceive. He is beyond every good that can be grasped by the intellect, beyond beauty, beyond goodness and virtue. God is completeness and the source of everything, and therefore He is superior to everything that exists. He is com -

pleteness and bliss. "In contemplating Himself God has everything He desires and He desires everything He has. He does not have anything from outside Himself." God is love and the source of love. "The life of the nature of the Supreme Being is love." God knows and realizes Himself as beauty, and God is love because He is beauty. As a Hellenist Gregory connects love with beauty and goodness. Goodness can also be an ethical concept, as is indicated by the relation of the words κάλλος and καλός.

The soul receives this vision of God through contemplating itself because in this contemplation it sees within itself the outline of the image of God and the living imprint of the perfections of the Divinity. The soul by nature is similar to these and can participate in them. We do not come to know the attributes of the Divinity through rational inference but by the contemplation of their reduced reflections within ourselves. We are images and we strive to return to our Archetype.

The Mystery of the Consubstantial Trinity as the Expression of the Completeness of Divine Life

The completeness of Divine Life is expressed in the mystery of the consubstantial and indivisible Trinity. Every "eloquent speech about this is unclear and says nothing." For polemical reasons Gregory tried to provide his doctrine with a firm foundation in Scripture, but Scripture itself had given rise to controversy because its testimony on the Trinity allowed for various interpretations. Gregory had to organize the relevant Scriptural passages into a unified dogma by exposing and refuting arbitrary and incorrect interpretations and by establishing the exact meaning of his terms. This is what Gregory has in mind when he says that his examination of the mystery of the Trinity is based on "general concepts."

Like Basil the Great and Gregory the Theologian, Gregory of Nyssa develops a theology of the Trinity which is midway be - tween the Hebraic doctrine and the polytheism of the Greeks. "The Jewish doctrine is destroyed by acceptance of the Word and belief in the Spirit, and the polytheistic error of the Greeks is done away with by the truth of the unity of the Divine nature, which invalidates their idea of plurality. After these corrections are made in the false premises of both these systems, let the Jewish conception of the unity of nature remain, and also the Greek distinction as to persons. The names of the Trinity are a remedy for those who are in error as to the One, as the doctrine of unity is for those who believe in many gods."

This synthesis of various individual truths was accomplished by Gregory through the elaboration of the distinction between the concepts "essence" and "hypostasis," a distinction which was common to all the Cappadocian fathers. At the same time Gregory also had to develop the concept of consubstantiality, especially in connection with the doctrine of the unchangeability and absolute completeness of the Divinity in order to effectively oppose the teachings of Eunomius. Gregory's trinitarian theo - logy was developed in the course of his polemic with the Eu - nomians and was not set forth as an integral system.

Gregory attempts to demonstrate the truth of the Trinity by examining the nature of God. God is not mute, not ἄλογος, and therefore He must have a Word, λόγος. Because God is eternal His hypostatic Word must also be eternal. This Word must be considered to be living, to be "in life," otherwise it would not be hypostatic and have independent being. There is no distinction in the properties of the Father and the Word, just as our words are not different from our intellects, of which they are the manifestation. "Nothing can be conceived of the Son which also does not belong completely to the Father." Otherwise the Divinity would be composed of dissimilars and Its unity and sim - plicity would be destroyed. God's Word contains that which can be discerned in God Himself, from whom the Word comes into being. The unity or identity of their properties expresses their unity of nature. At the same time the "Word differs from the One Whose Word He is." The very name of Word indicates a re - lationship, since it necessarily entails that there is a Father of this Word. "If this Word were not the Word of Someone, it would not be a Word."

The Word and the One from Whom the Word is have separate hypostases. Gregory usually refers to the Second Hypostasis as the Son in order to emphasize the parallelism and inter - relationship of the Divine names and to express both the in - divisibility and the distinctness of the hypostases. "The name Father indicates that He exists in a relationship and entails the concept of the Only-Begotten." "The very name of Father is a re - cognition of the hypostasis of the Only-Begotten." Gregory objects to "unoriginate," the "new name" introduced by Eunomius, "because it conceals from the listener the conception of the relationship and mutual properties of Divinity which is immediately conveyed by the names Father and Son." Gregory discusses the Spirit in a similar way and compares Him to our breath, which makes manifest the strength of our word and appears together with our word. This is also the way we should conceive of the Spirit of God.

Gregory avoids saying that God is the Spirit. The Spirit is an hypostatic name, not a substantial one. The Spirit of God does not merely "accompany the Word and manifest the Word's ac - tivity," nor is He merely transient, flowing in from outside and then pouring Himself forth until He is exhausted. This idea is blasphemous. The Spirit must be understood as the "Power of the Divinity which is realized in an independent hypostasis, indivisible from God in whom He abides, and from the Word of God whom He accompanies. He does not exhaust Himself by being poured forth but, like the Word of God, He exists hypo - statically." The One Who has a Word and a Spirit is not identical with Them. The Trinity of hypostases does not destroy the unity of the Godhead, the components of which can be distinguished but not divided. God is one and unique. He is the only good, a self-enclosed and individual monad, unchangeable by addition, an absolute unity, individual, full, and complete.

There are two different ways of counting. Counting and or - dering, even of created things, does not necessarily relate to essence and does not necessarily entail differentiation of es - sence. A man retains the state of being man even when he is counted. Gregory develops this idea in analyzing the names of God. Each Divine name designates a power or activity or energy of the Divinity. No activity is limited to any one of the hypostases but all operations are accomplished by the Trinity as a whole. The Trinity acts indivisibly and in unity and Its powers belong to all three hypostases in an equal degree. The Trinity manifests ac - tivity or energy which is not only common but single. "Every activity which extends from the Trinity to creation, no matter how it is named or conceived, comes from the Father, is extended through the Son, and is perfected by the Spirit." In discussing baptism and our eternal life Gregory writes: "We have been given life and it has been given by the Father and Son and Spirit. It is one life that we have received, not three. It is one and the same life which takes place in the activity of the Father, is prepared for us by the Son, and depends on the consent of the Spirit. This testifies to the unity of the Divinity in which we participate."

Gregory emphasizes that the operations of the triune Divinity are identical. Their activity is not only common or in kind but it is one and the same, in the same way that the essence of the Trinity is single. Gregory therefore discredits the misleading analogy of Divine activity and human activity. In human activity what seems to be a single action may really be composed of many different smaller actions. Or sometimes the actions of men can be encompassed in a general conception, even though each man acts independently from the others who are doing something similar. However, three philosophers or three rhetoricians are not one. Their activity is united by its common name only.

God's activity must be considered in a different way. The Divinity acts as a unity and Its actions are "a single movement and direction of the will which goes from the Father through the Son to the Spirit." "All of the Divine providence, guardianship, and vigilance over the universe are one, only one, and not three. It is all accomplished by the Holy Trinity. Our faith allows us to contemplate three Persons in the Divinity but Divine activity does not disintegrate into three parts in such a way that any action, examined separately, can be considered to come only from the Father, or from the Only-Begotten by Himself, or from the Spirit alone."

Gregory's teaching has a formal similarity to Origen's doctrine but its substance is quite different. In the first place Gregory denies that Divine actions are distributed among the hypostases, which Origen allows. Gregory also denies that the kingdoms of the Father, Son, and Spirit are different in extent or composition. He maintains exactly the contrary. Furthermore, Gregory's doctrine is completely free of Origen's subordinationism. In Origen's conception the activity of the Divinity diminishes in accordance with the descending order of the hypostases. Strength, power, and authority all become less. It is true that in Gregory's conception Divine activity is realized in creation according to the order of persons, "from the Father through the Son in the Spirit," and involves the distinction of the concepts ἐκ, διά, and ἐν. This distinction, however, takes place within the Divinity Itself and is in keeping with the distinct and unmerged structure of consubstantial Life. This distinction helps us to understand the mystery of the Trinity.

There are no interruptions and no intervals of time within the activity of the whole Trinity, just as the Trinity Itself is not divisible. "There are no gaps in this eternal nature," there is no emptiness, and there is "nothing that is unrealized." The bliss of this life is beyond temporal duration and there is nothing about it that can be measured. "Inside God there is nothing that is passing and there is nothing that will be past, but everything is always entirely present." The Divinity is not subject to time. It has no "once" or "when" because God is unchangeable. He never becomes; He always is. He is completeness and a "triune simplicity." Nothing in God comes into being. "That which was in Him is and always will be, and if there is something which was not in Him, it is not in Him now and will never be in Him."

This is the basis for Gregory's refutation of Eunomius, who at -
tempted to penetrate "beyond the generation of the Son," as if
hoping to distinguish the stages of eternity. To suggest that
something may have existed before the Son implies that it
existed before the Father. This is impossible, for God is "both
older and younger than Himself." If the Son is not eternal, then
there was a time when the Father too did not exist. The orthodox
conception of God must be outside of time. "Both before the
ages and after them the infinity of His life pours forth every -
where." "Time," writes Gregory, "flows in a sequence and either
contains in itself or passes by essence which is constant and
immutable and abides by its own principles."

All of God's names and all conceptions of Him "must be un -
derstood together with His eternity." This makes the conception
of temporal succession in the activity of the Divinity impossible.
Divine activity is simple, just as Divine nature is simple. Origen
also conceived of the Divinity as eternal and uncompound but
from this premise he concluded that the hypostases of the Trinity
must be subordinate. In his conception the Second Hypostasis
(and there is not point in distinguishing a third) is reduced to a
"participant" in the Divinity, as if generation, even eternal gen -
eration, would abrogate the simplicity of the Godhead. Gregory,
however, understands that a complete unity can be composed of
coinciding properties which are not divisible but also maintain
their distinctness, and that in this conception unity is simple and
not compound. Starting from the same premises as Origen,
Gregory was able to elaborate an orthodox doctrine of the Trinity.

Gregory develops the doctrine of the Trinity by considering Its
power. The Son and the Spirit are powers but powers which have
"essential existence." In other words, they are hypostases. Gre -
gory's definition of an hypostasis is similar to his brother Basil's.
"By these names (Father, Son, and Spirit) we recognize not
different essences but only different properties which enable us
to distinguish the hypostases so that we know that the Father is
not the Son and the Son is not the Father and that the Father
and the Holy Spirit are not the Son. Each Person is known by the
particular distinguishing properties of His hypostasis and each
Person is absolutely indivisible from and united to the other Per -
sons and cannot be conceived without Them." The hypostatic
names are correlative and to a certain extent they give in -
formation more by negation than by affirmation. They do not of -
fer us a complete understanding of the mystery of the Trinity,
especially since this mystery cannot be understood by analogy
with the created world, even though this world contains re -
lationships similar to those indicated by the names of the hypo -

stases. The hypostatic names indicate "properties," rela -
tionships, and modes of being. They designate how, but not
what.

In his definition of the properties of the hypostases Gregory
differs somewhat from the other Cappadocians, especially Basil.
Gregory primarily distinguishes the Father and the Son as the
Unoriginate and the Only-Begotten, ἀγέννητος and μονογενής.
These names indicate two modes of being. Gregory is not
satisfied with stating that the Son is begotten, but stresses the
name Only-Begotten in order to distinguish His ineffable mode of
being from that of the Spirit. Gregory is also not content with
calling the hypostasis of the Spirit the "Sanctifier," as Basil does,
nor is he satisfied with the term "procession," ἐκπόρευσις, which
is used by Gregory the Theologian. Gregory of Nyssa considers
that the distinguishing property of the Third Hypostasis is exactly
that He is the third. He is from the Father through the Son, δι '
ὑιοῦ. This through δία indicates the ontological status of the
Spirit, not just His position within the Godhead. "Through,"
however, does not imply causality, which is the attribute of the
Father, "from Whom" (ἐκ) the Trinity has Its Being. In this way
Gregory emphasizes the single source of the Trinity. However,
"through the Son" has almost the same force as "from the
Father" because "Father" is the name of the First Hypostasis in
relation to the Second.

The names Father, Son, and Spirit do not indicate essence or
nature. By their essence the hypostases are all equally named
God. Gregory emphasizes this in order to exclude from the Trinity
the concept of subordination. The name of God applies to all
Three in an equal degree as their common designation and not in
such a way that it is possible to call the Three "God and God and
God." There is only one Divinity and one God. It may seem that
the relation of the indescribable essence of the Divinity to Its
hypostases can be understood as the difference between the
general and the particular. This is possible only if the "general"
and the "particular" are correctly understood as they apply to the
Divinity. The Divinity must be recognized as unchangeable and
unchanging, and that which is "particular" within It (that is, that
which cannot be further reduced or separated) must be un -
derstood to exist within the perfect unity and absolute simplicity
of Divine Being, Being in which there are no sections and no
division. Gregory himself is not always careful to maintain this
qualification. Gregory follows Basil in elucidating the distinction of
essence and person by distinguishing between, on the one
hand, the concept of man in general, and on the other hand,
three particular men — Peter, James, and John. With respect to

the Divinity, however, it is not correct to assume that the general is only derived from the particular or abstracted from common elements among particulars.

The Cappadocian fathers reflect the influence of Aristotle in their use of terminology and their understanding of the "general" as a concept only, which relates to real individuals, is derived from the Aristotelian theory of individualism and pluralism. The Cappadocians, however, develop the idea of ultimate essence in a way different from Aristotle. Like Aristotle, they posit an ultimate totality of unfinished and unqualified matter. Aristotle considers that this lack of quality is an imperfection, but the Cappadocians apply this principle to the Divinity and conceive of it as ultimate completeness, a state superior to qualification. In their thought this is not chaos but the supreme totality of matter without subjection to qualification. The hypostatic distinctions presuppose a single and unified "substratum."

This is the reason for Gregory's strict attention to ontology. It is necessary for him to explain why there are three hypostases but not three Gods. After all, Peter, James, and John are three men. Gregory's attempts to answer this question become convoluted and ultimately he asserts that properly speaking Peter, James, and John are *not* three men. Part of the reason for this conclusion may be that Gregory is not careful to maintain the distinction between Divine nature and created nature. On the contrary, he considers the essence of both the Divinity and humanity on equal terms. His final answer is no more than a sophistic attempt to evade the question.

Gregory answers the question by stating that strictly speaking it is inexact and contradictory to say "three men." "Three" relates to things that can be distinguished and separated, whereas "man" is the name of an essence which is indivisible. It can be identified in individuals but the name "man" cannot be used to designate an individual. It is not a proper name, but a common name. Only proper names are counted, added, and indicated by a number. Enumeration, however, presupposes unity as the basis of addition. "Man" is one, since it has one and the same meaning for each of its hypostases. "This nature is one. It is united within itself and is an individual unity. It cannot be enlarged by addition or diminished by subtraction. It is one and it remains one. It appears among many individuals but it remains indivisible, inseparable, and integral. It is not given in pieces to those who partake of it."

Nature and essence are not changed by numeration. That which can be counted or added remains exactly what it is, whether it is counted or not. Neither is essence changed by the passing of time. Was David's being any less than Abraham's, even though he appeared on earth later than the patriarch by fourteen generations? Was David any less a man because he lived later in time than Abraham? Each of them is identically and equally man. "Man is a concept and is properly called one." Gregory states that since it is logical that concepts are invariable, the only way a concept can be counted is through the individuals in which it is realized. The "man" in three men is one and the same, just as the gold in a quantity of coins is the same. "No diminution or growth takes place, whether 'man' is discerned in many individuals or in only a few." Thus Gregory distinguishes the general and the particular as "what" and "how."

The essence "man" is part of the created world and, although it is indivisible, it is in a constant state of becoming and changing. It remains itself but appears and is realized accidentally in individuals. "Now in some, now in others, now in a greater number, now in a lesser number." "If anyone is a man, it does not necessarily follow that he must be Luke or Stephen." The additional properties which distinguish individual men are accidental ,συμβεβηκότες, and make no difference in the identity of their essence.

It is in this respect that Divine Being is different from human being. "In the Three Persons there is never any growth or diminution, development or change." We can count men, in spite of the fact that their essence is identical because they are distinguished and separated by many accidental and varying characteristics. "There is nothing like this within the Trinity because Divine essence is realized only in these Three Persons Whose names we have, and not in any others. The Trinity will never grow to be four or diminish to be two. No new person will ever be generated from the Father or proceed from Him or from any of the other Persons in such a way that the Trinity would become four, and none of the Persons of the Trinity will ever at any time cease to be in such a way that the Trinity would become two."

This means that the Divine hypostases are unchangeable and that They are necessarily entailed by the essence of the Divinity. They are the eternal, immutable, absolute realization of the nature of the Divinity. They are the constant and eternal images of the Being of the only God. They form a unity which is simple, uncompound, and unchanging. "The Persons of the Divinity cannot be divided from each other by time, or by place, or in will, or in operations, or in activity, or by or in any of the things to which man is subject." The hypostases are unblurred but their being is a cohesive and simple whole.

There is no reason to suspect Gregory of naturalism, and his terminology has nothing in common with that of the Western Stoics. It is true that he uses Tertullian's image of three flames and three lamps, but he is careful to avoid making misleading analogies between Divine essence and created nature. The Divinity and Its Three Persons cannot be compared with gold and individual coins because the realization of the created essence is accidental and arbitrary. Gregory is careful to exclude any pos - sibility of chance, accident, arbitrariness, instability, or potential alternative from his concept of the Divinity.

THE SHELTER OF THE UNIVERSE

The Source of the Existence of the World

God is the source of the world's existence and the ultimate goal of its striving and aspiration. In the beginning God created the heavens and the earth. This means that creation has its source in God and that its being has a beginning. Gregory writes: "The beginning of the world refers to that moment when God sud - denly, in one instant, created the foundation for all causes and substances." The Creator alone knows what the foundation of creation is and it is impossible for us to understand it. All we know is that creation originates "through change." The beginning of created being is "a movement and change from non-existence into existence."

Change and Becoming as the Nature of Created Existence

"The hypostases of created matter begin by change," and therefore creation is necessarily subject to change. By their very nature created things are constantly changing and becoming, and they will remain this way until they achieve fulfillment, com - pletion, and perfection. God's will for creation to arise is the only support that creation has in its fluctuating state. The world exists and endures only because its order is maintained by "the Power of the Wisdom and artistry of God, which is realized in everything and penetrates all created natures," and which "by dissolving Itself in the universe maintains the existence of all being. God did not only create the world at some definite point in time, but He continues to preserve it, and as the Almighty He sustains it by His presence, which is everywhere." "Nothing can maintain its being unless it abides in the One Who truly is."

The Presence and Transcendence of God

God abides in the world but does not merge with it, just as the soul does not dissolve and blend with the body in which it has life. Gregory's idea is similar to the Stoic conception of διοίκησις, but with the difference that in Gregory's conception God, in spite of His presence in the world, maintains both His transcendence and His inaccessibility. The properties of created beings are entirely different from God's, and "created natures and the es - sence of the Divinity are different and are not connected by their attributes." This is in spite of the omnipresence of the "un - qualified and indescribable Strength of the Divinity, which con - tains in Itself all the ages and all creation from all times." How is this possible? We do not know and we should not ask because this surpasses our understanding. What existed before creation? Why did creation arise? All we know is that the world was created by the power of the Word, for the beginning of the world was not mute ἀλογία.

Gregory's Attitude Toward the Biblical Narration of Creation

Gregory considers that the Biblical narration of creation is the record of Moses' contemplation on Mount Sinai and not the rational conjecture of some human mind. We must discern and correctly understand the true meaning of this narrative and together with Moses we must enter the mysterious cloud. Gregory goes further in his speculation than Basil.

God as Uncreated Essence and the Creation of Created Existence

The world is a structured and harmonious whole, and has been created by the Creator. God creates through His Wisdom, and this Wisdom is His will. God's activity is indivisible from the consent of His will. Gregory writes: "We must realize that the creation of the world was accomplished by everything in God: His will, Wisdom, might, and all His essential nature." Gregory delib - erately equates the "might" of God with His "substantial or essential nature" in order to anticipate two false conceptions which might arise about creation. Although it is true that the nature of created things is different from God's essence, this does not mean that God did not create the world from Himself. Nor is it true that God achieves creation through some type of "reserve" matter and not from matter which previously had no existence. What Gregory wants to stress is that "as soon as the Divinity desires anything, it is accomplished. Every Divine desire is realized at once and immediately assumes being through the might of the Omnipotent. Whatever God desires in His wisdom and artistry does not remain unrealized. Substance arises from the activity of the Divine will."

Gregory states that the foundation or source of matter as such is immaterial. It "arises from something conceptual, not material." Matter is an aggregate of qualities and there is nothing which can be conceived outside of this totality. Only a "sum total" of qualities comprises matter. "Each of these qualities by itself is only an intellectual concept" because not one of them considered individually, neither lightness, nor heaviness, nor density, nor color, nor outline, nor duration, is material. These immaterial qualities, these "foundations for causes and substances," are created by God in the beginning. Gregory stresses that this "beginning" is "instantaneous and without interruption." It is also the "beginning of temporal duration." Gregory follows Basil the Great and states that the beginning of time does not occur within time. The beginning of time is not yet time itself. The beginning of time means the beginning of movement and change. In a similar way, the origin of creation is the beginning of its process of becoming. The universe does not arise in its ultimate state but is gradually developing. The elements of the world arise suddenly and instantaneously, coming into existence from nothingness through the power of God. In this way the world begins its development.

At first the world was "empty and without distinction" because, Gregory writes, "when God initiated creation everything was still in its potential state. It was as if a seed had been planted which contained the future growth of the being of the universe, but as yet each thing did not exist individually." The earth was, and it was not, for "it was awaiting that which would give it order and qualification, for this is what is meant by coming into being."

In the words of the translation of Theodotion, "Everything was empty." What had been given to the world was the "strength to acquire qualities" but the qualities themselves were not yet present. Darkness was over everything and "none of the substances which fill the universe was as yet fully itself." Gregory denies, however, that it is only unqualified matter which originated at creation. Qualities themselves, and their various combinations, were also created, but they had not yet become stabilized. In order for this to occur a connective element had to be introduced into creation. This stabilization was accomplished when the "Divine artistry and power," power of movement and the power of rest, was emplanted in creation.

Creation and the Gradual Realization of Matter

Gregory interprets the Biblical narrative of the six days of cre - ation as a description of the ordering of the world and the gradual realization of created matter. "By the might of the Creator the foundation of all matter comes into being instantaneously and in totality," Gregory writes, "but the individual manifestations of what is visible in the world are realized according to a natural order and succession, over a certain period of time." The genesis of matter is followed by a "necessary series and a particular order." First fire appears, separating itself suddenly from the depths of unformed substance and illuminating everything with its radiance: "And there was light." "God said" indicates that the "Word of His wis - dom and artistry" is implanted in every substance. God by His mighty Word "establishes a radiant power in nature," and Moses calls everything which proceeds from the regular activity of this Divinely implanted power a work of God.

God's act of creation is instantaneous. Succession and se - quence, the passing of days and the cycle of the elements, are proper only to His creatures. In primordial chaos there is motion and the elements come to be distinguished by their different densities. Fire comes to the surface and strives to move upward until it reaches the "limits of perceptible creation." In the Bible this ultimate boundary is called the firmament. "Beyond this boun - dary," Gregory writes, "there exist intellectual creatures which have no form, or size, or limited place, of duration, or color, or outline, or quantity, or any of the things we discern beneath the heavens." At this point the path of fire forms an arc and describes a circle. This is the first day, and its achievement is the de - limitation of visible creation from intellectual creation.

Gregory describes the further ordering of the world as a process of division and apportionment. In the course of the next three days the "mutual separation of everything in the world is ac - complished," and each thing is assigned to its place. Dry land and water are separated, and the sun, moon, and stars are fixed in the heavens in accordance with the nature of their radiance. Every - thing takes its place in a definite order and maintains it "in per - petuity, by virtue of its nature." This could not all be accom - plished at once because "everything that has motion moves in time and therefore a certain duration of time is needed for everything to be harmoniously fitted together." For this reason the heavenly bodies are affixed only on the fourth day. Gregory emphasizes that they are not created anew but that they only assume their established place. It is likely that his conception of the natural place of each thing in the universe was influenced by Aristotelian physics.

Gregory adds little to Basil's commentary on the final days of the creation of the world. He only emphasizes that there are de - grees and a gradually ascending order to perfection in created matter. Lowest on this scale is inanimate matter, followed by vegetable life and then animal life. First there is matter and then there is the life which penetrates it. The forms of life are also gradated. "The power of life and animateness" which is common to all organic natures appears in three forms. There is a "power to grow and nourish" which is in plants; a "sensible power" or "power of perception" which is in animals; and an "intellectual power" or power of reasoning which is only in man. These are not three forms of a single principle but three separate degrees which relate to each other in an ascending order. Gregory's concept of the hierarchy of nature was also influenced by Aristotle. In accordance with this conception he describes the sixth day as the day on which everything achieved its proper end or goal, when "all the abundance of creation was established both on the earth and in the sea."

Rest and Motion

The earth is in a state of both rest and motion. The combination of these two opposing principles is responsible for the harmony of the world. Rest can appear in motion and movement can occur in immobility. "All things exist in each other and support each other. There is a cyclical force in the world which transforms everything from one state to another and constantly brings things back to what they were before. This force forms a circle which rotates around itself and constantly makes the same revolutions so that nothing diminishes and nothing is added but everything abides as it was in the beginning." This is the harmony of the world, a "musical proportionateness," "the first, archetypal, truest music." The world is a "harmonious and wonderfully com - posed song of praise to all the powers which govern it," and this music is accessible to the hearing of the intellect.

Time and Space in Incorporeal Being

Angels have a special place in creation. The angelic world is spiritual and incorporeal but nevertheless it is contained by time and space, since "nothing which comes into being through change can exist other than in time and space." This does not mean that angels occupy space in the same way that material bodies do, but only that their sphere is limited. Angels are not omnipresent, even though they can instantly appear wherever they choose. Gregory departs from Basil the Great by em - phasizing the restriction of angelic being by time. Gregory considers that angelic nature is mobile and calls it "vigilant" because in his conception everything should constantly and without interruption be striving towards God. This is especially true of spiritual life, which by its nature is a path of ascent to God. This life is realized in time and is therefore subject to succession and sequence. Perpetual motion is especially evident in the world of angels. "The nature of angels is in a constant state of development. It changes because the good things which angels enjoy are always becoming greater and no limits have been set to the unceasing growth of their bliss."

Gregory admits that the world of angels originated gradually, through a mysterious form of multiplication. The number of angels was established but was later diminished by the fall. At this time the hierarchy of angelic ranks, which is determined by rel - ative degrees of perfection, came into being. Gregory comments on the number of angels by referring to the parable of the lost sheep: "He leaves the ninety-nine for the sake of one." In Gregory's interpretation this means that God leaves the angels and comes to man.

Gregory describes angelic being as an endless hymn of praise. He adds that angels are not omniscient. Their knowledge is limited by the very fact that they are immaterial, and the Gospel has revealed that the only way these incorporeal beings know about the mystery of the Incarnation is through the Church (*Ephesians* 3: 10-12). Gregory considers that the Church enables angels to "better see the Invisible One." Men are able to form a conception of angelic nature because "we are of the same tribe as they." We are related by virtue of our souls, even though human souls are clothed in flesh.

Man as the Culmination of the Creation of the World

The creation of the world culminates in the creation of man. This is its fulfillment and completion. Man is not only a part of the world but, by having been brought into the world last, he is its lord and sovereign. God orders and adorns the world like a royal palace for the sake of man, and man is introduced into this completeness "not to acquire what is not in the world but to enjoy the things that are," partly as an observer and partly as a ruler.

Man's nature is double. On one hand he is the center of the universe, a complete microcosm of nature, a "small world con‐taining all the elements which fill the great world." God creates man last so that "man can encompass every type of life within himself." However, this is not man's chief dignity. "What do we gain by considering man the image and likeness of the world?" Gregory asks. "After all, the earth is transient and the heavens change, and everything they contain passes with them." He makes an ironic comment on pagan philosophers: "They say that man is a microcosm of the world but, in glorifying human nature with this resounding praise, they do not notice that they are endowing man with the properties of gnats and mice."

Gregory considers that man is sovereign because he is created in the image of God. Man is the medium through which God's works are accomplished in the world. Man contains both an intellectual nature and a nature which depends on the senses for perception. In commenting on the formation of man from the dust of the earth Gregory writes that the breath of God gave life to this dust "so that the earth could ascend to the Divinity and be united with It. Grace was given to the whole of creation when this earthly substance was mingled with the nature of the Divinity." Through man all the elements of the earth participates in spiritual life, and in this sense man contains the whole world. For this reason man did not originate by a single Divine word or command but God created Him solemnly and "with circumspection."

God creates man through His love for him and so that he can become a participant in Divine bliss. This is why God makes man in His own image and likeness: "so that man is an animate like‐ness of the eternal Divinity." Everything recognizes that which is similar to it and, "in order for us to become participants in the Divinity, there must be something in our nature which we have in common with the nature of God." God has thus given man the possibility of enjoying ineffable and infinite bliss. Gregory sees the greatest significance of the being of humanity in his con‐ception of man as the image of God. This is what distinguishes man from the rest of earthly creation.

The Image of God in Man

The image of God must be sought in that faculty of man which distinguishes him from the rest of nature; that is, in his "reasoning power," in his intellect, νοῦς. An image implies a reflection and "everything in man which reflects the perfection of the Divinity, every good which has been implanted in human nature," should be recognized as the image of God. Gregory considers that this doctrine is important for an understanding of man's ontological status and also of his ethical nature. His conception of God's image in mankind is dynamic and allows for the growth or diminution, the greater or lesser clarity and completeness of this image in individual man. The more man reflects the perfection of the Divinity, the more distinct is the image of God within him.

Man's similarity to God is revealed in all his faculties but its focal point is the human intellect. "When a sliver of glass lies in the rays of the sun, the entire orb of the heavenly body can be seen in it, not in its own magnitude, but to the degree that can be contained within the small piece of glass. In this same way, the images of the inexpressible attributes of the Divinity are radiant within the smaller sphere of our nature." The Divine image within man is a living link between man and God and enables man to develop his similarity to God. It is only through this effort that man can participate in Divine bliss. "The intellect is created in the image of the Most Beautiful and it remains in a state of beauty and goodness as long as it partakes, as much as is possible, in its likeness to its Archetype. As soon as it departs from this likeness, it Is deprived of the beauty in which it had partaken. The intellect is adorned by the beauty of its Archetype in the same way that a mirror expresses the features of the figure which is visible in it." The beauty of the intellect is reflected in all of man's faculties because "the communication of true beauty extends proportionately throughout the whole, for the superior nature beautifies that which comes after it."

The Image of God and Freedom of the Will

To be the image of God means to live in God and to have the "possibility of being beautiful." This possibility is expressed in certain attributes of human nature, most importantly in man's freedom of the will. Man's free will means that he is "independent of the forces of nature" and that he is capable of making his own decisions and choices. Free will is a necessary condition of virtue because "virtue must be freely chosen and voluntary. Anything that is compulsory or forced cannot be virtue."

Without free will there can be no intellect. "If intellectual natures lost their free will, they would also lose their ability to reason," that is, the ability to make distinctions and judgments. Furthermore, "if any kind of necessity controlled human life, this would destroy man's likeness to God. How can a nature which is subordinate to or under the power of necessity be called an image of the sovereign nature of the Divinity?" Free will is the reason that man desires good and love. "This is what the Creator ordained as the basic feature of human nature, for God is love and the source of love. Wherever there is no love the features of the Archetype are marred." "Man can recognize the Supreme Being and wants to share the eternity of the Divinity" because eternity has also been implanted in human nature. Man is called to be sovereign in the universe because of his likeness to God.

The Ontological Status of God's Image in Man

Gregory develops his doctrine of man as the image of God primarily in connection with his belief in the possibility of man's communion with God. He ignores the ontological problems of this concept. Gregory considers that the inaccessibility of human nature stems from the fact that man has been made in the image of the Divinity. "This image is a proper image as long as it lacks nothing which we consider to be a property of its Archetype. But as soon as the image is deprived of its likeness to its Archetype, it ceases to be the image of God. Therefore, since one of the properties we acknowledge in the Divinity is the property of inaccessible essence, it is necessary that the image be similar to its Archetype in this respect as well."

The fact that the essence of human nature is not com-prehensible to us does not make it impossible for us to recognize it and to attempt to define it in the same way that we also manage to speak about God in spite of the fact that His essence is unknown to us. However, the ultimate foundation for man's being is inaccessible to us. The ontological status of God's image in man is beyond our comprehension and this results necessarily from the unknowability of the nature of the One Whose reflection we are. We can only speak about the perfection of the Arche-type's reflection or about participation in the good things and bliss it offers, which are really the same things.

Gregory develops this conception from his belief that it is possible for man to achieve communion with God. "Man has been given being in order to enjoy the bliss of the Divinity and therefore he must have something in his nature which is related to the nature of the One in Whom he partakes. For this reason man is endowed with life, intellect, wisdom, and all the beauties of God, and each of these gifts inspires man with the desire for the One Who is thus related to him. All of this is expressed in the book of *Genesis* by the simple statement that man is created in the image of God." Man's likeness to God cannot be found in any one faculty or feature, although it is definitely a part of man's spiritual nature and not his physical or sensual being. However, the image of God has also mingled with man's senses and physical faculties of perception. This is the significance of the double nature of man.

Two Simultaneous Operations in the Creation of Man

Gregory distinguishes two simultaneous operations in the cre - ation of man. It has been written that "God created man." Gregory explains: "The indefinite character of this term indicates that it refers to all mankind. At this point God's creature was not given the name Adam, which he received only later. On the contrary, the name given to the newly created man refers not to one man alone, but to the whole race." The whole of humanity was en - compassed by the foresight and power of God from the very beginning. At creation God established the ultimate goal for each human being because He had complete foreknowledge about His creatures. The Biblical expression does not mean that only a single man was created as the sole representative of mankind or that each individual human came into being at once. Human nature in all its completeness was created in a single instant, in the same way that the whole world was created at once.

The first man was not created as a single, isolated individual, but as the source and first representative of the human race. At his creation the Divine will encompassed all future men who are consubstantial with each other and established for each of them a common foundation and a common end or goal , τέλος. Gregory also considers that at creation God decreed a finite number of individual men and that therefore human history will come to an end. God "in His foreknowledge made time com - mensurate with the human race so that the appearance of a definite number of souls will correspond to the continuation of time. The flowing motion of time will cease when the human race stops growing."

At creation God gave a single command but the creature which originated "at the first ordering" has a double significance. "By virtue of Divine foresight God encompassed all human nature in a single body," Gregory writes. He emphasizes that the image of God was given not only to Adam, the first man, but that "this image is endowed equally to the whole race." "The whole of mankind is named in this one man because for the power of God there is no past or future. God's activity comprehends both the present and what will follow it. Therefore all men, from the first man to the last, are a single image of the One Who truly is."

Every man contains the complete measure of human nature and therefore "Adam, the first man, also had everything which each of his descendants has," at least "as far as concerns his essential nature." The essence of man is identical in all men but their distinguishing properties are different and Gregory never implies that they are all contained in the first man. On the contrary, he emphasizes that descendants "pre-exist in their forebears by virtue of the common essence of humanity, which is never created anew and which is not divided according to the number of individuals who share in it." This essence exists neither before nor outside of its individual hypostases.

Gregory's Interpretation of Creation and the Distinction of the Sexes

Gregory differentiates the creation of the "common essence of humanity" from the creation of male and female. The distinction of sex has no relation to the image of God in man because this distinction is not present in the Archetype. "Therefore," Gregory concludes, "the establishment of our nature was a double operation. We were made similar to the Divinity but were also divided into different sexes." By this second operation man is linked with animal nature.

Man is created in the image of God, and for this reason there should have been no need for different sexes. The increase of the human race should have taken place in the same way that the "angelic race multiplies, in a way that is unknown to us." At the fall, however, man lost his equality with the angels and thus lost their impassive means of increase. God had foreknowledge of this fall, since "He saw beforehand by His all-seeing power that human wills would fail to follow a direct course to what is good, and that men would fall from angelic life." Therefore God "invented" for His image the distinction and division of the sexes, which has no source in the Divine Archetype. God "invented for our nature a means of increase which is suitable for those who have fallen into sin. He implanted in mankind that animal and irrational mode by which we now succeed each other instead of the mode which is fitting for the majestic nature of the angels." Gregory adds that this at least is his view of the matter.

Gregory's Differences with Origen

These conceptions are clearly influenced by Origen, and yet in many respects Gregory's thought is very different. Gregory denies the pre-existence and transmigration of souls and he rejects the idea that "there is some tribe or citizenry of souls which exists before life in the body." Gregory admits that there is a mode of increase in the angelic world. He conceives of time as a process of development during which the complete number of human hypostases will be realized and have existence. He emphasizes that a soul does not have existence without a body, or a body without a soul, but that both have a single source for their being. Man is not composed from two separate elements but he is generated as a body and as a soul simultaneously. The development of the human embryo is a single organic process which takes place by virtue of a "hidden element in the seed." "The soul is also present in the seed but it is not yet discernible." That which is animate generates that which is animate, flesh which is living, not dead. In conclusion Gregory writes: "We consider that it is impossible for the soul to adapt itself to other dwelling places."

Gregory does not share Origen's distrust of physical matter. Everything created by God is, in the words of the Bible, "very good." Therefore, "we should discern good in every thing." "Every element by itself is filled with goodness in a way that is suited to its nature." "Whether it is a myriapod, or a green frog, or an animal born from some filth, it is all very good." For Gregory matter itself is not impure, especially since it was created first. That which is proper to animals is not impure by itself but only as it appears in man because "that which irrational life has been given as a means of self-protection becomes a passion in man." Furthermore, Gregory agrees with Basil that the lower motions of the irrational soul in man should "each be transformed into a virtue" by the power of reason. Finally, in Gregory's conception the "second operation" in the creation of man, the distinction of the sexes, is also the work of God. "The ordering of nature has been established by God's will and law. It should not be con - sidered a flaw." "All of man's members have been designed for one goal: that mankind may continue to have life." Even man's animal and passionate mode of increase is not to be despised because it "ensures the succession of mankind." It is the way that "nature fights with death." "The sex organs assure mankind of im - mortality so that death, which is always striving against us, be - comes ineffectual and powerless. Nature is always renewing itself and compensating for the limitations of those who are born." This idea is foreign to Origen.

Gregory never specifies the exact moment at which this "se - cond operation," the actual differentiation of the sexes, occurs. Since in his conception the "fleshly robe of the body" refers to the physical status of man after the fall, it may seem that he considers that man in his pure state of equality with the angels did not share the corporeality of animal natures and was not ac -

tually distinguished by sex. Divine providence only foresaw the coming coarsening of human nature and its division by sex and allowed this to take place. However, it is unlikely that Gregory considered that man was fully incorporeal before the fall because this would contradict his doctrines of man's intermediate status in creation as the link between immaterial and earthly beings, and of man's calling to be sovereign in nature. Gregory probably agreed with the idea introduced by Methodius of Olympus and later supported by Gregory the Theologian that man's "fleshly robe" is an indication of the coarsening of human nature and the sub - jection of the body to death which took place after the fall and in which respect man is similar to the animals. This is not just cor - poreality but mortality and the "subjection to death." This mor - tality is a "robe which has been imposed on us from outside. It temporarily serves the body and is not a part of our nature." It is a robe, a shell, a "deathly mantle." Thus Gregory departs from Ori - gen by insisting on the integrity of man's being even in this life, and on the absolute simultaneity of the development of the body and the soul.

Gregory's view that there was no marriage before the fall, that the "conjugal state" is a result of sin, and that no marriage can be entirely pure, was also shared by a number of earlier theologians, especially those who were not influenced by the school of Alexandria. This conclusion was later supported by John Chry - sostom (although he ultimately altered his position), Theodoret of Cyrus, Maximus the Confessor, John of Damascus, and later by Byzantine theologians, until the statement of Patriarch Jere - miah to the theologians of Tübingen in 1576.

The Fall of Man and the Image of God

After man's fall it became difficult to discern his original features and to recognize in him the image of God. "Where is the soul's likeness to God? Where is that which is not subject to corporeal suffering? Where is the eternal life? Man is mortal, passionate, and ephemeral, and his soul and body are inclined to passions of every kind." Similarity to God can only be seen in attributes which are eternal. In these attributes the original Divine likeness again shines forth so that we can recognize the original law of human life, the law of hierarchy and proportion. Everything should be subordinate to the soul and the intellect and express their dignity and perfection. This is the meaning of impassivity, $\dot{a}\pi\dot{a}\theta\epsilon\iota a$. That which is impassive is that which is in opposition to the passions. The true significance of the state of passion is that in it the hier - archy is upset and overturned. That which is superior in man becomes subordinate to that which is lowest in him and "the baseness of matter is transmitted to the intellect itself." Impas- sivity entails incorruptibility, ἀφθαρσία. When the hierarchy of human nature is maintained, the life-giving rays of the Divinity are communicated to man's entire being through his intellect. Before the fall this protected man from mutability and ephemerality and gave him endurance and stability, immortality and unending life.

In Gregory's understanding God's command to man at creation to rule over the earth signifies not only that man is to have power over nature but also that he is to reign over irrational beings. Reason is to control irrationality as the culmination of the hier- archic and harmonious order of the world as it was originally created. Man is called to be lord over nature and for this reason he must be independent of it. This independence and freedom from the instabilities of the cycles of nature will be realized in paradise when man will experience spiritual bliss through par- ticipation in eternal life. Gregory does not describe paradise with allegory or fables. He does not reject the world but separates man from it and liberates him. Man has been summoned not to live in the world but to live above it.

THE FATE OF MAN

Freedom of the Will and the Mystery of Evil

The fate of mankind is determined by God and by man's free choice. Man was created with a free will and his original purpose in life was to strive to reach God. This goal was not accomplished. The efforts of the will grew weaker and the inertia of nature over- came man's striving to reunite himself with the Divinity. This led to the decay of human nature and the growth of disorder in the whole world. The universe ceased to be a mirror of the beauties of the Divinity and the image of God which had been engraved in it grew faint. This is how evil entered the world. Evil has no foun- dation in the will of God because it comes from things which do not exist. "By itself evil has no existence but exists only as the ab- sence of good." "Evil is the name of that which is outside of our conception of good." It is primarily as "that which has no exis- tence" that evil is opposed to the Good which truly exists and to everything in the world that originates through the will of God. "Paradoxically," Gregory writes, "it is in its very nonexistence that evil exists."

Evil is not merely an apparition but is the absence or insuf- ficiency of good. "Outside of free will there is no independent evil." The reality of evil is in the distortion of the will. It is a harvest which has not been sown and a plant which has no roots. Evil is a reality, although it is unstable and "has no independent hypo - stasis." It is a shadow which appears when the spirit is absent. This leads Gregory to conclude that evil will ultimately be destroyed. It is a tumor and an outer crust which will eventually fall from every nature which is good and enduring. Evil is not a phantom that will suddenly be dispersed but it is a reality that will be overcome only gradually and with difficulty and this will deter - mine the course of human history. In his conception of evil Gregory is closer to Origen than to Plato, from whom he borrows only his terminology.

The source of evil is in the corruption of the will. "Human nature is mutable and it began to move in the wrong direction." This movement of the will was not in accord with its nature and thus the will was harmed and destroyed. "The fall away from the One Who truly is," Gregory writes, "corrupts and destroys everything that exists." How did this turn of the will from existence to nonexistence become possible? How can that which does not exist and has never existed influence the will and give it motivation? The solution to the mystery of the first sin and the fall away from God lies in the fact that the original task of man was dynamic. Human nature was implanted with the aspiration to good, but not with a clear recognition of good. Man must find out for himself what is truly good and beneficial for him. The fall came about through deceit. Man was deceived by external appear - ances and was "mistaken in his desire for true good." In his foolishness he considered that things which delight the senses are good and thus he accepted the "phantom of goodness" as the truth. His judgment was deceived and he was guided by false standards. "A lie is a conception which somehow develops in the mind about something which has no existence, as if that which does not exist were real. The truth is an unquestionable un - derstanding of the One Who truly is."

Not only did man deceive himself but he himself was deceived because of the envy of the angel who was offended when man was created in the image of God. Thus the second root of evil and sin is found in the angelic world. The erring angel severed his natural ties with good and, like a stone, he sank to the bottom, dragged down by his own weight. He led man into error and "treacherously and deceitfully appeared to man and convinced him to bring death on himself and to become his own murderer."

The serpent tempted Eve with "the apparition of good," with sensual pleasure, "which is beautiful to look at and pleasant to taste." It is difficult to determine whether Gregory understands the forbidden fruit literally or allegorically but his interpretation of the Divine prohibition is clear: "Our forefathers were commanded not only to acknowledge good but also not to try to understand that which is opposed to good. They were to flee from that which is both good and evil at the same time and to enjoy good in its pure form, untouched by evil." The nature of evil is two-faced and deceitful. It is poison mixed with honey. The tree of the knowl - edge of good and evil received its name because "it produced fruit with a double nature, which was formed from opposing qualities." The knowledge of good and evil does not only mean that man must be able to distinguish between them. Man is allured and enticed to evil in the guise of good and this confuses him. The fruit of the forbidden tree was not purely evil (because it flourished in beauty), nor was it absolutely good (because evil was latent inside it). It was an ambiguous mixture of both.

Sensual temptation was born in the lower sphere of man's soul, in the faculty of desire, which managed to free itself from the con - trol of the intellect and distracted man's attention to the material world. The intellect lost its supreme authority and God's com - mandment was broken. Thus sin is the result of the dis - obedience of the will and the existence of evil is ethical and not only objective. It is not the senses as such, but the fascination of the senses, the "passion for satisfaction," and the "disposition to sensual and material things" which are evil and the root and source of sin and sinfulness. The mind has become similar to a mirror which was turned to the wrong side, so that "it does not represent the radiant features of good but reflects in itself the ugliness of matter." Matter becomes ugly at the moment that it is isolated from that which is superior to it.

By falling into sin man became subject to the laws of the world of matter. He became mortal and liable to decay. Death, dying, the succession of forms and generations, birth, and growth have all been part of the natural world from the beginning and in nature these processes are neither flaws nor diseases. Death is ab - normal and contrary to the law of nature for man alone, although Gregory also considers that death is a beneficent healing which leads man to resurrection and purification. This is because man is saved from corruption by sin at the resurrection when his original incorruptibility will be returned to him.

Gregory's Doctrine of the Limits of Evil

The restoration, healing, and transformation of man cannot be accomplished through natural forces. The effects of evil cannot be simply reversed and movement in the wrong direction is re -

sistant to change. Man's salvation requires a new creative action on the part of God. It is true that Gregory believes that evil will eventually exhaust itself and that it cannot be boundless and infinite because finiteness is a property of all being. It is only in striving for good that limitless motion is possible because this is a goal which can never be reached. Movement in the opposite direction cannot continue forever: "Since evil does not extend into infinity but is encompassed by certain necessary limits, it appears that good once more follows in succession after the limits of evil."

This reasoning stems from Gregory's belief in the absolute nature of the future restoration and in the impossibility of the ulti - mate stability and endurance of evil. Gregory foresees the second coming of Christ, our Savior, and when our final salvation is thus accomplished it will have no limits. Gregory does not mention the ultimate exhaustion of evil without referring to the manifestation of God in the figure of Christ. On the contrary, he sees the Word Incarnate as man's only hope for salvation from the "black and stormy sea of human life." Gregory, like Athan - asius, considers the redeeming work of Christ as a return to life and a victory over death and mortality. This is possible only through the union of Divine life with human nature. The power to destroy death is a property of life. "He Who lives eternally accepts corporeal birth not because He needs life but in order to return us to life from death . . . With His own body He gives to our nature the source of its future resurrection and through His power the whole of human nature will rise up."

Gregory's Legalistic Interpretation of the "Ransom"

Gregory suggests another reason for the necessity of Divine intervention to save the world from evil when, following the example of Origen, he speaks about ransom to the devil or, more specifically, ransom from the devil. The devil's power over man is legitimate because man sinned through his own free will and by this he surrendered himself to the devil and became the devil's slave. Therefore man cannot be "arbitrarily torn away" because this would "bring harm to our nature in returning to it its greatest good," which is our freedom. This action would "deprive the image of God of its honor." It would be unjust to use violence or superior force against the devil, who legally acquired man as a slave. Thus, man can only be liberated through the payment of a ransom.

The devil is crafty and would not exchange something good for something inferior. He chose Christ as ransom because he was impressed (not frightened) by His unique life and ability to perform miracles. He asked the price and was told that "if through death he could attain mastery over this flesh, then he would have control over all flesh." The deceitful one was deceived. "He swallowed the bait of the flesh and was pierced by the hook of the Divinity."

In developing this unsuccessful "legalistic" theory Gregory was influenced by Origen and in some respects his presentation is even more extreme. This doctrine is incompatible with the rest of Gregory's system of theology and is also self-contradictory. The basic idea that only God can legitimately save man from sin turns into a defense of God's deceit. Gregory shows that it is fitting for a deceiver to be deceived. "Here, by the reasonable rule of justice, he who had practiced deceit is given back that very treatment, the seeds of which he had sown himself of his own free will. He who deceived man with the bait of sensual pleasure is deceived by a human form." Gregory's defense is inconclusive and inap - propriate. This theory was later rejected in its entirety by Gregory the Theologian.

The Goal of the Incarnation

The basic goal of the incarnation of the Word is the "resur - rection and deification of man." Christ "becomes one with our nature and, in being united with the Divinity, our nature becomes Divine itself, is removed from the power of death, and is saved from the torments of the enemy." Athanasius and Irenaeus express themselves in similar terms.

Gregory is aware that for both Jews and Greeks the "human economy of the Word of God" might seem to be "impossible and even unseemly." Certain Christian heretical sects, especially the Arians and the Apollinarians, were guilty of the same error. Gre - gory sets forth his teaching on the unity of the two natures in the God-man in order to oppose these heresies. In doing this he concentrates his attention on the salvation brought by Christ. "It is both possible and proper only for the one who gave us life in the beginning to return this life to us when we are perishing." Furthermore, "how would our nature be corrected if the Divinity were united with some other heavenly nature?" The reality of our salvation makes it necessary for us to recognize the dual con - substantiality of Christ and the "unity of the hypostases" of the God-man. Gregory tries to avoid the expression "two natures." Instead he writes: "We acknowledge in Christ both Divinity and humanity. By nature He is Divine, and by economy He is human."

Gregory and the Unity of the God-Man

Gregory has no definite terminology to describe the unity of the God-man. Sometimes he talks about συνάφεια, a close union, and about μίξις, a mingling or combination, or κρᾶσις, a blending. He calls Christ the "Bearer of God" and sometimes he simply refers to ἕνωσις, a union or unity. Gregory's usage is frequently careless. He occasionally uses the term "mixture" to describe the organic unity of the body, and συνάφεια to describe the indivisible unity of the Trinity. The way in which the unification of natures takes place remains incomprehensible to us but it may be partially explained by the coexistence of the body and the soul.

Gregory develops his doctrine of the full humanity of Christ in his polemic with the Apollinarians. He stresses that Christ's assumption of human nature is complete. "No Christian will say that the man who was united with God was only half a man, but that his whole nature entered union with the Divinity." After all, "anyone who lacks something, without which his nature is incomplete, cannot be called a man." This is vital for Gregory's understanding of the redeeming work of Christ. The Lord came and was incarnate for the sake of salvation. "It is not a body which perished but a whole man who had a complete soul. In fact, it is right to say that the soul perished even before the body."

The Lord comes to save His sheep which is lost. "He finds it, and then He raises on His shoulders the whole sheep, not just its fleece" because "not only a part of the sheep was lost but the whole sheep had gone astray, and so the Lord returns it whole." Gregory makes another comparison: when we wash a garment we never do so in such a way that some spots remain while others are removed. On the contrary, we clean the whole cloth from one end to the other, so that the whole garment is of a single quality and all of its parts are purified by the cleansing. "So, since human life has been defiled by sin at the beginning and at the end and in all its parts, the purifying agent must penetrate the whole, and not in such a way that part of it is purified through this treatment while another part remains untreated."

For Gregory "man" is the name of an essential nature and he emphasizes the integrity of the composition of man: "A body without a soul is a corpse and a soul without reason is a beast." In order to oppose the teaching of the Apollinarians Gregory stresses the identity of the flesh of Christ "with the rest of humanity." "We know what His body was composed of when He lived among people as a man." Gregory realizes that the corporeal nature of Christ is disturbing to many: "His human birth,

His growth from infancy to maturity, His need to eat and drink, His weariness and need for sleep, His sorrow, tears, calumniation, trial, cross, death, and removal to the tomb: all of these things which make up the mystery weaken the faith of people whose minds are not elevated."

Gregory answers these doubts by developing an apology for human nature. None of the actions of Christ's life is unworthy of Him because it is only base passions which are shameful. "God is born not into anything flawed but into human nature." The com - position of man contains nothing which makes virtue impossible and there is nothing impure about birth itself. Voluptuousness and lust are impure but the birth of man into the world is not. "What can be unseemly about this mystery? God was united with human life through the very means which nature uses to fight against death." It is only passion, in the narrow sense of the word, that was not assumed by the Lord. Gregory speaks frequently and clearly about the true corporeality of Christ in order to expose the false doctrine of the Apollinarians about the "heavenly flesh of Christ," which was their explanation of the mystery of the In - carnation. Gregory considered this explanation false because because in their system creation would be brought no closer to the Creator and also because the Divinity has no need of deified flesh.

The human nature of the Savior develops according to the norm established for mankind before the fall. Furthermore, His humanity becomes deified through its union with God. This is the source of the salvation of human nature; it is its salvation, revivification, and restoration to its original state. Gregory writes that God the Word "becomes flesh because of His love for mankind and He assumes our nature so that by mingling with the Divinity humanity can be deified. In this way all the elements of our nature are sanctified." Once it is united with God, human nature can raise itself to His level, and that which ascends is that which has been raised up from destruction. "By commingling with the Divinity, everything that is weak and corrupt in our nature also becomes Divine."

Two Phases in the Deification of Human Nature in Christ

Gregory follows Origen and distinguishes two phases in the development or deification of human nature in Christ. The first phase is the period of healing through obedience which oc - curred before the Resurrection. Death, which had been intro - duced by the disobedience of the first man, is driven out "by the obedience of the second man," Gregory writes. The "True Healer" frees those who have been afflicted by disease because they have departed from the will of God "by means of reuniting them with the Divine will." The Divinity heals both the body and the soul. "Through the union of God with each part of man, signs of the superior nature appear in both these parts. The body is healed by contact with the Divinity and reveals the Divinity that was latent within it and through the strength of the Almighty the soul demonstrates its own Divine power."

However, it was still necessary for the Savior to suffer and die and to sacrifice Himself on the Cross. "In a solemn and ineffable rite, the like of which mankind had never seen before, the Savior gave Himself as an offering and a sacrifice for us. He was both the priest and the Lamb of God Who accepted the sins of the world." This indicates that the flesh had still not been given new life by the Divinity, and Christ's prayer in the garden of Gethsemane demonstrates that "His weakness was identical to ours." Gregory's commentary on Gethsemane is similar to Origen's: "The Lord spoke these humble words and expressed human fear in order to show that He truly shared our nature and by taking part in our weakness He testified to the reality of His humanity."

Gregory emphasizes that the Savior's death was unique. Death is the separation of the soul and the body, after which the body, having lost the "strength of life" it had in the soul, disintegrates. The Savior's death was a true death because His soul and body were separated. However, "since He had united both body and soul within Himself, He Himself was not separated from either of them." This was the source of the resurrection because both body and soul remained in communion with the Divinity, with Life. Even in death the deified body of the Savior was incorruptible and through the incorruptibility of His body mortality was destroyed. His soul entered paradise and was seated beside the Father.

It was necessary for the soul and the body to be reunited. "By the unity of Divine nature, which existed equally in the body and in the soul, that which had been separated was again joined together. Death results from the separation of united elements and resurrection comes from the unification of that which is divided." This was a resurrection of all the elements of human nature. The Lord gave to humanity the "power and potential, δύναμις, for resurrection." The Lord descended into hell, "into the heart of the earth," "to destroy that mind which was great in evil and to bring light to the darkness, so that mortality was consumed by life and evil and was turned into nothingness."

During the three days of His death the Lord destroyed "all the evil which had accumulated since the creation of the world." He destroyed it not by struggling against it but by His descent alone. "The simple and incomprehensible coming of Life and the presence of Light for those who were sitting in mortal darkness and shadow destroyed death and made darkness disappear." The death of the Lord was His resurrection and the resurrection of all mankind. This is the beginning of the second phase of the life of the God-man and the ultimate deification and glorification of human nature. "After the great mystery of death is fulfilled in it, the flesh reveals God in itself, and by dissolution it will turn into something higher and Divine. When it has become one with Christ the Lord, the flesh will change into that which He was even when He was revealed in the flesh." Man will become superior to every name which is proper to the Divinity (cf. *Philippians* 2: 10). "By mingling with the Divinity our corruptible nature will be transformed into the superior nature. It will participate in the strength of the Divinity in the same way that a drop of vinegar is blended in with the sea and loses its natural qualities in the infinity of the other, enduring substance."

In this way our salvation was achieved. "The kingdom of life arrived and the power of death was destroyed. There appeared a new birth, another life, and our very nature was transformed." Christ at His resurrection "resurrected with Himself everything that had gone to rest." He destroyed the bonds and affliction of death in order to establish for us a "path to birth through resurrection" and a "path to rebirth through death." Thus Christ is the Path, the Resurrection, and the Life, and through Him God creates a new heaven and a new earth. "The foundation of the Church is the foundation of the universe."

Man is a true participant in the death and resurrection of our Savior not because of his relation to the Savior or his con-substantiality with Him, but through faith. "Rebirth is achieved in two ways," through baptism and resurrection. Baptism is a new birth "which does not begin with corruption and end with decay but which leads the newly born into eternal life." Baptism is the first stage of resurrection, a way out of the "labyrinth" of this life. "I apply the figure of a labyrinth to our inescapable bondage to death, which imprisons the whole wretched human race." The symbolism of the baptismal rite refers to the "three days' state of death and the return to life of Christ." Baptism is the "imitation of death," the "imitation of the grace of the resurrection which was achieved after three days."

Baptism and the Imitation of Death

In death things that have been separated are purged of sin so that they can be reunited at the resurrection in purity. In the baptismal "imitation of death," in this "form of mortification, which is given by water," since water is the element closest to earth, the proper and natural place for all dead things, by the power of the Divinity and "by the will of God and the inspiration of the Spirit, which mysteriously descends for our liberation," there occurs "not a complete destruction, it is true, but a kind of break in the continuity of evil." This is the "beginning and cause" of that which will be completely accomplished at the "great resurrection." Baptism is "the beginning of our restoration to our original blissful state, which is Divine and far from all sadness." The water takes the place of fire, for "whoever is purified from evil by the mysterious water has no need for any other form of purification. Those who are not sanctified in this way must necessarily be purified by fire." Visible appearances are not changed at baptism. Old men do not become youths and wrinkles are not smoothe out. However, the internal man is renewed and "that which has been stained by sin and aged through evil habits returns to the innocence of a child through this sovereign grace." "We are restored to our original beauty, which was imprinted in us at our creation by God, the great artist."

At baptism man is required to demonstrate his faith and to re - pent, to turn away from evil and the false movements of the will. Man must give his faith freely, for only "inanimate and irrational beings can be forced to anything by the will of another." Grace calls to man, but man's will must respond. The grace received through baptism must be actively accepted by the will, and the signs of a newly born man are the "inclination to the best" and the "free movements of the soul" as it starts out on its new path. The old man disappears only through good works. Baptismal grace testifies that man has been pardoned and shown mercy, but not that he has truly become virtuous.

"The man who accepts the water of rebirth is like a young warrior who has just been enrolled as a soldier, but who as yet has demonstrated neither martial spirit nor courage." Great things are expected of him and only after he has accomplished his feats will he be worthy to be rewarded with bliss. "Faith requires the companionship of its sister, which is a virtuous life." At baptism man is reborn as a son of God and those who are thus reborn should demonstrate their similarity to their Parent. "Their relationship should be proved by their life." "If a man does not prove his noble lineage through his deeds, then it is a bad sign. He is not a legitimate son, but only a foundling."

Gregory claims that those whose lives after baptism remain similar to their previous lives demonstrate that their souls have not yet been cleansed of the impurities of the passions. "The water remains water because the newly born man does not show the gifts of the Holy Spirit because Christ, Who Himself united man with God, unites only that which is worthy of communion with the Divinity." The newly baptized man must show that he has freely chosen to live a new life. "In our rebirth the degree of beauty which the soul is given through grace depends on our own desire. The more greatly we strive to live a life worthy of God, the more greatly our soul will be glorified." Grace is manifested in the free choices of the will, but the will's activity is necessary for grace to be achieved. Their relationship is synergistic and har - monious.

Man's Call to Make Himself a Son of God

The path of man's quest for self-perfection is determined by his call to make himself a son of God. "When the Lord instructed us to say in our prayers that God is our Father, He commanded us to make ourselves similar to our heavenly Father by leading lives worthy of Him." In this sense it is possible to say that "Christianity is an imitation of the nature of God." The beginning of man's struggle is his love for God and love pours itself forth in prayer. "Whoever burns with love will never find satiety in prayer but will always be consumed with the desire for bliss." Christ's command to man to make himself similar to God by "imitation" is not beyond the limitations of our nature because man was created as the likeness and image of God. However, true similarity to God can be attained only by the man who is reborn, in whom the image of God has been restored and purified, and this is possible only through Christ, in Whom this renewal was accomplished. The process of imitation is endless because it is "making oneself into the likeness of One Who is eternal."

The ascent to God can take different forms. It is accomplished through victory over the flesh and the senses, liberation from "sensual and irrational movement" and the restoration of the sovereignty of the intellect, the "helmsman of the soul." "We can raise ourselves to God only by constantly turning our gaze to the heights and by having a continual desire for higher things." This victory is realized in impassivity, which, Gregory writes, "is the beginning and foundation for a virtuous life." Gregory's form -

ulation that "moderation is a property of virtue" and his con-ception of impassivity as a middle path are taken from Aristotle.

Virtue should not be excessive or extreme. The path of virtue is like a narrow mountain passageway leading between two equally dangerous chasms. The soul must overcome the inclinations of the senses but its struggle against them should not be immoderate because "too much attention to the body" can distract the soul from what is truly superior, and entrap it within a "circle of petty cares." Furthermore, men who are carried away by this struggle "are not in the condition to elevate their minds and contemplate higher things, since they are buried in their concern to master their flesh." The true goal of continence and fasting is not to overcome the body but to turn it to the service of the soul. Neither timidity nor audacity are virtues but only courage, which is the median between them. Man should strive for neither craftiness nor simplicity but wisdom, for neither sensuality nor aversion to the flesh, but for chastity. Even piety is an intermediate stage between superstition and atheism. The string should be tuned only to the degree proper for it, otherwise the sound it produces will not be pure.

Gregory had a great respect for virginity and praised it as the highest form of purity but he was also not averse to marriage. He stressed that man's goal should not be physical virginity alone but a "devout way of life," without which even virginity is no more than an "earring in the nose of a pig." "There can be no basis for denying the demands of nature or for condemning as disgraceful that which should be respected," he writes. He did not approve of the extreme asceticism of the Encratists. "They have been instructed by demons. They burn out strange symbols over their hearts and abhor the creation of God, as though it were impure."

The goal of ascetic discipline is not the mortification of the body but the mortification of the passions and sin, the subordination of the body to the law of reason, and the reconciliation of the body and soul. "Man must pacify the conflicting forces of nature within himself." A virtuous life is a gathering together and a simplification of the soul. By simplification Gregory does not mean that the soul's qualities should be effaced but that they should form a harmonious whole. In triumphing over the distractions and des-tructiveness of the passions man "saves himself from internal division, returns to a state of good, becomes simplified, and is a genuine unity, so that what is visible in him is the same as that which is hidden and that which he cherishes within himself is the same as that which he displays."

This integrity expresses itself as love, forgiveness, and charity. To whom does the Lord promise bliss at the Last Judgment, and for what? "Not because we have put on the robe of incorruptibility nor because we have washed away our sins but because we have accomplished works of love. He will read a list of those to whom we have given food, and water, and clothing." "As we forgive those who are in debt to us": this is the greatest virtue. It is superior to the limits of human nature because forgiveness is proper only to God, and whoever forgives "has made himself a second god." Charity expresses our recognition of the com - munity of all men and our acknowledgement that debts and sins are common to the whole human race. By charity we overcome pride and isolation.

All men are created in the image of God, all men bear the image of our Savior, and all men enjoy God's love. Love for our neigh - bor is inseparable from love for God, and one is not possible without the other. Love is an internal connection and a growing together with the beloved object. This connection is realized in the Church. In the *Song of Songs* the Church is symbolized "with the image of a cord," "so that all become a single cord and a single chain." Perfect love drives out fear and fear is transformed into love. "The one who is saved turns out to be a part of the great union of all in their affinity with the single Good." This affinity with the single Good, this unity with the Holy Spirit, is the foun - dation of universal human love. Only in spiritual life is humanity reunited, and the integrity of personal life is strengthened through the unity of life within a brotherly community.

The Eucharist and the Christian Life

The summit of Christian life is the sacrament of the Eucharist. The Eucharist is the food of incorruptibility, the antidote against the poison of death and the "all-healing power." "Our nature had tasted of something ruinous to it and hence we necessarily needed something that would save from decay that which had been destroyed." This antidote is that Body "which proved Itself to be stronger than death," which arose and was glorified. How is it possible that a single body which is separated into portions and distributed to the faithful does not remain divided but, on the contrary, reunites those who have been separated, "becomes whole in each of its portions and thus endures in each who receives it as a whole?"

Gregory answers by comparing the Eucharist to the food which nourishes the physical body. "The Word of God," he writes, "en - tered into union with human nature. When the Word lived in a body like ours He did not make any innovations in man's physical constitution but He nourished His own body by the customary and proper means and maintained its existence through eating and drinking . . . His body was maintained by bread and thus His body was once bread in reality. This bread was consecrated by the Word dwelling within the body. Therefore, for the same reason as that by which the bread in His body was transformed and received a Divine potency, so now a similar result takes place. For in that case the grace of the Word sanctified the body, the substance of which came from the bread, and so in a way the body which was sanctified was itself bread. So also in this case our bread, in the words of the Apostle, is sanctified by the Word of God and prayer (*I Timothy* 4:5], not in such a way that by the process of eating it becomes the Body of the Word but it is changed into the Body of the Word at once."

The Eucharist and the First Stage
of Resurrection

Thus, the flesh which had contained the Word of God receives again a portion of its "own substance," and through this portion this substance "is communicated to every believer and blends it - self with their bodies, so that by this union with the immortal, man too shares in incorruptibility." Through the sacrament of the Eu - charist all humanity is reunited in Christ and is resurrected. This is, however, only the first stage of resurrection. The Savior's victory over corruption and death is completely accomplished only at the last great resurrection of all mankind.

The Activity of Death Until the Final Resurrection

Death has been conquered by the resurrection of Christ but its activity has not yet ceased. It has been conquered because all men will be resurrected but it is still active because men are dying and will continue to die until the cycle of earthly time is com - pleted. Only then will the succession of the human race come to an end. Our time, which is ephemeral and transitory, will cease because the "need to come into being will be past and no one will ever again be destroyed." "The power which leads us into being and destruction will not exist." At that point the final re - surrection will be accomplished and all nature will be transformed into a new mode of life. Until then, however, the activity of death will continue.

Death is the separation of the soul and the body, and when the body has been abandoned by the soul it disintegrates into the elements which originally composed it. Each of its parts returns to its natural element so that not a single part is completely destroyed or turned into nothingness, and the body remains within the boundaries of this world. This is decay but it is not destruction or transition into a state of nonexistence. "The body does not disappear forever but breaks down into the elements from which it was put together. These elements then continue their existence in water, air, earth, and fire. Within these elements the components of the human body which have returned to them remain completely whole and unharmed."

The Soul's Identity with the Body

These elements retain certain signs which testify to their having belonged to a particular body because the soul imprints them with its own stamp as if they were wax. Gregory follows Origen in referring to the stamp which the soul puts on the corporeal elements of the body with which it is united as their "aspect" or "form," ἔδος. This stamp is the internal image or idea of the body and it does not change even after death. It is the unrepeatable and ideal image of the man and serves to distinguish the body from all others. It is distorted only under the influence of extreme passions which "cover it with the mask" of ugliness and disease. By this "form" the soul at the resurrection will "recognize its own body as being different from the other garments around it."

The soul is not effected by the decay of the wholeness man enjoyed during life because it is simple and incomposite and therefore cannot disintegrate. The soul is immortal and extends into eternity. The only thing about it that changes at death is its mode of existence. Even then its connection with the decaying body is not severed and the soul will be able to find all of its elements by virtue of its "cognitive power." It is like a watchman and "without any difficulty it will know where to find each of the elements of the body that once belonged to it."

The soul retains certain "signs of union" and "marks of the body" which have been sealed in it. It is as if the soul has been imprinted with a stamp. The new connection between the soul and the body is similar to their union before death when the "living power" of the soul penetrated all the parts of the body equally and identically and gave them life. During its earthly life the soul had a natural affinity and love for its companion, the body, and this friendly connection and "acquaintance" is mys - teriously preserved even after death. This vital connection is incomprehensible to us. It has nothing to do with the spatial placement of the soul in the body because the soul has no physical being and is not located in or limited to any definite part of the body. "By means of the movements of the intellect the soul spreads freely throughout the whole of creation" and sometimes even attains the mysteries of heaven.

"The communion of the intellect with the body," Gregory writes, "is a form of contact which is inexpressible and unim-aginable. It does not occur internally because that which is in-corporeal cannot be contained by a body and it is not achieved from outside because that which is incorporeal cannot surround anything with itself." The intellect is not in any particular place or part of the body. It is neither inside nor outside but it exists "in such a way that we cannot describe it or even conceive of it." Therefore, the spatial dispersion of the elements of the body after death does not hinder the soul from recognizing its connection with them. "A spiritual nature is not defined by space and therefore it does not feel the effect of distance." The connection between a soul and a body is absolutely unique and for this reason Gregory considers that the idea of the trans-migration of souls is absurd.

Death as a Moment of Becoming and Restoration

Death is a particular stage in the development of man. It is a moment of becoming or, more exactly, a moment of restoration. "The Creator did not intend for us to merely remain embryos," Gregory writes. "The final goal of our nature is not the state of in-fancy nor the successive ages which follow after it and change our appearance with the passage of time, nor even the des-truction of the body which occurs through death. All of these are only a part of the path which we are following. The ultimate goal of this movement is our restoration to our original state." Death is a path which leads us into a better mode of existence. In death the soul is freed from the body and can make itself more similar to its original state of beauty. The body is "melted down" and purified in the earth from debased passions and inclinations. It is liberated from the needs connected with the conditions of life on earth and it is completely changed and recreated for another life. "The artist of everything melts down the solidity of our body to form a new instrument for his grace." This is a time of expectation and preparation for the resurrection and final judgment.

This process is itself a type of judgment because not everyone will share the same fate and not everyone will follow the same path. There are differences among souls. Just souls will be glor-ified but sinful souls will be punished. Some souls, however, will join neither the worthy nor the condemned but will withdraw to an intermediate place. To this indeterminate group Gregory assigns the souls of those who have received baptism only immediately before death and have thus had no opportunity to bring forth its fruits. These are the "infants who are prematurely seized by death," who have earned no reward for themselves and who "by reason of their ignorance and lack of development are incapable of participating in the bliss of true life." These souls must under - go a period of development. This doctrine is a further indication of the high regard which Gregory had for man's active quest for virture and self-perfection.

Just souls will ascend to heaven but sinners will be cast down into hell. Although Gregory speaks about heaven and hell as actual places and even distinguishes different orders of heavenly dwelling, he ultimately considers that the concept of "place" is only a metaphor here, since "a soul is incorporeal and has no need to be in a specific place." On the contrary, heaven and hell are modes of existence which cannot be described or defined. They "do not submit themselves to words and are inaccessible to the intuition of reason." In keeping with his basic conception of man's life as a journey, Gregory describes the afterlife as a path which continues beyond the grave into eternity. He borrows this idea from Origen.

The blessings of heaven are indestructible. "Not only do they endure forever but they are like seeds which are constantly in - creasing and multiplying." There is "no boundary to interrupt the growth of heavenly bliss" and the bliss which is sought "is constantly and regularly superior to the strength of those who are seeking it." Furthermore, continual effort is proper to the soul and after death there is nothing to oppose the soul's movement. "It will always be ascending to the highest things and renewing its efforts through that which it has achieved." There is a certain or - der and consecutiveness in this ascent in accordance with the capacity of each soul to strive for the Good. This process of growth is similar to the maturation of an infant and its ultimate goal is the contemplation of God.

The Fate of the Unworthy and the Unbaptized

This ascent is not possible for those who are unworthy. They are spiritually blind and will be left outside of true life and bliss forever. They are driven off to the outer darkness and they carry with them the stench of their flesh which they nourished by their constant surrender to sensual passions. This is the result only of sins which have not been effaced by repentance, but confession is potent only on earth, and in hell it is ineffectual. Gregory de - votes particular attention to unbaptized souls which have not been sealed and which "do not bear any mark of the Lord." "It is only natural that such a soul will wander and circle aimlessly in the air. No one will look for it since it does not bear the mark of the Lord. It will long for rest and refuge but it will never find them. It will grieve in vain and its repentance will be fruitless."

In Gregory's conception, the sinner's torment consists primarily in the nakedness and hunger which result form the deprivation of the hope of bliss. The sinner is also consumed by an inexhaustible fire, the "furnace of hell" and the "untiring worm." This is the "outer darkness." These images are all symbolic but they also express a certain spiritual reality, for they indicate the continuation of man's earthly path and his process of purification. Gregory considers the fire of hell as as a fire of baptism and renewal. "There is a purifying power in both fire and water," and whoever fails to purify himself through the water of the sacrament "will necessarily be purged by fire."

The Possibility of the Eventual Salvation of the Impure and Unrepentant

Salvation can be attained even in the afterlife and the path of impure and unrepentant souls can lead to their eventual healing and purification from evil. All traces of past life are burned away in the fire. This process is not accomplished by means of external force because even in the purifying torments of hell man remains free. Repentance is awakened by the fire, and the soul, which had been held captive by material things, suddenly sees and realizes the vanity of everything it had wanted for itself, and it mourns and repents. The soul, Gregory writes, "clearly recognizes the distinction between virtue and vice through its inability to participate in the Divinity." Movement toward God is natural for the soul and when the soul turns away from evil it sees God, Who "calls to Himself everything which comes into being through His grace."

In other words, after the soul crosses the threshold of death, the deceitful nature of sin is revealed to it. The soul is shaken by this discovery and "with absolute necessity" it turns in a new direction. The will to evil, which had previously been strong in it, becomes weak and is soon exhausted. Gregory does not believe that the created will's movement toward sin can be eternal. He considers it highly unlikely that the will can maintain this insanity, especially when it is freed, even if only partially, from the fetters of the flesh. It seems to him that this is contradictory to the very nature of man, who has been created in the image of God. "The passionate desire for that which is foreign to it cannot remain in our nature forever. Everything which is not proper to us, which was not part of our natures at the beginning, will surfeit everyone and become a burden. Only that which is related to us and natural for us will always be desired and beloved."

"Evil is not so powerful," Gregory writes, "that it can overcome good. The foolishness of our nature is not higher or more enduring than the Divine Wisdom. Furthermore, it is impossible for that which is inconstant and changing to be better and more resistant than that which is immutable and has always been firmly established in good."

This explains why the free movement of the will with which this process begins is "necessary." The turn of the will away from evil makes purification possible. The fire can burn out sin, "impurities," "material tumors," and "the remainder of fleshly contamination. Gregory compares this purification to the excision of a wart or callus, but even this image is insufficient. Purification is a separation which is ordered by God. God in His love irresistibly draws to Himself everything which has been created in His image. Movement toward God is natural and easy only for the pure. Impure souls must be forced to this movement, which is agonizing for them. The soul which has been ensnared by its passion for the material things of this earth "suffers constantly and undergoes violent tension. God draws the soul to Himself because it is His own property. Whatever is foreign to the soul, or whatever has grown into its substance, has to be scraped away by force and this causes the soul unendurable agony."

The duration and intensity of this torment is determined by the "quantity of healing" needed for purification to be achieved. "The agony will be measured by the amount of evil in each individual." From this it follows that the torment ultimately comes to an end because the "amount of evil" or the "amount of unpurged matter" in the soul of a sinner cannot be infinite, since infiniteness is not a property of evil. Sooner or later the fire will destroy every impurity and vice. This process of healing "by fire and bitter medicines" may seem protracted and "commensurate with eternity" but nevertheless its duration is limited to time.

Gregory maintains a clear distinction between the terms ἀιώνιος (from αἰών) and ἀίδιος (from ἀεί). He never applies the second term to the torments and he never applies the first term to bliss or the Divinity. Ἀεί designates that which is superior to time or outside of time. It cannot be measured by the ages and it does not move within time." This is the sphere of the Divinity. Creation, however, abides within time and "can be measured by the passing of the centuries." Αἰών designates temporality, that which occurs within time. This distinction in terminology is the explanation for an apparent contradiction in Gregory's thought. He demonstrates that the torment of fire is only temporary by citing passages from Scripture which describe it as "eternal." This refers to the eternity of time and the totality of the temporal state. However, this is not the same as the state which is superior to time. There is no foundation for considering that Gregory be-lieved that the "eternal" torment foretold in Scripture is limited to unrepentant sinners only. Gregory would not accept even this re-stricted conception of damnation because for him the finiteness of the process of purification is a basic truth. It must end, no matter who is forced to undergo it. Other commentaries on this problem have not been conclusive.

Gregory's basic premise is that everything which has been created is finite. Time, which is the sphere of death (because dying is a process of change and can take place only in time), is also the sphere of purification, the purification of man for eternity through death. The body is purged through dissolution into its original elements and the soul is also purified and grows to maturity in the mysterious ways and dwelling places. When time is fulfilled it will end, the Lord will come, and the resurrection and judgment will be at hand. This will be the first restoration.

The End of Time and the Universal Resurrection

Time will end when the internal measure of the universe has reached its limit. Further origination will be impossible and the passage of time will be unnecessary. "When our race has com-pleted in an orderly fashion the full cycle of time," Gregory writes, "this current streaming onward as generation, succession will cease." The significance of the forward motion of time is in the succession of human generations, in which the "fullness of humanity," which has been predetermined by God, is realized. "It is necessary for reason to foresee an end to the multiplication of souls because otherwise there will be an endless stream of births into nature which will have no end." Measure and limitation are part of the perfection of nature. "When the birth of men has ended, then time will end, and in this way the renewal of the universe will be accomplished." This is not merely exhaustion or the natural end to that which had a natural beginning. This is fulfillment, the realization of completeness, and the reunification of this fullness.

The seven days of temporal creation will end and the eighth day will come, "the great day of the future age." A new life will begin, "continuous and indestructible, and it will never be altered by birth or death." Christ will come again and the universal resurrection will be accomplished. The Lord comes for the sake of this resurrection and "to restore the dead to incorruptibility." He comes in glory, born by hosts of angels who bow to Him as their King. "All the higher order of creation will worship Him" and "all the angels will rejoice that men have again been summoned to their original state of grace." This summons is the universal re - surrection, the renewal and gathering together of the whole of creation. "All creation, both the higher and the lower orders, will join together in their rejoicing."

This universal gathering will begin with the resurrection of the dead. It is our bodies which will rise up, for the soul never dies even though the body disintegrates. The soul will not arise, but it will return. "The soul will again return from its invisible state of dispersion to a state which is visible and has a focus." This is the restoration of the entire man, the "return of that which had been separated to an indivisible union." The bodies of all men will be restored to their original beauty and there will be no physical difference between the virtuous and the wicked. this does not mean that there will be no distinction between the purified and the unpurified, but this difference will exist only in their internal natures and fates. That which awaits men in the afterlife is pur - ification, the renewal and restoration of the body, and the re - surrection of all. But for some souls the path to purification will have to continue even beyond this.

Gregory's Doctrine of Apocatastasis

There is a certain inconsistency in Gregory's doctrine, which is apparently the rocult of his acceptance of certain features of Origenism and his rejection of others. In Gregory's conception the universal resurrection is a restoration, the "restoration of the image of God to its original condition." Through this men are again led into paradise. However, even at this restoration impurity is still in existence. It is only the mortality born of sin that has been brought to an end. Not every soul has been fully healed and purified, and yet it is the soul which contains the image of God. In Gregory's system true *apocatastasis*, universal restoration, is separated from the universal resurrection and delayed until some future time. This is both unexpected and contradictory, since according to this very system time has already ended and there can be no further succession or development. The whole of humanity has not yet been led into paradise. The just have been admitted into heaven but the impure souls cannot yet enter because paradise is achieved only through absolute purity. If the universal restoration is expected to take place at the end of time, this restoration cannot logically be separated into parts or stages, for this division would abrogate the integrity and completeness we would expect in a mode of existence that is outside of time.

In Origen's system this does not involve a contradiction be - cause for him the "resurrection of the dead" is not the final restoration or the ultimate fate of the universe. It is only a point of transition in the continuing flow of the ages. For Origen the fate of the body is not resolved at the universal resurrection because the resurrection is followed by further stages of existence in future ages. Origen does not separate the fate of the soul from the fate of the body.

Gregory accepts certain features of Origen's doctrine, although the basic significance of their eschatologies is different. Ac - cording to Gregory's system time has ended and the last things have been accomplished but suddenly it turns out that not everything has been brought to completion. The ultimate fate of all men should be realized simultaneously, but for Gregory this is not the case. In Gregory's conception the bodies of all men are purged and become radiant in unison. How can such a body remain incorruptible if it is reunited with a soul which has not yet been purified but which is still moribund and decaying? The strength of Divine life cannot be active in such a soul but the body without a soul will remain dead. Origen's system, on the other hand, maintains a distinction between the bodies of the righteous and the bodies of sinners, which is in accordance with his conception of the gradual overcoming of corporeal nature.

There are two possibilities. If the last resurrection is truly the restoration of the universe or, in the words of Gregory, a "catholic resurrection," then time and development have absolutely ended. Any souls which may remain unpurified are condemned to torment for eternity, the true eternity, which is superior to the limitations of human time. This idea was later developed by Maximus the Confessor. The other possibility, which is set forth by Origen, is that the general resurrection is not the ultimate restoration. The features of Origen's system which Gregory a - dapts are logically incompatible with his own premises. Further - more, Origen's conception is contradictory and cannot be defended. Gregory's attempt to achieve a synthesis between Origen's system and the eschatology of Methodius of Olympus, from whom he borrows his doctrine of the resurrection, is unsuccessful.

At the resurrection the body grows forth from the earth as if it were a new plant. Gregory compares this resurrection with the germination of seeds, the blossoming of trees, and the de - velopment of the human embryo. All of these analogies had long been a part of Christian tradition. "In the words of the Apostle," Gregory writes, "the mystery of the resurrection can be un - derstood as the same type of wonderful development that we observe in seeds." "Seeds" and "ears of grain" are among Gre - gory's favorite images. He distinguishes two stages in their growth. Their development originates in a state that is inde - terminate because "at first the seed is without form but once it is established by the ineffable artistry of God, it takes on form and develops and becomes dense." For this reason there is nothing exceptional about the growth of the seed of the dead body or its restoration to its previous form and "entire material state." Since every germination is achieved through dissolution and death, all growth is a resurrection and a victory over death.

Resurrection is made possible by the connection of the soul and the body in an individual organic unity but it is actually achieved only through the power of God. It is He Who authorizes the birth, renewal, and life of all nature. Resurrection is a miracle worked by the omnipotence of the Divinity but it is a miracle which is in accord with the basic laws of nature. It is one more mani - festation of the general mystery of life. Resurrection is the fulfillment and ultimate realization of nature. The bodies which are resurrected are the very bodies which have died. Otherwise this would not be resurrection but a new creation. The resurrected bodies are composed of their former elements which have been gathered from everywhere by virtue of the life-giving power of the soul. "In this way the different elements are gathered by the power of the soul, which weaves them together to form the chain of the body."

Resurrection is not merely a return to our former life or our pre - vious mode of existence. This would be a great misfortune and the soul would lose all hope of true resurrection. Resurrection is the restoration of the entire man. It is a renewal and a trans - formation to something better and more complete. However, it is one and the same body which makes this transition. Not only the unity of the subject, but also the identity of the substratum are maintained. This does not contradict the truth of the renewal and transformation. "The veil of the body, after it has been destroyed by death, will be recomposed and rewoven from the very same material elements, not into its previous coarse and imperfect state, but in such a way that the fibers of its being will be light and airy. It will be restored into the superior state of the great beauty which it had desired." That which returns to life is that which was enterred in the grave, but it will be different. All earthly life is a continuing process of change and renewal. "Human nature is like a constantly flowing stream," Gregory writes, and yet this does not turn individual men into an indefinite "crowd of people."

When man is resurrected he will not be any particular age nor will he be every age all at once. The concept of age will become invalid at the resurrection because it was not part of our original nature. "In our original life there was probably no old age, or child - hood, or suffering from various diseases, or any other deformity or imperfection of the body because it is not proper to God to create anything like that. All of these violated us when we were invaded by sin." These things will not be a part of our resurrection but neither will they prevent it. It is only our true nature that will be resurrected and not the vices and passions which have infected it. We will be renewed and liberated from this heritage and all the traces of our former lives of evil and sin. At the resurrection we will be transformed into a state of incorruptibility and immortality because resurrection is victory over death. The ears of grain will ripen to their maturity and be fruitful, and they will reach out to the heights of heaven.

Nothing that is connected with disease, the infirmity of old age, or ugliness will survive at the resurrection, neither wrinkles, nor deformity, nor immaturity. Resurrected bodies will not preserve their former organs and members which were made necessary by the demands of sinful life on earth. Death will purify our bodies of everything that is "superfluous or unnecessary for our enjoyment of our future life." This is especially true of the organs which we need to nourish ourselves and to perform the other functions of animal life or which are connected with the cycles of all material growth. Humanity will no longer be distinguished by sex. All the unrefined matter of our bodies will be overcome and the heaviness of the flesh will disappear. The body will become light and will naturally move upward. All of the attributes of the body: its color, form, features, and everything else "will be transformed into something Divine." Our bodies will lose their impermeability and their accidental distinctions will be effaced.

This is what Gregory is referring to when he says that we will all assume a single appearance at the resurrection. He writes: "We will all become the single body of Christ and we will all take on a single form and aspect because the radiance of the image of the Divinity will shine equally in all." This means that our appearance will be defined from within. "It is not the elements which will distinguish the appearance of each but the particularities of sin and virtue." Thus, the appearance of everyone will not be the same. The resurrection is the reinstitution of our original con - dition. It is not only the return to but also the gathering together of everything that was part of our previous life. It is not only *apocatastasis*, a restoration, but also *recapitulatio*, a summing up.

Gregory's conception of the final restoration is not the same as Origen's because Gregory did not believe in the pre-existence of the soul. For him the restoration is not a return to the past but the realization of something which had never existed and the accom-plishment of that which had not been fulfilled. It is completion, not oblivion. This is especially true for the body. In Gregory's conception the body is not replaced but it is transformed and in this way it truly fulfills its function as the mirror of the soul.

The resurrection is followed by the Last Judgment of the entire universe. The Son of God will come again because He is the Judge and the Father judges through Him. "Everything the Only-Begotten decrees at the Last Judgment is also the work of the Father" but it is the Son Who sits in judgment because through His own experience He can truly measure the circumstances and difficulties of human life. He will judge everyone, "whether they had great experience of the good and evil of human life or whether they had hardly begun to know it and had died in immaturity."

This is more a judgment of Divine love than of Divine justice. All of its sentences are properly merited, however, and are equal to that which each man deserves. Christ is the "Justice of God and He revealed this Justice to men." In a certain sense each man will be the judge of himself. Each man will awaken at the resurrection and will remember his past life and give it a true evaluation, so that everyone who appears to be judged will be fully aware of his good deeds and his faults. The judgment is a mirror in which all men will be reflected.

The full glory of the Son, which is equal to the glory of the Father, will be revealed at the Last Judgment. This judgment will be universal and "the whole human race, from the first creature to the full completeness of all who were ever brought into being," will gather together and stand before the royal throne of the Son. The devil and his angels will also be brought to Him for judgment. "Then," writes Gregory, "the instigator of the rebellion, who dreamed of usurping the dignity of the Lord, will appear before the eyes of all as a beaten slave, and he will be dragged to pun-ishment by the angels. All of his servants and the accomplices of his malice will be subjected to the punishment which is fitting for them." The ultimate deceit will be revealed and the true and only King will appear and both those who are victorious and those who are conquered will recognize Him and sing Him songs of praise.

Gregory devotes relatively little attention to the Last Judgment. The few depictions he has left of this terrible day are striking but they are intended more for edification than for serious con - sideration as dogma. The focal point of Gregory's eschatology is not the judgment because for him the judgment is not the final resolution of the fate of the universe. It is only a preliminary summation of history and a mirror of the past. The judgment is simply the beginning of the eighth day, which will continue beyond this process. Only the resurrection and the appearance of Christ in His glory are ultimate. The Son's judgment is more the revelation of the activity of humanity than its resolution and it accomplishes little that is new. The bliss of just souls has already been determined by the resurrection and the torment of sinners has begun even before the resurrection and will continue be - yond the judgment. The greatest significance of the Last Judg - ment lies in man's expectation of it because this conception motivates us in our efforts on earth to achieve religious and moral perfection. "The coming Judgment is a threat for us in our weak - ness. This magnification of our sorrows makes us fear pun - ishment and teaches us to avoid evil." "We make our description of this severe court as convincing as possible only in order to teach the necessity of leading a good and charitable life." Gregory has borrowed much of his doctrine of the Last Judgment from Origen.

Gregory sets forth a doctrine of a "universal restoration." "Par - ticipation in bliss awaits everyone," he writes. Some men achieve this through their actions in life on earth, whereas others must pass through the fire of purification. In the end, however, "after many ages evil will disappear and nothing will remain except good. This will be the completion of the return of all intellectual creatures to the original state in which they were first created, when there was as yet no evil." Eventually "evil will disappear from existence and it will again become nonexistence." Not a trace of evil will remain, and then "the beauty of our similarity to God, in which we were formed at the beginning, will again shine forth."

"There was a time," Gregory writes, "when all intellectual natures formed a single union and, by fulfilling the command - ments of God, they brought themselves into agreement with the harmony which the Source had established through His activity. But after sin had intruded among the first men, who until then, together with the angelic forces, had made up a single assembly, the Divine harmony of this union was destroyed. Something had made men susceptible to deceit and this caused them to fall. Man was deprived of communion with the angels, so that through the fall their intellectual harmony was abrogated. After this it became necessary for the fallen one to labor and sweat in order to fight to liberate himself from the power which had gained dominion over him at the fall. Man must rise again and he receives as a reward for his victory over the enemy the right to participate in the Divine assembly." In this assembly human and angelic natures will again be united and form a "Divine host."

This will be a great and universal feast and nothing will interrupt the unity of intellectual creation. Both the lower and the higher orders will rejoice in universal gladness and all will worship and praise the Father through the Son in unanimity. All veils will be raised and a common joy and glory will shine forth in all. This final restoration will include everyone: all people, the entire race of men, and the whole of human nature. Moreover, it will encom- pass even evil spirits and the "inventor of evil" himself will finally be joined to the triumphant gathering. He also will be saved because during the three days of his death the Lord healed all three vessels of evil: demonic natures, the female sex, and the male sex. Evil will finally be driven out "even from the race of the snake, in which the nature of evil first found a source for itself."

Gregory's doctrine of the universal restoration of everything to its original state is based on the teaching of Origen. Their com- mon point of departure is that Good is omnipotent because it alone has true existence and is the only foundation and goal of everything that exists. "There is always an immutable Divine har - mony in everything," Gregory writes. "Your indignation and the dissatisfaction with which you observe the necessary chain of the sequence of things are in vain, since you do not know the goal to which each individual thing in the ordering of the universe is directed. It is necessary for everything to follow a certain order and succession, in accordance with the true Wisdom of the One Who directs all, as it comes into harmony with Divine nature."

Gregory understands the opposition of good and evil as the opposition between being and will, between that which is nec - essary and that which is accidental. There is no evil. It does not exist but only occurs or happens occasionally. It is necessary for that which occurs to have an end, for "that which has not always been will not always be." That which originates can subsist eter - nally only if there is an eternal will for it to do so and only through that which itself exists eternally. It can exist only by participating in the One Who truly is and by communion in the eternal Good. Creation can be maintained in this way but this is not possible for evil because evil is not from God. It is the "absence of good" or nongood, and this is the same as non-existence. In Gregory's reasoning: "Since it is not proper for evil to exist without being willed, and since the eternal will is from God, evil will eventually be completely destroyed because there will be no place for it to exist." Gregory follows Origen in his reference to the Gospels: "God will be all in all." "By this Scripture teaches us that evil will be completely destroyed because if God is in all being, it is evident that He is not in evil being or sin." God is in everyone and for this reason no one can be excluded from the whole. "God is in everything" means that all are in God and partake in the Good.

Gregory manages to avoid one of the difficulties of Origen's system. In Gregory's conception time is not merely the falling out of eternity or the environment for sinful and fallen men. Nor does Gregory concede that creation had pre-existence or is eternal. On the contrary, creation is realized for the first time only within the process of history. This gives a completely new significance to the conception of *apocatastasis*, the restoration, and estab-lishes a positive value for the course of human history. This principle is undermined, however, by Gregory's insistence that nothing created has any essential value and that God is the only worthy goal of our contemplation and striving. This premise leads Gregory to conclude that we will ultimately achieve a state of ob-livion. "The memory of that which existed after our original state of prosperity and of that which caused man to sink into evil will be effaced by that which will be effected when time runs out. Our memory of this condition will come to an end when it is com-pleted. Our final restoration in Jesus Christ will efface our memory of evil." However, without the memory of evil there will be no remembrance of our struggle against it and our victory over it.

Gregory openly or by implication proposes that creation will find its ultimate completeness only in God. Creatures will be oblivious of themselves and of everything which is not similar to God. All that men will see in one another will be God, and a single image of God will be in everyone. This doctrine contains elements of his-torical docetism and is connected with Gregory's underestimation of the human will. This is why Gregory denies the permanent existence of evil. Man's will cannot fail to yield when ultimate Good is revealed to it because even in opposition the will is weak. Furthermore, in Gregory's conception the will is determined by reason, which can be mistaken only when it is deceived and cannot persist once its error is revealed. According to Gregory, a clear vision of the truth will necessarily turn the will towards that truth.

Gregory's doctrine of the necessary movement of the free will is an attempt to unite the concepts of human freedom and necessity. This is the basic concern of his eschatology. The will is subordinate to the law of the basic goodness of all nature and the eschatological process is defined as the gradual elimination of the consequences of evil. This is the significance of the fire of purification. Gregory's doctrine shows the influence of the traditions of the school of Alexandria, and it is very different from the teaching of Basil the Great. It should be noted that certain features of Origenism are also present in the system of Gregory the Theologian, who accepts the idea of baptism through the purifying fire but does not support the doctrine of the general restoration.

Gregory's Doctrine of Apocatastasis and Later Church Theologians

The contemporaries of Gregory of Nyssa did not respond to his eschatology. It was first evaluated by Barsanuphius, who died about 550. He considered that Gregory was an uncritical disciple of Origen. Gregory's theology was later examined by Maximus the Confessor, who interpreted his doctrine of the universal restoration as the turn of every soul to the contemplation of God, which is the realization of the "totality of the faculties of the soul." "It is fitting that just as all nature will, at the appointed time, be made incorruptible through the resurrection of the flesh, so also will the damaged faculties of the soul efface the flawed images contained within it in the course of the ages. The soul will reach the boundary of the ages without having found peace, and it will finally come to God, Who is without limit. Thus it will recognize the Good but not yet participate in it. It will return to itself all of its faculties and it will be restored to its original state. It will then become clear that the Creator is not the author of sin." Maximus distinguished between ἐπίγνωσις, the knowledge of Divine truth, and μέθεξις, participation in the Divinity, which requires a definite movement of the will. Gregory's conception differs from this because Gregory makes no distinction between the consciousness of Good and the inclination of the will towards it.

Maximus' interpretation did not satisfy his contemporaries. Several decades later Patriarch Herman suggested that the elements of Origenism in Gregory's theology were interpolations. Although his theory is unacceptable because of the organic integrity of Gregory's system, his views were seconded by Patriarch Photius and are representative of the way Gregory was understood in the eighth and ninth centuries. The reticence of Justinian in his epistle on Gregory to Mennas, Patriarch of Con - stantinople, as well as the silence of the fathers of the Fifth Ecumenical Council, can be explained by the circumstances in which they were writing. They were primarily concerned with refuting those Origenist doctrines which stemmed from Origen's premises of the pre-existence of souls and the originally pure spiritual nature of all creatures, which were rejected by Gregory. It is with this in mind that the fathers of the council pronounced their anathema on "those who accept the pre-existence of the soul and the *apocatastasis* that is connected with it." Because of Gregory's generally accepted authority and sanctity, the sixth century opponents of Origenism were disposed to remain silent about those of his views which were, if not coincident with, at least reminiscent of the "impious, impure, and criminal teachings of Origen." However, Gregory's Origenism was not entirely with - out effect on his authority, and he was read and cited less frequently than the other "chosen fathers."

CHAPTER SEVEN

ST. EUSTATHIUS OF ANTIOCH

I
LIFE

Little is known about the life of Eustathius. According to Jerome he was a native of the town of Side in Pamphylia. Neither the year of his birth nor the year in which he was consecrated bishop is known. For this reason it is difficult to make any conclusion about his age. By about 319/320 Eustathius was serving as bishop of Beroea in Syria. It was during these years that, according to Theodoret, he received a letter from Alexander of Alexandria containing an epistle to Alexander of Solun against Arius. Eustathius was elevated to the see of Antioch immediately before the convocation of the Council of Nicaea. The Arian con - troversy had already broken out and Eustathius was drawn into the struggle. It later became apparent that not everyone had supported his appointment to the Antiochene see.

At the Nicene Council Eustathius was one of the principle defenders of "consubstantiality," and this explains the hostility he was later shown by the anti-Nicene faction. In Antioch he carried on an intense struggle with the Arians and their sym - pathizers. To a certain extent this struggle was literary. The dog - matic works of Eustathius were highly regarded and Athanasius called him a "confessor." However, his enemies continued to intrigue against him and he was soon charged with Sabellianism. In 330 a fairly large council gathered in Antioch, which was presided by Eusebius of Nicodemia and Theognis of Nicaea, both of whom had just returned from exile. At this council Eustathius was deposed. Sozomen has written that "this was because of his defense of the Nicene Creed," but it is difficult to establish with certainty the pretext for his deposition. Eustathius was banished "to the western limits of the state," and he set off in the company of many other clerics. The exact location of his exile is not precisely known but it is thought that it was Trajanopolis in Thrace. In 337 the banished defenders of the Nicene dogma were allowed to return but by that time Eustathius had already died.

II
WORKS

Eustathius was a prolific writer but only one of his many works has survived in its entirety. This is the long exegetical work *On the Witch of Endor, Against Origen.* Only fragments of his other writings have been preserved, and in many cases their authenticity is doubtful. Theodoret refers to a commentary written by Eustathius on the controversial text of *Proverbs* 8: 22, and quotes sections from its introduction. Fifteen other excerpts from this commentary have survived in the works of different writers. Fragments of a commentary on the *Psalms* have also come down to us. Eustathius was the author of a long denunciation against the Arians which was composed of no less than eight books, but of these only several excerpts have survived in the works of Facundus and in the library of Photius. Apparently a great part of this work was exegetical in character.

Jerome mentions another book *De anima* [*On the Soul*], from which eleven fragments have been preserved in the works of other writers. Apparently it was written in opposition to Arius. Jerome also refers to a "great number of letters" but these have not survived. A recently published homily on the resurrection of Lazarus is probably not the work of Eustathius. The remainder of the works usually ascribed to Eustathius do not in fact belong to him.

It seems that Eustathius' literary works were primarily intended as polemics against the Arians. He was well suited for this type of activity because his command of Scripture was augmented by his thorough knowledge of secular philosophy.

III
THOUGHT

ANTIOCHENE EXEGESIS

As an exegete Eustathius was a resolute opponent of the allegorical method of interpretation. He always based his commentary on the "letter of the narrative." He made great use of Biblical parallels, and he demonstrated that the speech of the Witch of Endor is composed of earlier prophecies about Saul. His analysis of this text is detailed and perceptive. Eustathius' remarks on Origen are ironic: instead of developing the image of the long-suffering Job as a model of patience, "he is shown spending his time like any other old man, cheerfully thinking about the names of his daughters."

CHRISTOLOGICAL THOUGHT

The only other aspect of the theology of Eustathius which can be evaluated is his Christology. No definite information about his doctrine of the Trinity has survived. Eustathius always stresses the complete humanity of Christ. Christ has two natures. By His Divine nature Christ is consubstantial with the Father and, although He is an "individual person," He abides immutably with the Father. He is the Divine Word and Wisdom and through Him everything is created. He is the "most divine Son of the living God, Who is generated from the uncreated essence of the Father, and He is the true Image of the Father." In opposition to the Docetists Eustathius emphasizes the reality of the Incar - nation, and to oppose the Arians he insists that Christ has a human soul. "The intellectual soul of Jesus is consubstantial with the souls of men, just as His flesh, which comes from Mary, is consubstantial with our human flesh." He usually stresses the human nature of the Incarnate Word by referring to Him as the "man Christ" or the "man of Christ." The man Christ is the "image of the Son," the temple of the Divine Wisdom and Word, and His "human abode and dwelling-place." God the Word "bears" upon Himself His own humanity, which "without interruption abides in Him." At Christ's resurrection His humanity is "elevated and glorified." This is an "acquired glory" which the "God-bearing man of Christ" previously did not have. Apparently the emphasis of Eustathius' soteriology is on the moral significance of Christ. In one fragment he refers to the Savior as the "source of the most beautiful path of righteousness."

In all of these respects Eustathius is close to the later "Antio - chene" theologians, and especially to Diodore of Tarsus. The obscurity of his language was noted even by his contemporaries. However, at the Third Ecumenical Council (Ephesus, 431) the authority of Eustathius was used to oppose the doctrines of the Nestorians, and this by itself invalidates any attempt to ascribe to him the extreme views of the Antiochene dyophysites.

CHAPTER EIGHT

DIDYMUS THE BLIND

I
LIFE

Didymus lived a very long life and died at the age of 83 or 85. The approximate dates of his birth and death are 313 and 398/399. He lost his sight in childhood but this did not prevent him from completing the usual course of studies with such dis- tinction that he was entrusted with the directorate of the school at Alexandria, probably by Athanasius, at a very young age. The remainder of his life was calm and untroubled, and the Arian controversy left him untouched. He lived not in Alexandria itself but in a small town outside the city where he was able to devote himself to ascetic discipline in solitude. He was predisposed to contemplation and meditation by his physical blindness.

Didymus spent a great deal of time with the Egyptian hermits and he had many disciples among them, including Palladius, the author of the *Lausiac History*, Jerome, Rufinus of Aquileia, and Evagrius. Asceticism and theology are closely united in Didymus, and in his theological works his reasoning frequently overflows into prayer. An intense feeling of belonging to the Church and membership in a larger community add an element of personal involvement to his theology. Even from theologians he demands good works, inner concentration, and piety. The life of Didymus passed without interruption in ascetic exercise and scholarly labor. Students came to him from everywhere, especially from the West.

Didymus is significant for his erudition, not for his independent thought. He did not develop his great knowledge into a spec- ulative synthesis, but expressed it in the form of a confession of faith. We know little about his activity as a teacher, but apparently his method was primarily based on exegesis. In his theology he is close to Origen, with whom he shares many points of view. Didymus' doctrine of the Trinity, however, is free of the extremity and vagueness of Origen's teaching, as was admitted even by Jerome.

The Trinitarian theology of Didymus was developed under the influence of the Cappadocians, especially Gregory the Theo- logian. Besides this, Didymus was familiar with the writings of Athanasius, and apparently also those of Cyril of Jerusalem,

Tertullian, and Irenaeus. He was well informed about heretical doctrines and in general his contemporaries were struck by his great erudition and his memory. His knowledge of the secular sciences was broad if not detailed, and he made frequent re - ferences to classical poets. Apparently Didymus had no particular interest in philosophy, and he did not concern himself with problems of metaphysics. For him, as for Origen, philosophy is no more than a preliminary study. Since Didymus considered that the abuse of philosophy was the root of all heresy, it is unlikely that he devoted much time to studying the works of philos - ophers. The elements of philosophy which are contained in his system were probably adapted through theology. He had a high opinion only of Plato, but his attitude toward Neoplatonism was cautious and reserved. In general Didymus as a scholar is a typical representative of the school of Alexandria.

Didymus died in the last years of the fourth century as peacefully as he had lived. It is only later that he became a subject of controversy and was suspected of unorthodox views and Origenism. The first to raise this charge was Jerome, although he excluded Didymus' Trinitarian doctrine from his condemnation and always maintained great respect for Didymus as an exegete. At that time the authority of Didymus remained unshaken, even in the West. The theology of Ambrose is drawn almost directly from Didymus, who also exerted a significant influence on Cyril of Alexandria and on the Trinitarian doctrine of Augustine. The question of Didymus' orthodoxy became a point of contention only in the sixth century during the Origenist controversy. At the Fifth Ecumenical Council (Constantinople, 553) an anathema was pronounced on his eschatology. It is unclear whether this ana - thema extended to Didymus himself, but in any event his name was discredited. As a result of this his literary remains disap - peared almost completely and only fragments and excerpts have survived in various later collections. The excavations at Tura in 1941 were thought to have produced some of his works but it is still uncertain whether these are authentic.

II
WORKS

Didymus was a prolific writer. The only one of his books which has come down to us complete and in its original form is his long composition *On the Trinity*. A single manuscript of this work, not in very good condition, was discovered only in 1759. It was probably composed in his old age in the period shortly before the Second Ecumenical Council (Constantinople, 381). This book

226 Eastern Fathers of the Fourth Century

should be considered in conjunction with a treatise *On the Holy Spirit*, which has survived only in a Latin translation by Jerome. In spite of its general reliability this translation does not allow us to make definite conclusions about Didymus' terminology. It was written before 381, and until the eighteenth century it was the only known work of Didymus. The fourth and fifth books on the Holy Spirit, which have been attributed to Basil, can probably be ascribed to Didymus, as can the *Homily against Arius and Sabellius* which has survived under the name of Gregory of Nyssa.

The references and citations of ancient authors allow us to reconstruct a partial list of the many compositions of Didymus which have been lost: *On Dogmas*; *On the Death of Young Children*; *Against the Arians*; another book known as the *First Word*; and others. Many of the fragments which have survived cannot be precisely classified. Of particular importance is Did - ymus' commentary to Origen's *On First Principles*. According to Jerome Didymus here tried to provide an orthodox interpretation for Origen's doctrine of the Trinity but he indiscriminately ac - cepted certain heretical features of Origenist theology, especially concerning the fall of the angels, the fall of souls, the resur - rection, the world, and the universal restoration. Rufinus made use of Didymus' commentary in his translation of *On First Principles*.

From the exegetical works of Didymus only fragments have been preserved in various later collections. It is not always possible to positively identify these because the sign "Δι" can refer not only to Didymus, but also to Diodore or Dionysius. According to Palladius Didymus was the author of an exegetical work on both the Old and New Testaments. This is apparently true because we have fragments of Didymus' commentary on *Genesis*, *Exodus*, the *Book of Kings*, *Isaiah*, *Jeremiah*, *Hosea*, *Zechariah*, *Psalms*, *Proverbs*, *Job*, *Ecclesiastes*, the *Song of Songs*, and *Daniel*. From the New Testament Didymus wrote on the Gospels of *Matthew* and *John*, and from the letters of Paul he commented on *Romans*, both *Corinthians*, and *Hebrews*. Jerome made great use of Didymus' exegesis himself and com - pared him to Plato, Aristotle, Cicero and Origen as an exemplary commentator.

III
THOUGHT

EXEGETICAL THOUGHT

Didymus is primarily an exegete. He naturally expresses himself in Biblical images and locutions and his system is basically a system of Biblical truths. For him the Bible is a Divine and spiritual book, a book which has been "anointed by God." He dis - tinguishes the Old and New Testaments only as two different aspects "in our reflection." The Old Testament is a temporary dwelling-place and the foreshadow of the truth which prepares us for the complete revelation of the Gospels. However, those who spoke in shadows were not deprived of knowledge of the truth and they themselves were its symbols. This is especially true of the Psalmist and the Prophet Isaiah. For this reason Didymus' method of commentary is always allegorical and he agrees with Origen in seeing the task of the exegete as the penetration and revelation of the higher spiritual truth contained in the literal images of Scripture. It is a path of allegory and ascent ἀναγωγή. In this respect Didymus always remained a true disciple of Origen but he was much more attentive to the literal meaning of Scripture, particularly in the New Testament. He frequently provides philological analyses, especially in the case of variant readings.

TRINITARIAN THOUGHT

The theological writings of Didymus are primarily devoted to the Trinity. This can be explained not only by the historical cir - cumstances in which Didymus was working but also by his personal experience. In his opinion it is only an orthodox con - fession of the Trinity that makes a man a true Christian. The truth of the Trinity is not revealed in the Old Testament but merely indicated in mysterious ways. Possibly only in *Psalm* 109 is it expressed clearly and openly. This is the main imperfection of the Old Testament in comparison with the New.

The Transcendence of God

Didymus' doctrine of God is based on Origen's transcen - dentalism. God is higher than everything and is inaccessible even to the gaze of the seraphim. We can speak about Him only in images or through negation. Whenever anything is said in relation to the essence or nature of God it is necessary to emphasize that His essence is superior to essence. In defining the Divinity by negation Didymus frequently uses the "without quantity." Cyril of Alexandria is the only other theologian who is known to have used this expression. The intellect can only be amazed before God and knowledge of Him is possible only through the revelation of Scripture. However, Didymus does not separate God from creation. The Divinity is continually active in our world and in the all-penetrating providence of God Didymus sees a justification for man's prayers about earthly things.

Didymus' Imprecision in Use of Terminology

The terminology Didymus uses in his examination of the Trinity reflects the influence of the Cappadocians, and he speaks clearly about three hypostases and one essence. However, his writing still maintains traces of the former identification of the concepts οὐσία and ὑπόστασις. This is especially evident in his use of the Nicene formula "from the essence of the Father." At the same time he frequently refers to the generation of the Word "from the hypostasis of the Father," by which he indicates that the gen - eration of the Son is a hypostatic property of the Father. It seems that Didymus uses the concept of hypostasis to emphasize the independent reality of the three persons. It also appears that he follows the Cappadocians in identifying ὑπόστασις and ἰδιότης, but this is less clear. He does not use the term πρόσωπον. Thus, in spite of the influence of the Cappadocians, the language of Didymus is not entirely free from the obscurity and indefiniteness of earlier theological usage. On the whole Didymus does not strive for precision in his formulations. This is a general feature of the school of Alexandria.

The Unity of Persons

The unity of the three persons of the Trinity is forcefully expressed by Didymus in many different definitions. He refers to one Kingdom, one Power, one Dominion, one Will, and one Desire. He stresses the unity of Divine activity, and from this he arrives at the conclusion of the consubstantiality of the Divinity. This is a common feature of the fathers of the fourth century. All of his definitions are encompassed in his conception of a single Divinity which is identical to Itself. Didymus develops the idea of the consubstantiality of the hypostases among themselves and also of the Trinity as a whole. From ὁμοούσιος he forms the word ὁμοουσιότης. Consubstantiality for him means identity of essence and thus for ὁμοούσιος he frequently substitutes ταυτοούσιος. In order to oppose the teachings of the Arians Didymus makes clear the equal dignity and power of the hypostases of the Trinity. For this reason he rejects as misleading the formula "through the Son" on the grounds that it gives an impression of inequality within the Trinity. Instead of this, the names of the hypostases should be united with the conjunction "and." In this connection Didymus constantly insists on the "dominion" of both the Son and the Spirit.

The Hypostatic Properties of the Son and Spirit

Didymus was influenced by Gregory the Theologian, who was the closest to him of the Cappadocians, and he defines the hy - postatic properties of the Son and the Spirit as "generation and procession." The distinction of these modes is inaccessible even to the angels, and Didymus stresses that Divine generation is incommensurate with the generation of creatures. The Father is the single source or root of the Divinity. Didymus has no ex - pression which is analogous to the phrase "through the Son" used by Gregory of Nyssa. Instead, he speaks about the pro - cession of the Spirit from the immortal source of the Father, and in this way he avoids any suggestion of inequality among the hypostases. Didymus considers it vitally important to stress the perfect equality of the persons of the Trinity.

The Consubstantiality of the Son

In defending his doctrine from heretical attacks Didymus attributes the following words to the lips of the Word: "The Father is God, and I am also, for I am His true and beloved Only-Begotten Son. The Father is the Lord and I am also. I am the Lord of everything, the heir of the living Father, and the master of the inheritance, for I rule that which is Mine both as the Creator and as the true Son. I became the heir through the Incarnation. The Father is the Creator and I am also. For I have said to you: 'He is the Emperor and He has arranged a wedding for his Son the Emperor.' The Father is unchanging and I am also. It has been said of Me: 'You abide in the ages and Your years will never pass away.' The Father is impassive and I am also and I give par - ticipation in this impassivity to those who are Mine. The Father is eternal and I am also, for there was never a time when the Father did not possess His name, the personal radiation of His glory, the image of His hypostasis, and the image of His Divinity, and that is

I. The Father is Life, Light, Goodness, Strength, Truth, and Wisdom, and everything that is worthy of God. I am also the Savior,
the sun which shines on righteous men and sinners and which
does not return evil for evil. The Father loves men and I love
them. I have given Myself for you, have accepted the outer form
of a slave, and from you I have endured ridicule and humiliation
and the Cross." A stronger testimony to the consubstantiality of
the Son can hardly be imagined.

The Trinitarian theology of Didymus is completely free of Origenist heresies. He is close to the doctrines of the Cappadocians, but their similarities are not restricted to external
details of theology alone. The immediacy and vividness of
Didymus' own contemplation are evident in his writings on the
Trinity, which are frequently developed with the intensity of
prayer.

CHRISTOLOGICAL THOUGHT

The most striking feature of Didymus' Christology is his insistence on the reality and completeness of the human nature of
the Savior. This also can be explained by historical circumstances, since at this time Didymus was involved in polemics with
the Manichaean Docetists and with the Apollinarians. He was also
trying to refute the Arian denial of the completeness of the
human soul in Christ. At the same time Didymus stresses the
absolute indivisibility of these two natures, which were united
forever when the Word assumed flesh or, more exactly, when He
became man. Didymus does not examine the way in which the
two natures are united, but he makes clear that within this union
they remain unblurred and unchanged. For some reason he
avoids the words μίξισ, κρᾶσις and συνάφεια and . Instead, he
restricts himself to the indefinite term "a single Christ," which
indicates the two natures, divine and human, in Him Who is one
and the same. For this reason there is a single worship of Christ,
Who has two natures. In connection with this Didymus always
refers to the Virgin Mary as the Bearer of God (apparently the
term *Theotokos* had already been used by Origen and Pierius of
Alexandria), and he also stresses her continuing virginity (Athanasius had expressed this with ἀεὶ παρθενος]. The second,
human generation of the Word from the Virgin, is a mystery which
in the opinion of Didymus can only be compared to His eternal
generation from the Father.

Didymus most frequently refers to Christ as the Savior. He
emphasizes that the primary significance of our salvation is our
liberation from sin and our victory over the devil and the power of

death. This was apparently a feature of Origen's system. Didymus also opposes the disobedience of Adam to the obedience of the Second Adam, an obedience which extended even to the sac - rificial death on the cross, which he considers vital to our redemption. The first gift of salvation is victory over death and eternal life. Didymus does not deal with deification but speaks only about the return or the restoration of the image and the likeness. He also focuses on the ransom.

DIDYMUS AND THE APOCATASTASIS

Didymus' doctrine of *apocatastasis*, if it was in fact a part of his teaching, remains unclear. He speaks about a "universal sal - vation," but this by itself is inconclusive. He seems to have hes - itated on the problem of the salvation of fallen angels and to have limited the redemption achieved through Christ's assumption of the flesh and full humanity to mankind. The fragmentary nature of the surviving documents does not allow us to make definite con - clusions, but most likely Jerome was right when he accused Didymus of confessing the ultimate restoration of the devil. Ap - parently Didymus also accepts the pre-existence of souls and he sees the afterlife as a process of purification. He insists that everything which has a source or a beginning is mutable and must have an end, and from this he concludes that the material world will ultimately be destroyed. He rejects metempsychosis and metasomatism, and his teaching on resurrected bodies as heavenly bodies is clear. Didymus suggests that in the future world there will be no evil men, not because their essence will be destroyed but because evil "as a quality" will cease to exist. He understands the Day of the Lord as an internal illumination of the soul. All of these doctrines reveal the influence of Origen. It should also be noted that Didymus seems to have sensed that the last days were at hand and to have expected the coming of the Antichrist.

THE CHRISTIAN LIFE

Didymus places great emphasis on the necessity of disciplined effort and striving. It is not enough to be without sin. Virtue must be a constant habit and a condition. A man's life as a Christian begins with the sacrament of baptism, which cleanses him of sin and returns to him his freedom. After his rebirth through baptism a believer is free and without sin, and the path of good works is open before him. Didymus considers the highest virtue to be wisdom or gnostic knowledge. This knowledge is not abstract or intellectual but is expressed in virtue and in the discipline of the soul. Didymus sees an example of a true philosopher in Job, whose image in his interpretation takes on Stoic features. Wisdom can be acquired only by renouncing and mortifying the flesh. Didymus presents the life of the true Christian as a marriage with Christ, which was also a favorite image of the Egyptian ascetics. Sanctified souls participate in the Word to the degree that they are united with Christ in such intimacy that they can be spoken of as christs and gods. In this expression Didymus is more reminiscent of Methodius than of Origen. Didymus places high value on virginity but he makes clear that this path is not for everyone. He emphasizes that marriage was sanctified and dignified by the birth of Christ.

INCORPOREAL BEINGS

Didymus expresses his personal views on angels with particular vividness. Angels are incorporeal and "intellectual beings," but Didymus ascribes to them "heavenly bodies" which are similar to the bodies of righteous men who have achieved perfection. Angels are creatures which have been created for service. Didymus describes their participation in the fate of the visible world, which is the reason that men are justified in invoking them through prayer and in dedicating churches to them.

THE "TRUE" GNOSTICS

Didymus follows the example of Origen in opposing Gnostics, men for whom a higher knowledge is possible, to men who can never attain the truth, who do not comprehend the spiritual meaning of Scripture, and who are incapable of defending themselves against heretics by giving a clear confession of their faith. The philosophy possessed by true gnostics is Divine. When Didymus is compared with previous Alexandrians, it becomes evident that the distinctions he makes in this respect are moderate.

CHAPTER NINE

ST. AMPHILOCHIUS OF ICONIUM

I
LIFE

Amphilochius was closely connected with the great Cap-padocians and apparently was related to Gregory the Theologian. He was born between 339 and 345 in Caesarea in Cappadocia, where his father was a rhetorician. He studied with Libanius in Antioch and then went to Constantinople as a rhetorician and lawyer. About 370 he returned to his native land and for several years lived in the home of his parents, in spite of the fact that he was always attracted by the monastic way of life. At the end of 373 Amphilochius, against his will, was consecrated bishop of Iconium. His elevation was probably due to the influence of Basil the Great. Amphilochius was responsible for a very large area (he was the first metropolitan of the new province of Lycaonia) and he frequently relied on Basil for advice and help in his pastoral duties. He turned to him during his struggle with the Pneu-matomachi and received in answer Basil's tract *On the Holy Spirit*, which was intended for the instruction of the dissenters. He was also the recipient of Basil's *Canonical Rules*. Basil, for his part, had a high opinion of Amphilochius. Amphilochius began to study theology only after he became bishop. It is unlikely that he devoted much attention to problems of speculative theology because he was not interested in philosophy and he had no background in it. This is evident in all of his theological writing. His theology is simple, even to the point of naïveté, and it is always based on Biblical material.

In 381 Amphilochius traveled to Constantinople for the Ecu-menical Council, where he was recognized as the "witness of the faith" for Asia. He returned to Constantinople several times in the following years. This was a period of intense religious con-troversy and Amphilochius was forced to defend himself against the Arians, Apollinarians, and also the Messalians (or Euchites), in opposition to whom he summoned a council in Side. On the whole Amphilochius was a gifted administrator in both Church and civil affairs. It is possibly due to his influence that the govern-ment took such severe measures against the Encratists. During the last years of his life Amphilochius maintained close contact with the religious circle of Olympiada (Olympias) in Constantinople. Apparently he died shortly after 394 but the precise time of his death is unknown.

II
WORKS

Very few of Amphilochius' works have survived. Eight homilies have been preserved, including one celebrating the Feast of the Purification of the Lord [*In occursum Domini*], which is the oldest known sermon on this feast. His *Oration at Midpentecost* [*In mesopentecostem*] is also significant, for it is one of the earliest references to the feast of Midpentecost. It is connected with the liturgical work of the Cappadocians and their effort to organize the yearly cycle of Church services. The homiletic works of Amphilochius display his talent as a rhetorician. His style is expressive and striking and is reminiscent of Gregory the Theologian. In his commentaries on the Gospel Amphilochius strives for historical accuracy and his main goal is to bring the historical figure of Christ to life for his listeners. There is good reason for giving Amphilochius a prominent place in the history of homiletics and for seeing in him a predecessor of John Chrysostom, who was perhaps immediately influenced by him.

In addition to homiletic literature, an epistle written by Amphilochius to the council of Iconium of 376 has survived, as well as a didactic work, *Epistula iambica ad Seleucum*. From the other compositions of Amphilochius only twenty-two fragments in all have been preserved. Apparently he wrote many other works, including tracts against the Arians, on the Holy Spirit, and on the apocrypha (widely read in certain heretical sects). He also wrote a commentary on *Proverbs* 8: 22 and on a series of Christological texts. Recently a long fragment of a work against the Encratists was discovered.

III
THOUGHT

TRINITARIAN THOUGHT

Amphilochius was not an independent thinker. The content of his theological works was determined by his needs as a pastor and teacher in his struggle against heresy. This does not mean that his theology is lacking in originality. On the contrary, it is clearly inspired by a calm and sincere faith. Amphilochius' doctrine of the Trinity is similar to the teaching of Gregory the Theologian, and he defines the hypostatic properties of the Son and the Spirit as generation and procession. At the same time, he emphasizes the unity of the Trinity by designating the hypo - stases with the new term "mode of being," τρόποι τῆς ὑπάρξως. This expression had not been used by the Cappadocians in their theology. Amphilochius was the first to apply it in this sense, so that in his system the names of the Trinity indicated not essence, but relations or "modes of being." By this conception the three hypostases are defined in such a way that their equality is maintained. In this innovation theology acquired a valuable philological tool and by the beginning of the fifth century this term was generally accepted in theological usage.

INNOVATIVE CHRISTOLOGICAL TERMINOLOGY

Amphilochius also developed innovative terminology in his Christology, which is based on the concept of "two natures in one Person." From this Amphilochius concludes that Christ has a "double essence" and a double consubstantiality. He anticipated later theological usage by introducing the term "hypostasis" in his writing about Christ. He was clear in his insistence on the com - pleteness of the human nature in Christ, which led him to con - clude that Christ has two wills. Amphilochius stressed that the two natures are indivisible and yet unmerged in their union: "I speak about one Son from two natures, unblurred, unchanging, and indivisible." This is significant for his doctrine of salvation. He who suffers for mankind is a man and men are saved through this human suffering. Men are liberated from death not by an act of authority but by the compassionate suffering of a fellow man. At the same time the curse placed on mankind can be removed only by God, and for this reason Amphilochius sees the hypostatic focus of the person of the God-man in His Divine nature, which has been implanted within the temple of human nature.

CHAPTER TEN

ST. EPIPHANIUS OF CYPRUS

I
LIFE

Epiphanius was born in Palestine around 315. Exactly where he studied is unknown but from his works it is evident that he was an extremely well-read man. He knew five languages: Greek, Hebrew, Syriac, Coptic, and some Latin. Epiphanius was an as - cetic from his early youth. He was a close friend of Hilarion and visited the monasteries in the Egyptian desert. When he re - turned home, he founded a monastery near his native town of Eleutheropolis, which he directed for many years. He was a well-known figure far beyond the borders of Palestine, and in 367 he was elected bishop of Constantia (Salamis) in Cyprus. There he became renowned as an ascetic, thaumaturge, and defender of orthodoxy. From 370 he was involved in polemics with the Apol - linarians. Epiphanius developed a close friendship with Jerome on the basis of their common interest in ascetic discipline, and through Jerome he became involved in the Origenist con - troversy in Palestine.

In 394 Epiphanius made a pilgrimage to Jerusalem, where he came into conflict with John of Jerusalem on the subject of Ori - gen. Epiphanius' conduct throughout the course of their violent argument was defiant and provocative. He soon left Palestine, but the Origenist controversy had broken out in Egypt as well. Theophilus of Alexandria managed to convince Epiphanius that this quarrel with John Chrysostom was essentially a struggle against Origenism. Epiphanius then set out for Constantinople, where he regarded Chrysostom with extreme suspicion and refused to have anything to do with him. However, it seems that Epiphanius was eventually enlightened as to the true state of affairs. He decided to return home, and his parting words are reported as: "I leave you your capital, your court, and your hypocrisy." He died on the voyage home in 403.

II
WORKS

Epiphanius displayed a zealous interest in the detection and denunciation of heresy. He considered that the uncovering of false teachings was his main task and calling in life, and his chief compositions are dedicated to the dissection of heretical doctrines. His most important work is the *Panarion* [*Medicine Chest*; usually cited as *Haereses*] which was compiled in 375-377. This survey of all known heresies is not so much an examination as a vituperation. Epiphanius collected everything concerning heresy contained in the previous denunciatory literature of Justin, Hippolytus, and especially Irenaeus, and he supplemented this with material drawn from his personal experience. Unfortunately he presented his own material carelessly and without discrimination, and all too frequently he allowed himself to be guided by his extreme suspiciousness. Furthermore, Epiphanius had a poor knowledge of Greek philosophy and confused the Pythagoreans with the Peripatetics, and Zeno of Elea with Zeno the Stoic. He was overly credulous of malicious rumors and in his narrow dogmatism he was instantly on the alert at the faintest hint of any difference of opinion, even on minor questions. He was distrustful of the major theologians of the fourth century, and he was especially hostile to the Alexandrians. Epiphanius regarded Origen with total horror and absolute disgust, and considered that his teachings were not merely false but "the worst of all heresies."

A large part of Epiphanius' writing is based on his memory and on rumor. This explains his constant inaccuracy, particularly in chronology. His denunciations are the weakest feature of his work, largely because he had absolutely no sense of history. In the most ancient times there was neither heresy, nor paganism, nor Judaism, and from this Epiphanius concludes that "the faith of the first men was similar to Christianity and was the same as that which was revealed later." He ascribes the knowledge of the Trinity to Adam and all the just men of the Old Testament until Adam, and he begins his enumeration of Christian heresies even before the Flood, transforming all dishonest men into heretics. The exact number of heresies must be eighty because this is what has been revealed in the *Song of Songs* : "I have sixty princesses and eighty concubines and young women past counting (6: 8)." The first heresy was barbarianism and the coarsening of morals which occurred before the Flood. The second heresy was Scythianism, which lasted until the building of the Tower of Babel. This was followed by Hellenism, with its philosophical sects, and then Judaism. Epiphanius' exposition of the theoretical viewpoints of different heresies is limited, and his attention is mainly devoted to their moral aspects. In his biased presentation the lives led by heretics are dismal. The *Panarion* is important as a collection of facts relating to heresies, but the material Epiphanius has provided must be used with great caution.

Epiphanius had completed an earlier volume in 374, the *Ancoratus* [ἀγκυρωτός]. The title expresses the conception of the true faith as a reliable anchor for man in his voyage through the sea of life, which is filled with the temptations and deceits of demons and heretics. The rules of faith contained in it are primarily directed against contemporary false doctrines, but the views of ancient heretics are included as well. Epiphanius is primarily concerned with setting forth the dogma of the Trinity and emphasizing the divinity of the Holy Spirit. In conclusion he cites two expositions or creeds of faith, one of which, designated as the "creed which is taught in the Church in the holy city" (that is, Jerusalem), coincides almost literally with the creed of Constantinople. The history of this creed is still unclear.

Epiphanius' Biblical commentary was written during the last years of his life. His book *On Weights and Measures* [*De mensuris et ponderibus*] (of the ancient Hebrews) is intended as an introduction to the study of the Bible. Epiphanius discusses the canon of the Old Testament, its various translations, the geography of Palestine, and deals with "measures and weights" in passing. Only part of the book has been preserved in the original Greek, and the rest is known in a Syriac translation. Another book, an allegorical interpretation titled *On the Twelve Precious Stones* [*De XII gemmis*], treats the twelve precious stones adorning the breastplate of the High Priest of the Old Testament. It was dedicated to Diodore of Tyre, not Diodore of Tarsus. The Greek text is shorter than a Latin translation which has survived. It is possible that Epiphanius wrote on other Biblical subjects but these writings, if they existed, have not come down to us. These works have a certain interest for the archaeologist and the Biblical scholar. As an exegete Epiphanius was not a defender of literal interpretation but was more inclined to symbolism and allegory in his explanation of the Old Testament texts.

Certain works which have been ascribed to Epiphanius on the veneration of icons deserve particular attention. They were frequently cited by iconoclasts, especially at the council of 754, but the defenders of the veneration of icons, the iconodules, considered them spurious. This was also the judgment of the fathers of the Seventh Ecumenical Council (Nicaea, 787), who wrote that "we reject these writings, but we consider the holy father Epiphanius a teacher of the universal church." The patriarch Nicephorus wrote specifically against these books and we can judge them for ourselves on the basis of the few fragments which are contained in his denunciations. It is almost certain that they do not belong to Epiphanius, despite the conclusions of some modern scholars. Apparently an episode which is presented as if narrated by Epiphanius himself in a letter to John of Jerusalem is a later addition. This has long been known in Jerome's translation, and in Nicephorus we have the Greek text. According to the narration, in a Church in a city in Palestine Epiphanius saw a picture of a man, either Christ or a saint, on a curtain. In irritation he tore the curtain to pieces and gave it to be used as shrouds for the poor. In return he presented the church with an unadorned cloth.

It is not without reason that these writings against the veneration of icons have been incorrectly attributed to Epiphanius. He was not a supporter of iconolatry or of the use of icons in general. In his *Testament* he commands that icons "not be brought" into churches or burial vaults. Commemoration should be realized in the heart, and there should be no need for its reinforcement by visual images. Epiphanius was not alone in this opinion. It was shared by Eusebius of Caesarea, who also denied the admissibility and the possibility of the representation of Christ, thus rejecting both the historic and graphic aspects of iconography. The writings of Epiphanius which can be found in his genuine works contain an implicit rejection of any form of sacred representation. Images are always anthropomorphic and effect the senses, and for this reason they distract the mind from God and turn it to creation. Epiphanius denounced the Gnostics for their use of images, which were all the more reprehensible because they depicted Christ as the Gnostics actually conceived Him, as as simple man.

III
THOUGHT

Epiphanius was more of a symbolist than a realist, and his rejection of visual images was in keeping with his psychological orientation. This was, of course, poor theology, but such a "theological opinion" does not discredit Epiphanius' authority in the Church. To a certain extent this way of thinking is an understandable result of the historical conditions of the fourth century, which was a period of struggle against paganism and active defense of the "consubstantiality" of the Word. Given these circumstances, the transition from symbolism to realism in iconography might well have seemed to be heretical.

CHAPTER ELEVEN

ST. JOHN CHRYSOSTOM

I
LIFE

Chrysostom's life was neither calm nor easy. He was an ascetic and a martyr. It was not in the desert that his feats were accomplished but in the chaos of the world, in the pulpit of the preacher, and on the episcopal throne. His martyrdom was bloodless. He was tormented not by external enemies but by his brothers who proved false to him, and he ended his life in chains, in exile, under interdiction, and persecuted by Christians for his faith in Christ and the Gospel, which he preached as a revelation and the law of life.

Chrysostom was primarily an evangelist and a preacher of the good news of the Gospel. He was also a teacher who had a lively interest in contemporary issues, and the true significance of his teaching can be fully understood only in its historical context. He condemned the Christians of the fourth century who claimed to be living according to the precepts of the Gospel and warned them that they had relaxed their efforts prematurely. This prophet of universal love frequently spoke harshly and severely because it seemed to him that he was preaching and bearing witness before men who were dead. For him the injustice and the absence of love in the Christian world assumed catastrophic, almost apocalyptic significance. "We have extinguished our fervor and the body of Christ has died." The light yoke of love seemed an unbearable burden for the indifferent world. This explains Chrysostom's ultimately bitter fate, for he was driven out for the sake of the truth which he preached. "For this the world will hate you."

Chrysostom was a native of Antioch, and he remained a typical Antiochene in his spiritual temperament and in his religious outlook. The exact year of his birth is unknown but it was probably sometime between 344 and 354. Chrysostom came from a wealthy and prominent Christian family. Both by birth and education he belonged to the intellectual Hellenistic circles of the society of his aristocratic gentility. Chrysostom did not renounce his cultural heritage even when he rejected the world and everything in it.

Chrysostom was a true Hellenist. He studied with the famous Libanius and received a broad and brilliant education. He was not a thinker or a philosopher, and in the classical sense he is best defined as an orator and a rhetorician. The classical rhetorician was a teacher, moralist, and preacher, and Chrysostom was just such a man. Chrysostom's Hellenism is most apparent in his language and style. As an orator and stylist, he can be compared with Demosthenes and even Xenophon and Plato, for the brilliance of the classical Athenians is revived in his writing. Even his contemporaries recognized him as an Atticist. It is incorrect to consider that his Hellenism is purely external or formal because it has penetrated all aspects of his style. It is true that Chrysostom was apparently never stirred by the philosophical problems of Hellenism and he was never forced to reconcile the Hellenist in himself with his Christianity. This, however, was characteristic of the intellectual outlook of the Antiochenes and of the "historical" culture of Asia Minor, which was always more "philological" than "philosophical."

Chrysostom always remained a Hellenist and this is especially evident in his moralism. In a sense moralism was the natural truth of the classical world. This explains and justifies the acceptance and transformation of Stoicism by Christian ethics, in which nat - ural truth is elevated to new heights through Divine grace. In Chrysostom the transformed elements of Stoicism are particularly apparent. He constantly tried to teach moral wisdom and nobility, and moral judgments and evaluations are present everywhere in his writing. However, he saw the full realization of natural truth only in the ideal that is revealed in the Gospel.

None of this implies that Chrysostom was not a mystic. "Mor - alism" does not exclude "mysticism." It is true, however, that his mysticism had a moral significance. It is a mysticism of con - science, of goodness, of good works and virtue. Ethical con - siderations are less clearly expressed in Chrysostom. He con - sidered beauty more as an ethical than an aesthetic phe - nomenon, and he saw beauty primarily in active goodness. For him the Gospel is most significant as a book about the beauty of virtue as revealed in the image of the God-man, and this de - termined the course of his own life. Chrysostom's moral character was formed very early in his youth. The example of his mother was reinforced and strengthened by the lessons of his devout mentors, including Meletius of Antioch, Diodore, and the ascetic Carteria.

Chrysostom was not satisfied by any secular vocation, and even before he was able to withdraw from the world he began to practice ascetic discipline in the home of his parents. Only after the death of his mother in 374 or 375 did it become possible for him to retire to a monastery not far from Antioch and became a friend of Theodore of Mopsuestia. He spent two years there, followed by two years in the desert. His novitiate was of short duration, however, and he returned to the world in order to continue his austerities amid the world. Chrysostom always con - sidered asceticism more as a spiritual orientation than as a specifically regulated form of daily life. And this state could be achieved primarily through renunciation, through internal free - dom and independence from the external circumstances and conditions of life in the world. In this sense Chrysostom remained an ascetic throughout his life.

Chrysostom returned to the world to preach the necessity of ascetic renunciation. It was not his intention to exhort men to make an external withdrawal from the world by leaving their cities. "I frequently prayed," Chrysostom wrote in these years, that the need for monasteries would pass away, and that I would be able to find even in cities such goodness and such order that no one would ever again have to flee to the desert." Chrysostom wanted to transform life in the cities and towns so that it would accord with the principles of the Gospel and with the spirit of "the higher philosophy." To this end he became a pastor and preacher.

Chrysostom was made deacon in 381 by Meletius of Antioch, and he was ordained priest by his successor Flavian in 386. Chrysostom discusses his new vocation in his famous six books *On the Priesthood* [*De sacerdotio*] (which actually deal with episcopal duties). The exact dates of these works are unknown but they were probably written before his ordination. Chrysostom takes the ideas of Gregory the Theologian as the point of de - parture for his own exposition, which has two main emphases. In the first place, he describes the highest goal of the holy calling as the performance of the sacraments. "Sacred service takes place on this earth but it also has a place among the heavenly powers." This is because the priesthood has been established by the Spirit of the Comforter Himself. How can it be that we remain on earth when we see the Lord Whose body is offered to us, and when we become incarnadined with His blood? The priest par - ticipates at the sacrificial table, which stands in the heavens. He is given the heavenly power of the keys which has not been received even by the angels.

In the second place, Chrysostom sees the priest as a teacher, mentor, preacher, and pastor of souls. He devotes most of his attention to the teaching responsibilities of the priesthood, and in this respect he places the priest even higher than the monk. There is more love in pastoral work than in monastic isolation, and the pastor's service to his neighbors is a service of active love. "The whole universe would be upset if we were to think that only monks need severity and discipline in their lives, while the rest of us can live freely," he writes.

As a priest and pastor Chrysostom himself was first of all a preacher. It is difficult to enumerate all of the themes with which he dealt. From among the homilies delivered in Antioch particular mention should be made of the *Homilies on the Statues* [*Homiliae 21 de statuis*] and also of a long series of exegetical homilies on *Matthew* and *John*, on the epistles to the *Corinthians*, *Galatians*, *Titus*, possibly *Ephesians* and *Romans*, and probably also on *Genesis*. The orations against the Jews and against the Anomoeans were written at this same time. Chrysostom never concerned himself with abstract themes. His homilies are lively and based on actual experience because they are intended for living people, and the presence of the audience and the preacher himself can be sensed in them. Chrysostom usually concludes his homilies with appeals to the wills of his listeners and with practical exhortations. His primary goal is to teach love but he also tries to encourage integrity and responsibility. Chrysostom spoke with authority, but this authority was based on the convictions of his faith. He emphasizes that personal transformation can be achieved through the strength of the spirit and even more through the strength of love. It was love which kept Chrysostom in the world with his flock.

In 398 Chrysostom was elevated to the see of Constantinople. The clergy, the court, and the laity were all united in summoning him for his recognized ability as a pastor and teacher. Chrysostom continued to preach in Constantinople, and Sozomen remarks that it was his habit to take a place among the congregation at the reader's ambo so that his listeners could sit closely around him. His sermons were more like conversations than speeches. During this period Chrysostom wrote commentaries on the *Acts of the Apostles*, the *Psalms*, and many of the epistles of Paul. A large number of his homilies were recorded by stenographers as they were being delivered, and these records preserve the liveliness of the spoken word. At this time Chrysostom saw his main task in the reformation of the morals of lay society. It was his impression that he was preaching to people for whom Christianity had become no more than a fashionable garment. "From among so many thousands," he said, "it is impossible to find more than one hundred who are truly saving their souls, and I am not even sure that there are that many."

Chrysostom was troubled by the very fact that there was such a large number of "Christians": "This is all the more fuel for the fire." He spoke with bitterness about their prosperity: "In matters of piety, freedom from oppression is the worst form of persecution.

It is worse than any other persecution. No one understands or senses this danger because safety gives birth to carelessness. It weakens the soul and lulls it to sleep, and the devil destroys sleeping men." The preacher's voice became harsh and severe because around himself he saw only chaff fit for the fire. Chrysostom was deeply concerned with the immorality of his society. He was troubled not only by debauchery, but even more by the tacit lowering of standards and ideals which he saw in the laity and in the clergy. Chrysostom fought with both words of denunciation and acts of love. "No one would remain a pagan if we were true Christians," he said. He spent a great deal of time in charitable work and organized hospitals and refuges for the homeless. He demanded practical activity from everyone and this caused dissatisfaction and opposition not only in Constantinople but in other dioceses as well.

The hostility against Chrysostom manifested itself on several occasions, and his altercation with the empress Eudoxia was only the final pretext for the ultimate outburst. Chrysostom had enemies everywhere, especially among the clergy and in particular among the wandering monks. He also had opponents in the wealthy society of the court. The shameful history of Chrysostom's deposition and condemnation at the "Synod of the Oak" is too complicated to be recounted here. Traitors were found even among the bishops, who were led by Theophilus of Alexandria, and others who were actively hostile included Acacius of Beroea, Severian of Gabala, and Antiochus of Ptolemais, all of whom at some time had been insulted by Chrysostom. The accusations against Chrysostom were many, and he was also charged with Origenism. He was deposed and his sentence was confirmed by the emperor. His exile was of short duration and at his return he was greeted by popular rejoicing. However, the hostility against him had not died down. The very fact that he had returned without obtaining a revocation of the synod's decree was used against him because, according to the fourth canon of the Antiochene council, this made him liable to be deprived of his rights, even if his sentence was unjust. Chrysostom recognized neither the legitimacy of the synod which condemned him (and in this he was not alone) nor the legitimacy of the Antiochene canon, and he demanded the convocation of a new council so that he could exonerate himself. The bishops condemned him for a second time. He carried on with the duties of his office but the unrest continued to grow. In June of 404 he was again exiled and sent first to Cucusus in Lower Armenia and then to Pityus, a wild area on the eastern end of the Black Sea. Chrysostom did not survive the hardships of his journey and died while traveling on September 14, 407.

The injustice of Chrysostom's condemnation soon became evident, and in 417 Atticus, bishop of Constantinople, read-mitted his name to the Church diptychs, claiming that this was the will of the people. Cyril of Alexandria protested violently: "If you include John among the bishops, why not include Judas among the apostles? And if there is a place for Judas, then where is Matthew?" By 419, however, Chrysostom was rehabilitated even in Alexandria. In 438 his remains were brought to Constantinople and interred in the Church of the Apostles. The sentence of the "Synod of the Oak" was revoked by the general testimony of the Church.

II
WORKS

The literary heritage of Chrysostom is enormous. It is difficult to determine its exact extent because with time Chrysostom's repu-tation became so great that the homilies and orations of other writers were ascribed to him. Some writings can be unques-tionably identified as the work of Chrysostom, and some writings clearly do not belong to him, but there are still many compositions which are doubtful, especially those which cannot be definitely attributed to another author.

The majority of Chrysostom's writings are sermons, homilies, and orations. Among these his exegetical works are of particular importance. The remainder are on a variety of different themes, but mention should be made of the homilies for feasts and saints' days, all of which were intended for oral delivery. Another cate-gory of Chrysostom's writings consists of exhortations and in-structions which were intended for private reading. Particularly significant are his compositions on ascetic themes and his books on the priesthood, which were written in his younger days. About 236 to 240 of his letters have been preserved, all of which date from the period of his second exile. They provide important material for an understanding of Chrysostom's personality and religious attitudes.

The problem of Chrysostom's liturgy is extremely complex. The oldest copy, which is contained in the eighth century Barberini euchologion, does not mention his name, but there is a ref-erence to his liturgy which dates from the sixth century. It is dif-ficult to determine exactly what should be ascribed to Chry-sostom from the later liturgy known by his name. In this respect comparison with the liturgical material contained in his homilies, especially the earliest, is helpful. In any event there is no doubt that he was deeply concerned with the regulation of the divine service, and particularly with the rite of the Eucharist.

Chrysostom's influence was enormous. He became the "universal teacher and prelate" in actuality even before he was distinguished by this title. He was called Chrysostom, "Golden Mouth," as early as the sixth century, and by the eighth century this epithet was generally accepted. Chrysostom's exegetical works in particular have been considered exemplary and authoritative. Almost all of the later Byzantine commentators, especially Theophylact of Bulgaria, were greatly influenced by them. The history of Chrysostom's influence is one of the brightest chapters in the history of Church literature and patristic tradition.

III
THOUGHT

CHRYSOSTOM AS TEACHER

Chrysostom was a gifted writer with a lively and authoritative style. He had the temperament of an orator, and this is the secret of his power of persuasion. He loved to preach: "I have commanded my soul to undertake the duties of a preacher and to fulfill the commandments for as long as I continue to have breath and God sees fit to extend my life, whether there is anyone to listen to me or not." Chrysostom understood pastoral work primarily as a service of teaching and persuading. A pastor is an authority, but his jurisdiction is realized through words which attempt to convince, and this is the basic difference between spiritual power and secular power. "The emperor forces; the priest convinces. One acts by command; the other by persuasion."

The Importance of Spiritual Freedom

A pastor must focus his attention on the free will of the individual. "We have been commanded to bring salvation to people by the strength of the word, by gentleness, and by persuasion," Chrysostom said. He saw the greatest meaning of the life of a Christian in freedom, which expresses itself in good works and ascetic discipline. The individual's freedom and self-motivation are constant themes in his homilies, for it is in free will that he sees man's "nobility" and the image of God which he has

been given. Chrysostom was a consistent voluntarist and con -
sidered morality a matter of will. He identified the source of sin as
the movement of the will, which was also the source of virtue. It
was his opinion that Christ "came not to destroy nature, but to
correct our wills." Each action of God's grace in man takes place
"in such a way that it brings no harm to our power over our -
selves." In other words, God Himself acts not through com -
pulsion, but through persuasion. "He comforts, advises, and
warns us away from possible evil but does not force us to do
anything." A pastor should follow the Divine example.

His Opposition to Any Form of Coercion

By temperament Chrysostom was a maximalist and on occasion
he could be harsh and severe. However, he was always an
opponent of force and coercion in any form, even in the fight
against heresy. He was against the use of civic measures and
political pressure in matters of faith and morality. "It has been
specifically forbidden for Christians to correct those who have
fallen into sin by force," he said. "We are not fighting to bring
death to the living but to bring the dead back to life, and in our
struggle we must be meek and humble . . . I persecute not by
deeds, but by words, and I want to cast out not heretics, but
heresy . . . I am accustomed to endure oppression, but not to
oppress, and to bear persecution, but not to persecute. Christ
was victorious in being crucified and not in crucifying others. He
did not strike out, but He accepted blows." Chrysostom endured
the condemnation of those who did not think as he did, and in
this respect his oration *On Imprecation and Anathema* is a typical
expression of his attitude. He saw the true power of Christianity in
meekness and endurance, not in force. It is himself with whom
each man should be severe, and not with others.

His Moral Ideals Drawn From Dogma

Chrysostom's sermons were mostly written on moral themes
but there is no reason to overemphasize this or to call him a
teacher of morality and not of faith. On the contrary, he frequently
dealt with doctrinal problems, especially in his early years in An -
tioch, and even more importantly, it was from his dogma that he
drew his moral ideals. This is clearly evident in his exegetical
homilies, and especially in his commentary on the epistles of
Paul. Chrysostom had several favorite dogmatic themes which he
continually returned to. In the first place, his teaching about the
Church is inseparably connected with his doctrine of redemption

as the sacrifice of Christ the High Priest, Who ascended to heaven through the Cross. From this he developed the teaching of the Church as a source of new being, not just as new life. Chrysostom also spoke frequently of the Eucharist as both a sacrament and a sacrifice, and for this reason he has been called the "teacher of the Eucharist."

Chrysostom never elaborated a system of theology, and there is no point in looking for dogmatic or theological formulations in his writings. His Christology and Mariology in particular are not en - tirely free from the ambiguity and one-sidedness which char - acterize the language of Antiochene theology. Chrysostom was a witness of the faith, and this explains why his works were so significant in ancient times, especially in the West. His writings are filled with the voice of Church tradition.

Chrysostom set himself a specific task. His activity was aimed not at overcoming unorthodox opinions, but at making people who professed themselves to be Christians understand that the truths of faith are the truths and commandments of life, and that these must be put into actual practice by the individual. At that time too many people had forgotten this. Chrysostom demanded that men live according to their beliefs, and he assumed that the truths of faith were known to his audience. There was no point in trying to go further if men's hearts were indifferent and if the seeds of faith had not yet been implanted in their souls. It is true that Chrysostom himself had no particular interest in speculative theology, but by no means was he exclusively a moralist without any interest in dogma. His own theological beliefs were primarily based on the writings of the apostle Paul, whose teaching cen - tered on Christ and salvation, not morality. Even Chrysostom's "evangelism" had a doctrinal significance because for him all life was connected with the image of Christ not only as a prophet but more importantly as the High Priest and the Lamb. This is related to his mystical attitude towards the sacraments.

It should be added that for Chrysostom it is only a pure life which testifies to pure faith. Moreover, it is only through a pure life that true faith is possible at all, for an impure life usually gives rise to false teaching. Faith is realized and fulfilled only in love, and without love it is impossible to attain faith, or contemplation, or knowledge of the mysteries. Without love, rational theology is no more than an endless labyrinth.

Chrysostom saw before him men who were struggling but who had not yet fully awakened, and he wanted to rouse them to spiritual live and love. In this sense he was an individualist. He had little feeling for worldly intercourse or society but always focused on individual persons, who for him were united only in the Church. This individualism is the reason for Chrysostom's sensitivity and perceptiveness. He never resorts to commonplaces or abstractions but is always concrete and graphic, teaching through examples and applying his material to specific instances. He uses few conventional rhetorical devices, surpassing in this respect even Gregory the Theologian. He never forgets that he is a spiritual pastor, not an orator, and that his goal is not to expound or develop a particular objective theme, but to touch men's hearts and to influence their wills and intellects. For this reason the logical and formal structure of his homilies is of secondary importance but they are held together by an internal integrity. Chrysostom's homilies are a unique dialogue with a silent interlocutor about whom the preacher occasional gives some information. They are never monologues and they are always directed at an audience.

On Poverty and Wealth

Chrysostom frequently spoke about poverty and wealth, themes which were set for him by life in the large, noisy city. For him, these and all other social themes had primarily a moral significance, and he dealt with them in relation to the rules of Christian behavior. He judged the life around him on the basis of its morality. Everywhere he saw injustice, cruelty, suffering, and misery, and he understood that this was caused by the spirit of greed and by social inequality. He warned against idle luxury and also against wealth as a source of temptation, since money threatens to corrupt the man who possesses it. Wealth by itself has no value but is only a theatrical mask which covers the true image of man. However, the wealthy man comes to value his riches. He begins to deceive himself and he becomes attached to something which is good in appearance only. In Chrysostom's opinion there is danger not only in wealth which has been ac-quired by dishonest means but in all forms of personal property. These are not harmful in themselves but they may stimulate the will to desire things which are perishable and transient. "The love for wealth is an unnatural passion," Chrysostom writes. "The de-sire for wealth is neither natural nor necessary. It is superfluous." This movement of the will is dangerous and riches are a dan-gerous burden. "Wealth is harmful for you not because it arms thieves against you, nor because it completely darkens your mind but because it makes you the captives of soulless pos-sessions and distracts you from the service of God."

The possession of wealth involves an unavoidable contra-diction. By the spirit of greed men are attached to material things, but God teaches us to despise things and to renounce them. "There is harm not only in trying to gain wealth but also in excessive concern with even the most necessary things," Chrysostom writes. "Christ has demonstrated what kind of harm can come from the passion for money but His commandment goes even beyond this. Not only does He order us to scorn wealth, but he forbids us to be concerned that the food we eat is the best we can possibly get: 'Do not worry your soul about what you eat'." This does not exhaust the subject. "It is not enough to despise wealth," Chrysostom writes, "but you must also feed the poor and, more importantly, you must follow Christ." Thus an-other contradiction is revealed: the worldly drive of greed and the desire for the accumulation and preservation of material goods is opposed to the command of the Gospels to "give all you have to the poor." Against this background we see with greater clarity the injustice of the social inequality in the world. In the face of poverty and misery, all wealth is an unjust and dead thing. It testifies to hard-heartedness and the absence of love.

It is from this point of view that Chrysostom disapproves of the magnificent decoration of churches. "A church is not a place in which to melt gold or forge silver," he writes. "It is a triumphant as-sembly of the angels. Therefore it is souls which we demand as an offering because it is for the sake of souls that God accepts our other offerings. It was not at a silver table and it was not from a golden vessel that Christ offered His blood to His disciples to drink but nevertheless everything there was precious and called forth reverence, for it was filled with the Spirit. Do you want to honor the body of Christ? Do not scorn to see Christ naked. What good does it do you if here you honor His silken coverlings while outside the Church you continue to tolerate the coldness and nakedness of others? What good does it do you if the altar of Christ is covered with golden vessels, while Christ Himself suffers hunger? You make a golden goblet but you offer no cooling water to go with it. Christ as a homeless pilgrim wanders and asks for shelter, but you, instead of accepting Him, adorn your floors, your walls, and the tops of your pillars, and you put silver har-nesses on your horses. But Christ remains bound in the dun-geon and you do not even want to look at Him."

It seemed to Chrysostom that each thing that one man puts aside is taken away from someone else who needs it, for there cannot be a man who is rich without another man being poor because of it. "The source and root of wealth must definitely be hidden in some act of injustice," he writes. Chrysostom did not consider that poverty as such was a virtue. Poverty attracted his attention as a form of need and suffering, and he considered that

Christ is present among the poor, since He comes to us in the image of a beggar and not in the guise of a wealthy man. Fur - thermore, when poverty is voluntarily chosen for the sake of God and accepted with joy, it can be a path to virtue. This is primarily because a man without possessions is freer than a wealthy man and has fewer attachments and worries. It is easier for him to live and to strive to perfect himself.

Chrysostom knew also that poverty could be a heavy burden not only in terms of external and material things, but internally, as a source of envy, spite, and despair. For this reason he tried to fight against poverty, but his attention was always occupied with its moral implications. In this respect he functioned as a spiritual pastor, not as a social reformer. Although it is true that he did have an ideal vision of society, this ideal was primarily moral. It was the ideal of equality because inequality makes true love im - possible.

The basic premise of Chrysostom's thought is that strictly speaking there can be no such thing as "personal property" because everything belongs to God and to Him only. All things are given by Him as a gift in the form of a loan. Everything is God's, and all that man can claim as truly his own are his good works. Everything God gives is intended for common ownership. "If the good things we enjoy belong to the Master of all of us, then they all belong equally to our fellow slaves. That which be - longs to the Master belongs to everyone in common. Do we not see a similar arrangement in great houses?"

"The possessions of the Emperor, the city, the squares, and the streets, belong to all men, and we all use them in an equal degree. Look at the economy that God has arranged. He has created some things that are for everyone, including the air, sun, water, earth, heaven, sea, light, and stars, and He has divided them equally among all men, as if they were brothers. This, if nothing else, should shame the human race. The Emperor has made other things common to all, including the baths, cities, squares, and streets. There is not the slightest disagreement over this common property but everything is accomplished peacefully. If someone tries to take something and claim it as his own personal possession, then quarrels arise. It is as if the very forces of natures were complaining, and as if at that time when God was gathering them from everywhere they were trying with all their might to separate among themselves, to isolate them - selves from each other, and to distinguish their own individual property by coldly saying that 'this is yours but that is mine'. If this were true, quarrels and bitterness would arise, but where there is nothing of this sort neither quarrels nor disagreements occur. In this way we see that for us as well a common and not an individual ownership of things has been ordained, and that this is according to nature itself. Is not the reason that no one ever goes to court about the ownership of a public square the fact that this square belongs to all?"

It seems to Chrysostom that in this respect even the animals are better than men. "They hold everything in common, the earth, and springs, and pastures, and mountains, and forests, and not one of them has more than the others. But you, O man, the most gentle of animals, have become more fierce than the beasts. In a single one of your houses you store up enough to feed thousands and even many thousands of the poor. How can this be, when we have one common nature, and much else in common besides this? We share a common heaven, sun, moon, choir of stars, air, sea , fire, water, earth, life, death, youth, old age, sickness, health, and the need for food and clothing. Our spiritual goods are also common to all: our holy altar, the body of our Lord, His sacred blood, the promised Kingdom, the bath of renewal, the purification of sins, truth, sanctity, redemption, and ineffable bliss. Is it therefore not madness for those who share so much in common, their nature, grace, covenant, and laws, to have such a passion for wealth that it causes them to forget their equality and to exceed the savageness of beasts? This is all the worse since they must of necessity soon leave these things behind them."

Chrysostom sees the source of inequality in man's free will and desire for personal property. Free will determines how an in - dividual will manage the gifts he had been given, and Chry - sostom considers that this is the heart of the problem. He does not recommend poverty for all men and, although he denounces superfluous luxury, it is primarily inequality to which he is op - posed. Chrysostom demands equality and justice. Material goods are given by God and for this reason there can be no cause to abominate them. However, they must not be used to the personal advantage of one man in such a way that another man suffers for lack of them. Chrysostom believes that the problem can be solved by love because "love seeks nothing for itself." It seems to him that this solution was realized by the earliest members of the Church in the manner described in the *Acts of the Apostles*. "They renounced property and rejoiced greatly because in this way they gained blessings that were even greater. The cold words 'mine and yours' did not exist, and there was joy at the altar . . . The expression 'mine and yours', which is so harsh and has caused so many wars in the world, was driven out of that holy Church, and men on earth lived like angels in heaven. The poor did not envy the rich, for there were no rich, and the rich did not despise the poor, for there were no poor. At that time things were not the way they are now. Now those who have property give to the poor, but at that time it was not so . . . All of them were equal and all wealth was shared among them." This example has been frequently cited by the supporters of com-munal monasticism who absolutely reject the right to personal property.

Chrysostom wanted to realize the example provided by mon-astic communities in the world, having in mind a comparatively small society in Antioch or Constantinople. In his homilies he tried to demonstrate how the voluntary renunciation of property and its equal distribution could provide for the needs of all. This is the way in which the property of the Church was organized at that time. It was held in common and was distributed by the bishop. Part of it was devoted to upkeep of churches and to the support of the clergy, but most of it was the "property of the poor." Chrysostom emphasized that such a socialization of property could be truly effective only if it was voluntary and if it was the expression of true self-renunciation and love.

All of this would presuppose a high degree of moral devel-opment and perfection. It would be the ultimate and ideal expression of Christian charity. However, Chrysostom was con-tent to limit his demands to generous almsgiving and works of charity. His conception of charity was very broad, extending from material contributions to consolation and comfort. "Is it not also an act of great charity when a soul, which is overwhelmed by grief, threatened by extreme danger, and held in thrall by the flames (of passion), is freed by someone from this affliction?"

Charity Essential for Christian Life

For Chrysostom it was unanimity, the feeling of belonging to a community and of common responsibility and concern, that were vital. For this reason he considered that works of charity were in-dispensable and essential for Christian life. "If someone does not show charity, he remains outside the wedding feast and he will perish. It is not by lifting up your hands that you will be heard. Stretch out your hands not to heaven, but to the hands of the poor." In commenting on the Savior's words about the Last Judgment Chrysostom writes: "There is no other virtue that He mentioned except the performance of works of charity, for charity comes from love, and love is the goal and meaning of Christianity."

Chrysostom's homilies on Christian charity reach the heights of true mysticism. "Do you wish to see the sacrificial altar of the All-Merciful? It has been built by God Himself, not out of stone, but out of a material which is lighter than heaven: out of rational souls . . . This altar was created from the very members of Christ, and the Body of the Master Himself serves as your altar. Worship before it, for you make your sacrifice on the Body of the Master. This altar is more awesome than both the new and the ancient altars . . . But at the same time you honor that altar because it receives the Body of Christ. You fail to pay attention to it when it is threatened by destruction. That kind of altar you can find anywhere, both on the streets and on the public squares, and you can make your sacrifices on it at all times because it is here that the sacrifice is sanctified.

On Civil Authority

Chrysostom's writings on civil authority also deserve attention, since it was frequently necessary for him to speak about this sub - ject, especially in Constantinople. In his conception authority entails inequality and is a form of enslavement. It has been established by God, but only as a result of sin. In paradise there was no authority because there was no inequality and man was free, but sin has made authority indispensable for the regulation of life in society, and without it there would be no order or peace. However, those who are in power are sinful just like everyone else, and for this reason authority often becomes harsh and unjust. This does not detract from the legitimacy of this authority, and everyone must remain obedient to it. It is only in the Church that secular authority has any limitations, for it cannot enter the Church's confines. Those who serve the Church are summoned to console the injured and the sorrowful. "Courts instill fear, so let priests give comfort. The authorities act by threats, so let the Church give encouragement," Chrysostom writes. "God has arranged for our salvation by means of both one and the other. He has armed the authorities so that they can instill fear in those who are audacious and He has consecrated priests so that they can comfort those who grieve."

At the same time it is also the duty of the priesthood to en - lighten those in authority and, when necessary, to denounce them for their abuses. "The ultimate authority of the priest is higher than that of the emperor," Chrysostom writes. "Therefore even the emperor bows his head under the hand of the priest. In the Old Testament it was the priests who anointed the emperors. However, the priest has been given only the right to speak out fearlessly, and he is not allowed to use force. In Chrysostom's eyes civil authority always remains inviolable, but he considers that it is nevertheless under the higher jurisdiction of the Church. In this respect his remarkable orations *On the Statues* and also his intercession on behalf of Eutropius, are typical. He himself considered this incident a "brilliant victory" for the Church and a "most glorious monument." Hostility and hatred were dissipated at the very threshold of the Church and violence was averted.

On Slavery

Chrysostom had no definite scheme for the external re-formation of society. He recognized and accepted the existing order and wanted not to rebuild society but to transform men. He believed in the triumphant strength of the spirit, and this explains his attitude towards slavery. He recognized it as an unnatural state but did not reject it or demand its abolition. This was not because such a demand would not have been fulfilled: on the contrary, Chrysostom frequently, especially in his severe standards of moral behavior, called for things that were not possible to realize. However, he saw a faster and more direct route to the overcoming of slavery in his advocacy of meekness, concern, and love. He reminded slaveowners of the dignity of man and of the equality of all people before Christ. He called slaves to a higher freedom and exhorted them to submit for the sake of Christ, as this would mitigate their earthly dependence. Chrysostom believed that every blow received in life on earth should be seen in relation to the life of the spirit. No external conditions can effect life in Christ and with Christ, and this is the source of eternal joy and bliss.

CHRYSOSTOM AS AN EXEGETE

Scripture as the Indispensable Source for Doctrinal and Moral Instruction

Chrysostom's work as both teacher and homilist is primarily based on Biblical exegesis. He insists that Scripture is the basic, indispensable, and completely adequate source for both doc-trinal and moral instruction. "He who is in agreement with Scrip-ture is a Christian," he writes, "and whoever is not in agreement with it is far from the truth." Chrysostom constantly exhorts each and every man to read the Bible with attention. "Do not wait for another teacher . . . You have been given the word of God, and no one will teach you as this will." Laymen in particular need to read the sacred books. "Monks who are removed from the cities are in a safer position but we who live amidst the sea of sinful desires and temptations need this divine medicine so that we can heal ourselves from the sores which afflict us and guard ourselves from further harm. With Scripture we can destroy the fiery arrows of Satan."

Everything contained in Scripture offers us instruction and healing, "and in one short passage in Divine Scripture we can find great strength and an ineffable wealth of ideas." A man who reads the Bible diligently will constantly discover new depths, and he will hear the voice of God which speaks with authority in every human soul. "The sight of the Gospels alone makes us more able to abstain from sin," Chrysostom writes, "and if we supplement this with attentive reading, then it is as if the soul enters into a mysterious and holy place. It is purified and becomes better, for through these writings it enters converse with God." The holy books are a message which has been written for men by God for all eternity, and this explains the effect that can be gained by reading the Bible. When the all-loving Master sees how eager we are to understand the depths of His Divinity, He enlightens and illuminates our minds and reveals the truth to our souls.

Chrysostom's understanding of Divinely inspired Scripture, in - cluding its list of names, salutations, and dates, is almost literal. Scripture contains nothing that is superfluous or has no definite purpose, not even a single iota or a single word, and frequently the addition of even one letter can alter its meaning, as is demonstrated by the renaming of Abraham. Chrysostom con - siders that the human weakness of the authors of Scripture is a sign of God's lenience towards men and His accommodation for them. He tries to discover the Divine significance of even mis - takes and discrepancies, since in his conception the "differences among the Evangelists" are an intentional part of God's plan. "If they were in complete harmony about everything, in relation to the time and the place and the words which were spoken, then none of their enemies would believe that they did not write without consulting among themselves and reaching an agree - ment beforehand, or that their agreement is true and genuine. Now the very fact that the Gospels contain discrepancies in minor details should allay all suspicion and should triumphantly justify our faith in those who wrote them."

The sacred writers wrote and spoke "in the Spirit" or the Spirit spoke in them, but Chrysostom carefully distinguishes the in - spiration of the Spirit from possession by It. Inspiration is a form of enlightenment. The consciousness and intellect remain clear and that which is revealed is fully understood. This is the es-sential difference between prophecy and mantic divination and this is why the sacred writers never lose their own identities. Chrysostom emphasizes the individual personality of each writer and the circumstances of the composition of the individual books. The image of Paul in particular is clearly present before him. The entire Bible forms a single whole because it is all from God. The individual writers are only the implements of a single great author.

His Scriptural Studies with Diodore of Tarsus

Chrysostom in his youth studied not only with Libanius but also with Diodore, and it was in his school that his understanding of the Bible and his exegetical style were formed. Chrysostom always spoke about Diodore of Tarsus with great feeling and gratitude. "He led an apostolic life of poverty, prayer, and the service of the word." "His tongue flowed with honey and milk," and he was a trumpet and a lyre. Chrysostom as an exegete was not an innovator, but followed within a firmly established tradition.

There is much in the history of Antiochene theology which remains unclear. Antioch became a center of Christianity very early but we can distinguish only unconnected links within its uninterrupted chain of tradition. Mention should first be made of Theophilus of Antioch, who was significant as both a writer and a thinker. Later we meet the name of the presbyter Malchion, who headed the Hellenic school and was one of the chief de-nouncers of Paul of Samosata. This is approximately the period in which the renowned teacher Lucian was active. At this time the presbyter Dorotheus was also teaching in Antioch. Eusebius, who heard his interpretation of Scripture in Church, described him as a learned man and a specialist in the Hebrew language, who had read Hebrew books and also received a Hellenistic education. Thus it is evident that even in the third century Antioch was a major center of Biblical study and that its unique exegetical style had already been formed. The Antiochenes were characterized by a cautious and frequently hostile attitude toward allegorism in exegesis. This is especially true of Eustathius of Antioch, who entered the struggle against the Arian disciples of Lucian.

In general, it was the polemical need to oppose false doctrines that was responsible for the formation of the fourth century school of Antiochene theology best represented by Diodore of Tarsus. He was connected with Lucian through his disciple

Eusebius of Emesa, who had also studied in Edessa. Diodore was an ascetic and a defender or orthodoxy, first against the Arians and later against the Apollinarians. He wrote on a variety of themes but was primarily an exegete. From the Old Testament he commented on the *Pentateuch*, the *Psalms*, and the books of *Samuel*, and also on difficult passages from *Chronicles*, *Proverbs*, *Ecclesiastes*, the *Song of Songs*, and the prophets. From the New Testament he wrote on the *Gospels*, the *Acts*, and the first letter of John. Only a few fragments of these writings have been preserved. We also have his short tract *On Contemplation and Allegory*, in which he sets forth the principles of his exegesis.

Diodore distinguishes among history, contemplation, and allegory. In his conception the Bible is neither an allegory nor a parable. Biblical narratives and pronouncements are always realistic and relate immediately to what is being described. For this reason Biblical commentary should be "historical" and a "pure exposition about that which took place." Allegorical interpretation, on the other hand, is removed from the direct meaning of the narration and "changes the subject" because it assumes that what is meant is not the same as what is said. Allegory must be distinguished from "contemplation," which reveals the higher meaning within history itself. Contemplation does not abrogate historical realism but presupposes it. This is the method that the apostle Paul used in his explanation of Biblical texts.

Apparently Diodore was interested in defending the realism of the Bible as a means of opposing the "Hellenism" he saw latent in allegorical interpretation. At the same time he also refused to acknowledge "Judaism" or strictly literal commentary, which in his view penetrates no further than the individual words. Many things are expressed in the Bible through hyperbole. Its narrations and locutions clearly exceed the measure of time, and this indicates the presence of a secondary meaning which is most frequently prophetic and foretells something else. What Diodore means by "contemplation" is primarily a type of exegetical divination, the discovery of prototypes. He is far from literal rationalism because for him the Bible is a sacred book which reveals a single Divine grace in many forms.

It is difficult to determine how Diodore applied these principles. The historical and literal method of interpretation was ultimately no more reliable than allegorism. On this subject Bolotov has aptly remarked that "the Alexandrian school was in danger of creating its own Scripture, but the Antiochene school, in remaining very close to the letter of Scripture, forgot that there should be a 'theory' to follow the 'history'."

The Additional Influence of Eusebius of Emesa and the Cappadocians on Chrysostom's Exegesis

This danger was realized in the work of Theodore of Mop - suestia, who was a pupil of Diodore. Chrysostom, apparently, avoided Theodore's excesses and was closer to Diodore. It is possible that Chrysostom incorporated his teacher's commentary in his own exegetical work, and there is no doubt that he was influenced by the interpretations of Eusebius of Emesa. On the other hand, he also made use of the writings of the Cap - padocians, who were closer to the Alexandrian tradition.

In general Chrysostom's exegesis is consistently realistic. The events in the Bible either teach us something or prophesy other events. This "typological" commentary is quite different from allegorism, and the doctrine of "types" or images is the essence of Chrysostom's understanding of the Bible. Sacred books have a religious significance for every believer and for everyone who reads them at all times and in all places, and this diversity of read - ership must be matched by the multiplicity of meaning in Scrip - ture. This is especially true for the Old Testament, where pure "historical" interpretation inevitably turns out to be "Judaism." Here the concept of "typology" is especially important. However, genuine "typologism" is possible only on a realistic basis. It is not surprising that it was in the Antiochene school that the doctrine of prototypes and prefiguration was fully developed. In Chry - sostom this doctrine is partially explained by the influence of the theology of St. Paul, which to a certain extent was instrumental in the development of all Antiochene exegetical theology.

Scripture is the word of God and it contains a kind of depth or three-dimensionality. For this reason the exegete must pen - etrate beneath the surface and go beyond the literal meaning. Chrysostom's primary motivation in using this approach is that the literal level of the Bible is often incomplete or unclear. When God speaks to man, He has to "adapt Himself and take into account the weakness of His audience," Chrysostom writes. This is his explanation for the anthropomorphism and anthropopathism in the Bible. "A father does not maintain his full dignity when he prattles with children." This is also how Chrysostom accounts for the occasional reticence of the New Testament. The Savior did not reveal His divine nature to Nicodemus "because this would have been premature and incomprehensible for the listener." For this same reason the apostles frequently speak about Christ as a man, refraining from revealing more than this until the time is right. All of this demonstrates that certain Scriptural passages need to be interpreted, especially in the Old Testament. This is true not only because the time had not yet come for full revelation. The main reason for the obscurity of the Old Testament is that it is directed towards the future. It is a form of prophecy.

Chrysostom frequently uses the term image or type, τύπος. He writes: "Do not expect to find a complete reality in an image. Look rather at the similarity the image has to the reality, and at the superiority of the reality in the New, and therefore only by starting from the New Testament can we recognize the "truth" or meaning of the Old. "An image should not be completely dif - ferent from the truth because in that case it would not be an image. But it should also not be completely equal to the truth because in that case it would be the truth itself. It should be contained within the boundaries of the truth, not having all the truth within itself and yet not completely distant from it. For if it had everything, then it would be the very truth, but if it had nothing (of the truth), then it would not be an image. It should have something in itself and also leave something to the truth."

A prototype or prefiguration can be identified as individual incidents which indicate other events in the future. "Typology" differs from allegory in that it explains events, not words. An allegorical approach to Scripture sees only parables or pure symbols in the Biblical narration. It distinguishes not two levels of reality, but two understandings of one and the same symbol. For allegorists, the Old and New Testaments are two systems of interpretation or two conceptions of the world but not two stages in the economy of history. Their method is not based on real events. Historical realism does not aim at transforming the Bible into a history of the world, and even Theodore of Mopsuestia cannot be regarded as an historical positivist. In his under - standing the entire Bible is a book about the Messiah and Christology, and the Old Testament is a prefiguration and proph - ecy of the future. He sees the Bible as full of allusions and presentiments, and this is even more true of Chrysostom. It cannot be denied that there is a certain degree of allegorism in his typological interpretation. However, it is not words which are symbolic, but facts. Thus the sacrifice of Isaac signifies the cross, and the lamb of the Old Testament prefigures Christ. The migration into Egypt and the subsequent Exodus foretell Joseph's flight to Egypt with the Infant and his later return to Palestine. Of course, this type of interpretation allows for the same kind of conventionalism and arbitrariness that can arise in the allegorical method.

Chrysostom discerns another system of Biblical prototypes in the words and means of expression themselves, especially in the speeches of the prophets. The prophets speak in a language of images which is, properly speaking, symbolic. However, the actual prophecies contain many meanings and relate to whole series of events, each of which reveals another. They often apply to things which have already taken place in the past. In this way Moses was prophesying when he revealed the nature of the creation of heaven and earth, and Jacob foretold Judas, and Christ as well, at the same time. The *Psalms* and the New Testa - ment also have a double meaning. The Gospels are historical, but in addition to this the events narrated in them are prefigurations of the future fate of the souls of believers who will come to Christ. Furthermore, the Savior Himself spoke in parables, and it is this which justifies the validity of seeing the Gospels as a guide for moral behavior. All of this explains the religious significance of the "historical-grammatical" method of exegesis. It was not merely an intellectual and empirical interpretation of Scripture, and the "scientific nature" of Antiochene commentary should not be exaggerated.

The erudition of the Antiochene exegetes was no greater than that of the Alexandrians. Neither Chrysostom nor Theodore of Mopsuestia knew Hebrew. Therefore both of them followed the Greek text, which they regarded as the ultimate authority, and the problem of the discrepancies between the Hebrew and Greek recensions remained unresolved in their work. Chrysostom's historical perspective in his interpretation of the Bible is not sufficiently broad. He limits himself to only brief references to the authors of the books, their goals, and the conditions in which they wrote, and then immediately begins his examination of their thought. Chrysostom's commentaries on the new Testament are among the best of his writings, as was recognized even in an - cient times, and the reason for this is the tremendous sensitivity with which he perceives even the slightest nuances in the Greek. Chrysostom's orientation as a philologist is apparent when he asks such questions as who is speaking, to whom, and about what? He examines the various shades of meaning in synonyms and explores possible alternative locutions. He always tries to derive the meaning of Scripture from Scripture itself, and his references to tradition are relatively few. For Chrysostom, as for Origen, the Bible is self-sufficient.

Both Alexandrians and Antiochenes alike tried to grasp and interpret the "inner" or "spiritual" significance of Scripture. Their disagreement was limited to their methods and did not extend to their goals. This divergence in methodology can be partially ex -

plained by the difference in the philological traditions from which they developed. The distinction and struggle between "alle - gorical" and "historical-grammatical" approaches can be observed even among the ancient interpreters of classical texts. However, this divergence is primarily connected with the difference in the way that the religious significance of history was perceived by them. It is very indicative that Diodore of Tarsus accused the Alexandrian allegorists of not understanding history. However, their ultimate goal always remained the discovery and explanation of the meaning of Scripture, whether that meaning was found in the word or in the event.

In their approach to the moral significance of Scripture the Alexandrians and the Antiochenes were very similar to each other. Furthest from the Alexandrian tradition was Theodore of Mopsuestia, but as a result of his views on theology and his particular brand of humanism his Biblical exegesis is almost de - void of religious significance. It was in his extreme doctrines that the Antiochene school was condemned. However, the most valuable aspect of the realism of the Antiochene exegetes, their interpretation of Scripture as history, was retained. It is this which is the most outstanding feature of the work of Chrysostom.

CHAPTER TWELVE

JACOB APHRAATES

I
LIFE

We have little definite information about the life of Aphraates, and we know him primarily through his works. In ancient times he was called the "Persian Sage." Aphraates lived in Persia during the era of Saphur II, and he has left a record of the persecutions suffered by Christians at that time. Aphraates was a bishop, and Jacob was his episcopal name. The exact location of his see is unknown, but in 344 he acted as a spokesman for an ecclesiastical council. The year of his death has not been definitely established.

II
WORKS

The name of Aphraates has been connected with a book or orations or homilies. There are twenty-two of these, in ac - cordance with the number of consonants in the Syriac alphabet, and together they form a systematic exposition of faith. In a certain sense this is an ascetic work, although the author also deals with problems of philosophy. These orations are mainly interesting for the fact that they contain no traces of Greek influences. They are a confession of the oldest form of Syrian Christianity and are untouched by Hellenism. The book was composed in two stages: the first ten homilies were written in 336-337; and the remaining homilies in 343-344. The last oration describes the persecutions in Persia and was written ap - proximately in August of 345.

III
THOUGHT

A CONFESSION OF FAITH

Aphraates speaks in the name of the Church, not as an individual, and he always supports himself with Scripture because Christ and the Spirit speak through the holy writers.

Aphraates devotes most of his attention to Christ, the Messiah who has come to us. His confession of faith is brief: "We only know that God is One, and that the Messiah who has come is One, and that the Spirit is One, and that faith is one, and that baptism is one. It has not been given to us to say more. If we say more we are mistaken, and if we doubt this, we will be helpless." Elsewhere he writes: "This is our faith. If a man believes in God, the Lord of all, who created heaven and earth . . . and who created Adam in His own image, gave the law to Moses, sent his Spirit to the apostles, and sent his Messiah into the world, and if a man believes in the resurrection of the dead and in the mystery of baptism . . . then this is faith in the Church of God." Faith gives birth to love and hope, and man purifies himself through works of light and works of faith so that he may become a temple of the Messiah and so that the Spirit will be implanted in him.

DOCTRINAL INTERESTS

Aphraates should not be considered only as a moralist who had no interest in dogma. Testimony to his doctrinal beliefs can be found in his homilies. His faith is concrete, although his language is occasionally obscure. Aphraates speaks about baptism in the name of the Three, "with the invocation of the three great and glorious names." He teaches that Christ is the Son of God, and that He is God, and that He is God generated from God and from the essence of the Divinity, light from light, and the Emperor and the Son of the Emperor. The Spirit is the Spirit of sanctity who is glorified together with the Father and the Son. He is revealed in both testaments and He dwells within us. Aphraates calls the Spirit our Mother who is at the side of our heavenly Father because the gender of *ruah* is feminine (there is no neuter gender in the Semitic languages). Christ came to save us from sin, and, being without sin Himself, he died as a living sacrifice for our sins. We have assimilated the fruits of the death on the Cross because Christ assumed our nature, and in ascending to the Father He brought our nature with Him. Aphraates carefully distinguishes the Divine from the human in Christ, but he sees Him as a single person. He speaks of the Eucharist in concrete terms and call it a sacrifice.

APHRAATES' UNIQUE ESCHATOLOGY

Aphraates' eschatology is unique. In his conception Christians are composed of a body, a soul, and the Spirit, which they re - ceive at baptism and which abides in them until they fall into sin or die, when It returns to God from whom It proceeds. It denounces sinners before Christ but prays to the Savior to resurrect righteous men and to reunite their souls with their bodies. At death the immortal soul falls asleep and is buried together with the body. Those who have died are only sleeping and, since they have vague presentiments of the fate that awaits them, some sleep joyfully but others are in torment. Six thousand years after its creation the world will reach the ultimate boundary of its existence, and the dead will arise in the very bodies in which they were enterred. The Spirit will await the righteous at their tombs, and the last trumpet sounds It will be united with them, trans - forming their bodies, absorbing their souls, and making them completely spiritual. The bodies of sinners, however, will remain earthly. Only moderate sinners will be judged at the Last Judg - ment. Great sinners, for example idolaters, will not be called to judgment, but as soon as they are resurrected, they will return to hell where they had been abiding. At the Last Judgment the damned will descent to hell and each will receive forever the retribution he has merited. The just will also receive their blissful reward forever, also in accordance with their works. Aphraates has left a vivid description of future paradise. On the whole his doctrine is simple, naïve, and almost fantastic.

HIS STRICT VIEWS ON MARRIAGE AND VIRGINITY

Aphraates was an advocate of strict morality and especially of virginity. He did not condemn marriage entirely, but apparently he rejected the idea of marriage after baptism, and at baptism he expected married couples to part. He seems to have considered that virginity, abstinence, and fasting were included in the baptismal vows. Aphraates' understanding of the words "a man leaves his father and mother" (*Genesis* 2: 24) is interesting in this respect. In his conception this implies that in entering marriage a man abandons his Father who is God and his Mother who is the Holy Spirit. Therefore, he concludes, "If a man's heart is inclined to marriage, let him enter this union before receiving baptism so that he will not break his vows during the time of his struggle. If a man fears and trembles before this struggle, let him return to where he came from, so that he will not break down the spirits of his brothers as he has broken his own."

THE "SONS OF THE TESTAMENT"

In one of his homilies Aphraates speaks about the "sons of the Testament," *b'nai Q'yâmâ*. We know of the "daughters of the

Testament," *bnâth Q'yâmâ*, from ancient Syrian martyrologies. This was not a monastic order but a type of regulated society for laymen. It is possible that in Aphraates' conception the idea of the "Testament" and the Church are the same, and this organ-ization should be considered along with the orders of virgins, widows, and other minor clerical ranks which existed among the early Christians. Aphraates tries to include all the members of the Church within these orders. He considers that it was better for the weak to defer their baptism than for the discipline of the faithful to be made less severe. Apparently the members of this lay society lived together, had their own church, and were under the direction of the bishop or clergy in general. Aphraates makes no particular demands on them except for the vow of virginity, and for the most part limits himself to offering basic moral in-struction. They should take their example from the figure of Christ, and a true "son of the Testament" rejoices in the only One who is from the bosom of the Father. The "Testament" is a type of betrothal with the heavenly Bridegroom, and the first com-mandment is to imitate the poverty of Christ. Aphraates ad-vocates spiritual vigilance as a means of preserving the soul, and then good works as a means of helping the poor. He especially recommends the reading of Scripture.

The "sons of the Testament" continued to exist within the Syrian church as an independent organization even after actual monasticism had been established. Rabbula composed a canon for their regulation at the beginning of the fifth century. It seems that this was a type of ascetic discipline for laymen. From Rab-bula's canon it is evident that they did not take vows of poverty, although they did isolate themselves from the world. By the sixth century this ancient institution was absorbed by various monastic orders. John of Ephesus uses the name "sons of the Testa-ment" to indicate either the minor orders of the clergy or monks in their novitiate.

CHAPTER THIRTEEN

ST. EPHRAEM THE SYRIAN

I
LIFE

It is difficult to separate the truth from the legends which have grown up around Ephraem the Syrian, and only a very few facts are definitely known about his life. He lived approximately between 306 and 373. He was born in Nisibis and his parents were probably Christians, not pagans. He practiced ascetic dis - cipline from his earliest youth, and was very close to Jacob, bishop of Nisibis. He entered the clergy but never rose above the diaconate. However, he played an active role in the life of his native city. In 363 Nisibis was ceded to Persia and Ephraem withdrew to Edessa, where he devoted himself to literary activity and to teaching in what was known as the "Persian School." Apparently it was Ephraem, who had probably taught Biblical studies earlier, who founded the Biblical school in Edessa. Lucian studied in Edessa with a certain Macarius, and Eusebius of Emesa was also a pupil there, but it was Ephraem who first organized the school.

We can form a conception of Ephraem's teaching from the Biblical commentary he has left, but we have no other reliable in - formation about the early years of the school of Edessa which later became so famous. Although it is unlikely that the school experienced any great changes, most of what we know of it re - lates to a later era when the Greek influence was predominant. During this period the school was similar to the Hebrew schools in which the pupils lived in dormitories and formed a kind of fra - ternity. The main subject of study was Sacred Scripture. Stu - dents learned to explicate the Bible by writing down and mem - orizing the exegeses of their teachers. In this way the "school tradition" came into being. Study was probably similar to this during the life of Ephraem, and it is his teaching that was ac - knowledged as the "tradition" until the middle of the fifth century.

We have no other reliable information about Ephraem. His later life in particular is obscure. An encomium to him has been as - cribed to Gregory of Nyssa, but probably does not belong to Gregory. According to tradition Ephraem was present at the Council of Nicaea, traveled through Egypt and Pontus, and visited with Basil the Great, but none of this can be proven. Little biographical material can be drawn from Ephraem's own writings, and furthermore the mass of compositions which have survived under his name have not yet all been definitely attributed to him, since his name was freely used by later scribes. The exact year of Ephraem's death has not been established.

Ephraem was primarily an ascetic, but at the same time he had an outstanding gift for lyricism. He is least significant as a thinker. His theological writings, which are euphonic and melodious, are the work of a lyric poet. They are sincere and intimate. Ephraem's orations are also lyric, and it often seems that he is singing rather than speaking. His abundant images are vivid and often extremely complex, and they frequently evolve into independent dramatic scenes. Besides this, Ephraem had the gift of tears. "Weeping for Ephraem was the same as breathing the air for other men. His tears poured forth both day and night." These were not tears of fear or guilt, but of tenderness and compassion.

Ephraem's severe personal asceticism did not make him harsh in his relations with other men. Even in his exhortations to repentance he does not denounce sinners but tries to soften their hearts and to move their souls. His cosmic imagery is especially remarkable. It is Ephraem's talent as a poet that accounts for his exceptional influence and the broad and immediate popularity of his works. Jerome has written that "in some churches (in the East) his writings were publicly read after the books of Scripture." And Theodoret has remarked that the holidays honoring martyrs are made more solemn by the hymns of Ephraem. According to Sozomen his works were translated into Greek, which Ephraem himself did not know, even during his lifetime.

II
WORKS

The most important of Ephraem's writings which have come down to us are his commentaries on the Bible. They were written during the later years of his life in Edessa. Apparently Ephraem explicated all of the canonic books but only his writings on *Genesis* and *Exodus* (up to 32: 26) have been preserved entirely and in their original forms. A few fragments from other exegeses have survived in the ninth century collection of Severus of Edessa, and the Biblical text of these has been altered to the *Peshitta*. Commentaries on the *Diatessaron* and the epistles of Paul (with the exception of the epistle to *Philemon*) have been preserved in Armenian translations. Ephraem also composed exegetical homilies on individual subjects drawn primarily from the Old

Testament, including the state of man before the fall, Joseph and his betrayal by his brothers, and the prophet Jonah and his mission to Nineveh. These are more like hymns than sermons. Besides his Biblical commentary, Ephraem's prose works include several dogmatic and polemical books.

The majority of Ephraem's writings are poetic and have a metri - cal form. Syrian versification is based not on the length of syllables but on their total number. Long vowels are not distinguished from short vowels, but words are broken up into distinct individual units, and in this way speech becomes measured. In addition to this, Syrian poetry makes use of a device similar to the "parallelism" of Hebrew poetry. Two or more verses are joined together to form a stanza, which can frequently be broken down into shorter lines, some of which function as refrains. Acrostics are also common. This form corresponds to the general character of Syrian poetry, which is didactic. Apparently the first Syrian poet was Bardesanes ("Bar-Daisan"), who used metrical forms in his sermons. According to Theodoret Ephraem decided to fight him with his own weapons. "Some time ago, Harmonius, the son of Bardesanes, composed several songs, and by uniting his impious teaching to these pleasant melodies he afforded his listeners great enjoyment as he led them to perdition. Ephraem therefore borrowed their melody but joined it to his own orthodox doctrine and in this way he provided his listeners with instruction that was as enjoyable as it was useful." Some of Ephraem's poetry, his *memre*, or orations, were intended for oral declaration or to be read aloud. In distinction to these, some other works, his *mad(h)ràse*, or, literally, instructions, were written for choral singing with the accompaniment of harps.

Ephraem utilized verse forms in the fight against heresy and al - so to glorify God. He wrote a great deal on dogmatic and polemic themes, and has left orations against Marcion and Manes (or Mani), against Bardesanes, against Julian the Apostate, and against the "sceptics" or Arians. Ephraem's "Nisibeian verses" were written early in his life. His funeral hymns and penitential hymns are particularly remarkable for their lyricism. Mention should also be made of his "Testament," which has been pre - served only in a later revision.

III
THOUGHT

HIS ATTITUDE TOWARD SCRIPTURE

Ephraem's most outstanding characteristic as a teacher is his close adherence to the Bible. His attitude to Scripture is reverent, for the Divine books have been given to us from God through the Holy Spirit. They are the means of our salvation. The mysteries of the holy books and their wonderful harmony are accessible only to those who approach them with faith. On the twenty-two streams a tree grows forth which bears many fruits, and its branches extend beyond the bounds of the earth. Ephraem uses the Old Testament text of the *Peshitta* and only rarely cites the *Septuagint*, probably referring to a Syriac translation or relying on a glossary. Occasionally he mentions the Hebrew text or Hebrew commentary, but he never quotes these directly.

Ephraem begins by examining the literal meaning of the Biblical text before exploring the significance of the events and characters of the Old Testament, including Adam and Eve, the patriarchs, the flood, and so forth, as prototypes and prefigurations. He interprets the narrative of the six days of creation literally, and in the tradition of Hebrew exegesis he understands the "Spirit of God" in *Genesis* 1: 2 as a powerful wind which moved and warmed the waters. God created man not by a simple command, in the way that He created the rest of the world, but with circumspection, through a kind of exchange of ideas among all the members of the Trinity. Man, like other incorporeal spirits, is created by God with a free will and a free choice between good and evil. In order for man to recognize God as his Creator and Master, God gave him His first commandment and prohibition. In Ephraem's conception the forbidden tree is a simple tree, but there is no other command that God could have given. God could not have told the first man not to kill, or steal, or commit adultery, or that he should love his neighbor because as yet there were no other people.

FREEDOM, THE IMAGE OF GOD, AND THE FALL

Man's likeness to God is revealed in his freedom. Because man contains the image of God within himself, man's thought possesses a kind of omnipresence and is capable of embracing all places. The first man was adorned with a "robe of glory" and with "heavenly garments" and the bliss and grandeur of man's state before the fall surpass description. We lost these through the lust and arrogant disobedience of the first Eve, but they are returned to us through the second Eve, the Virgin Mary. Our first paradise is restored to us in the Church, and the tree of life is here replaced by the Eucharist. Ephraem interprets all Messianic references as prefigurations.

THE EXEGETICAL MIXTURE OF POETIC SYMBOLISM AND LITERAL INTERPRETATION

Ephraem's writings are characterized by an unsystematic com - bination of literal interpretation and poetic symbolism, and the Bible is transformed from a book of history to a book of parables. However, he succeeds in demonstrating the organic integrity of both Testaments, which together form "a single body of truth." This is a single word "which was spoken by a single pair of lips for various generations." It contains both the weaker rays and the full light, both the image and the fulfillment. It is two harps which are played by one Artist. The single path has three parts: from para - dise to Zion, from Zion to the Church, and from the Church to the Kingdom of Heaven.

Poetic form does not always foster clarity. In addition to this, the Syriac language of Ephraem's time did not yet possess a theo - logical terminology. Finally, Ephraem had a tendency to be satisfied with definition through negation and to avoid more detailed examination. "I openly admit the insignificance of my being and I do not want to try to know my Creator because the Inaccessible One is awesome by His very nature." He limits his inquiry to that which has been revealed and does not try to discover that which is hidden or which is not clearly expressed in Scripture and in the canons of faith.

DOGMATIC THOUGHT

However, a wealth of dogmatic material can be drawn from the works of Ephraem. First of all, he emphasizes the importance of an orthodox confession of the Trinity, for "without this it is impossible to live a true life." The Trinity is a mystery but we have been enlightened by the testimony of God so that we can distinguish the names and recognize the indivisible unity and equality of the Divinity. There is neither separation nor merging in the Trinity, but "there is a great order." The Divine names are not merely names, but they designate actual persons. "If there is no person, then the name is only an empty sound." The persons can be contemplated in the Divine names. The Son of God is the proper Son of the Father and everything that belongs to the Father belongs also to the Son. The incomprehensible gen-eration of the Son is natural and eternal, and in this same way the Father manifests the Spirit, Who proceeds eternally from His own essence. This Trinitarian dogma is brief and simple, but never-theless it is completely clear. Possibly its lucidity is explained by the presence of Jacob, the bishop of Nisibis, at the Council of Nicaea. "The truth is written in few words," Ephraem remarks. "Do not try to make long explanations."

Ephraem's Christological beliefs are also clearly presented. Primarily, in opposition to the Docetists, he defends the com-pleteness of the Incarnation. In connection with this he develops his teaching on the Mother of God as the Virgin Mother. "Mary would be superfluous if Christ came to us as an apparition and God would be jesting in showing people the birth in the manger." Christ is both God and man at the same time. "He is entirely of the lower order and entirely of the higher order, entirely in everything and entirely one." Ephraem refers to "mingling" and stresses the indivisibility of this union and the unity of the Person of Christ. He says little about redemption but his basic idea is clear: "Christ becomes similar to us in order to make us similar to Himself. The Immortal One comes down to mortals, makes them immortal, and ascends again to the Father." He places particular emphasis on the sufferings of the Savior and on His descent to hell, from which He leads forth Adam as the dead rise from the dust and glorify their Savior.

Ephraem's depiction of the last days is both poetic and lively. His description of the institution of a new Easter through the Eu-charist, and the true transformation of the Eucharistic gifts into the food of incorruptibility, is particularly vivid. Against this back-ground his realistic attention to detail is especially striking, and he remarks that the bread which the Savior offered to Judas had first been moistened in water, which removed His blessing from it. All of this is closer to mystical poetry than actual theology.

Ephraem in his anthropology primarily stresses man's freedom, which he sees as the source of responsibility and the desire to strive for God. This striving is a victory over necessity and nature, and it is also a liberation from the "power of the stars" and the ele-ments. The very question as to whether man is free proves that he is because "questions and scepticism arise from freedom." "A nature which is deprived of freedom cannot ask questions. Questions are the work of freedom. Only a free nature can in-quire." Man's own internal experience testifies to his freedom.

The world is created by God and "there is nothing on earth that has not been authorized because the source of everything is God." Therefore evil is not from nature or from material sub - stance, and "there would be no evil if it were not for the will." At the fall freedom was distorted but not destroyed. Man must make a choice, and "the nature of freedom is identical in all people," so that if one man can be victorious, then this is possible for every - one. Man is created in the image of God, and this is revealed in his freedom and in his capacity to accept God's gifts. At his cre - ation man was endowed with immortality, wisdom, and knowl - edge, and he was clothed in light. At the fall he became mortal, and the first sin is still reverberating in us like an echo. Only Christ liberates men from this condemnation to death.

Ephraem's writings on the Church are vivid and emotional. The Church is the Bride of Christ, the Courtyard of the Shepherd, and the House of God. This house stands on two columns, which are the visible world and the invisible world. Ephraem describes the continuity in the order of things from Adam to Christ, and also the continuity of the apostolic tradition, which has been transmitted through consecration and the laying on of hands. For Ephraem the Church is a place of sanctification which is realized through the sacraments. The first of these is baptism, the sacrament of forgiveness and adoption. The baptismal font is another Jordan, a boundary between life and death, and only the man who crosses to the other shore becomes a "citizen of the spiritual world." At baptism man "is led to freedom in the name of the Trinity." This sacrament is accomplished through anointing with oil, and Ephraem compares this to the Eucharist. Sinners can again wash away their pollution by repentance, and especially by sincere sorrow and tears. "I dress myself in tears and thus I am adorned." Tears magnify the beauty of the outer garments. At the same time Ephraem speaks about the power of the keys, a power which has been given to the Church. The basic principle of his doctrine is that "the entire Church is a Church of those who are perishing and of those who repent."

Ephraem frequently speaks on eschatological themes, which obviously appealed to his poetic imagination. His description of the Last Judgment is similar to the dogma of Aphraates: the righ - teous are superior to judgment; average men will be judged, but sinners are beyond judgment. The doctrine of the resurrection of all is essential for Ephraem, and he considers that without faith in the resurrection it is impossible to be a Christian and useless to participate in the sacraments, since it is the sacraments, and especially the Eucharist, which testify to the resurrection. At the resurrection everyone will be made incorruptible but the bodies of sinners will be dark and they will exude a terrible stench. Everyone will pass through the fire. Righteous men will be un-harmed, but sinners will remain in the flames. Just souls will enter the realm of bliss only after the resurrection because outside of their bodies they are insensible and cannot go beyond the boundary of earthly paradise. It is at this boundary that the souls of pardoned sinners will remain after judgment, but the souls of the righteous will then achieve the heights of blessedness. This will be their ultimate and eternal fate.

Ephraem's writings contain many outstanding images but few original ideas. However, his exposition of general Church doc-trine is vivid and artistic, and this is the main significance of his dogmatic writing.

Date Due

BJJJ

PRINTED IN U.S.A.   CAT. NO. 24 161   BRO DART